W9-ALV-021

SMOKE AND MIRRORS:

LIFE IN THE CFL WITH RICHIE HALL

SMOKE AND MIRRORS:

LIFE IN THE CFL WITH RICHIE HALL

Richie Hall with Guy Scholz

Bestselling Author of *Gold on Ice and Between the Sheets I & II*

"When I did my SI blog on the CFL, I asked insiders who is one of the best defensive coaches. Richie Hall's name always came up. If there is a defensive genius in the CFL it might be Richie Hall."

- Peter King of *Sports Illustrated*

Smoke and Mirrors:
Life in the CFL with Richie Hall

© 2017 by Richie Hall and Guy Scholz

Ebook ISBN: 978-0-9958193-1-3

Paperback ISBN: 978-0-9958193-0-6

No portion of this book may be duplicated or used in any form, by any electronic or mechanical means (including photocopying, recording, or information storage and retrieval), for any profit-driven enterprise without prior permission in writing from the publisher. Brief excerpts may be shared subject to inclusion of this copyright notice:
© 2017 by Richie Hall and Guy Scholz. All rights reserved.

Additional copies of this book may be ordered by visiting the PPG Online Bookstore at:

✦PolishedPublishingGroup

shop.polishedpublishinggroup.com

Due to the dynamic nature of the Internet, any website addresses mentioned within this book might have been changed or discontinued since its publication.

"A book that shows how under-sized Richie Hall, one of football's nicest guys, has endured and succeeded through 30-plus seasons as a CFL coach and player, tough professions that typically don't demand any sort of kindness."

Darrell Davis: 2006 inductee into the media wing of the Canadian Football Hall of Fame and a long-time Saskatchewan Roughriders beat writer for the *Regina Leader-Post*

"From his time as a Grey Cup-winning player to his emergence as a championship coach, Richie Hall has been a CFL fixture. Beloved. Respected. He has earned his stature by making his life and life's work about guiding others, helping them become better people, better players. This book is a splendid telling of Hall's spiritual journey."

Allan Maki: *Globe and Mail* and member of the CFL Hall of Fame media wing

"Richie Hall as a successful player and assistant coach —even as a fired head coach — has had an enduring relationship with those whose lives he's touched. Only trying to be a good team-mate, good coach and good person, Hall quietly became part of the fabric of football in the heartland of the CFL."

Terry Jones: *Edmonton Sun & Journal*; media member of the Hockey, CFL Hall and Curling Hall of Fames

"There has always been an infectious enthusiasm about Richie Hall dating back to his days as a player in the Canadian Football League and now as a coach. He draws you in with his caring personality and, inevitably, you leave any conversation with the man feeling upbeat and energetic. That's part of what made him a successful player and it's critical in his role as a coach. This book helps captures all of that and, just as important, of Hall the man and his life story."

Ed Tait: Director of Content for bluebombers.com. Member of the Canadian Football Hall of Fame media wing, and Media Roll of Honor with the Manitoba Sportswriters & Sportscasters Association

"If everyone in this choir (world, team etc.) was just like me, what kind of choir would this choir BE?"

-Richie Hall

Richie, Janice, Richard Sr. (Daddy), Michael, Jean (Mommy)

DEDICATION

This book is dedicated to Mommy (Jean Hall), Daddy (Richard Sr.), Janice, and Michael, who have supported, encouraged, challenged, sacrificed, and loved me throughout this journey of life. God is so amazing with all the blessings He's provided. I love you all so very much and I like my family.

Love Richie

To my son Reed Scholz, who we named after the greatest Roughrider of them all. He's my hero. So full of compassion, conviction, and character. As his namesake was known for toughness and clutch play, Reed exemplifies this in the arena of life.

Guy

TABLE OF CONTENTS

Forward: Glen Suitor   01
Prelude   05

FIRST QUARTER: IT ALL BEGINS
Chapter 1:   57 Days in '89   10
Chapter 2:   1989 Part Deux!   19
Chapter 3:   An Old Soul in a Young Body   26
Chapter 4:   He Who Walks with the Wise Becomes Wise   34
Chapter 5:   Underdog Meets Pint!   40

SECOND QUARTER: BOMBERVILLE
Chapter 6:   Come to Winnipeg and Hang Out   48
Chapter 7:   We'll Go till the Hay is in the Barn   55
Chapter 8:   Bridging that Gap   62
Chapter 9:   Playmakers   70
Chapter 10: Tomahawk Chop   77
Chapter 11: Testosterone Ballet   84
Chapter 12: Football IQ   90
Chapter 13: Don't Muddy the Waters   98

HALF TIME: THE ECLECTIC WAYS OF MR. HALL
Chapter 14: Jazzing It Up   114
Chapter 15: The Boston Way   118
Chapter 16: Granite to Gridiron: Embracing the Prairies   127
Chapter 17: Magnetic Kindness   134

THIRD QUARTER: MUSINGS FROM THE VALLEY
Chapter 18: Musings from the Valley—Uno!   140
Chapter 19: Musings from the Valley—Deux!   147
Chapter 20: Musings from the Valley—Trey!   153
Chapter 21: Musings from the Valley—Quatre!   159

FOURTH QUARTER: PRAIRIE LESSONS
Chapter 22: Calgary   168
Chapter 23: Regina I   176
Chapter 24: Edmonton   184
Chapter 25: Regina II   192
Chapter 26: Winnipeg   202

Epilogue   216
Overtime: November 2016—Takeaways and Faith   219
Acknowledgements   224
Biographies   228
Index   231

FOREWORD

by Glen Suitor

I actually felt like I knew, and respected, Richie Hall before I even met him personally. It was in the late '80s; I was a member of the Saskatchewan Roughriders at the time and Richie was an all-star with the Calgary Stampeders. The Stamps were in financial trouble, and team owners had just been turned down when they looked for a bailout from local government. I will never forget the picture at the top of the sports section. It was a shot of a very emotional Hall, at what looked like a rally to save the Calgary Stampeders. The article was all about the financial difficulties of the Stamps, and the gloom and doom that were unfortunately commonplace at the time for the CFL. However, what caught my attention was this relatively new import player from Colorado State (I immediately went and read his bio) who was so emotionally involved in a league and a country that he had only been part of for a few years.

At that time a football player born in San Antonio, Texas, and playing his college football at Colorado State couldn't just Google the CFL and find out what kind of league it was, or where the games were played. Canadian players grew up with a great understanding of CFL football, and were often the poster boys for the league. It was unusual for an import player to be front and centre in a newspaper story, and it was even more unlikely that an import player would be that passionate about fighting to save this Canadian team, and by extension the league.

I was impressed to say the least, and found myself watching more film on Richie, and following his career a little closer. I quickly found out that he was an all-star for a reason, and watching him on film, or even playing against him, didn't really reveal the fact that he stood just five foot six inches tall. Guys that small weren't supposed to make it in pro football. But what was weird was, even though I was on the opposite sideline, or at times trying to tackle him on a punt return, when we played against each other, he never looked like an undersized player. In retrospect, I guess if you make big plays, and play big, you are a giant on the field, no matter what the tale of the tape actually reads. Richie made big plays as a player, and played big. His height didn't matter; he was a player, and it didn't take long before I found out he was also a great teammate, and a coach in the making.

I honestly didn't realize Richie was undersized until I met him personally when he became my teammate in 1988. He was traded to the Roughriders that year, and our friendship began immediately. I'm sure as you read testimonials in his book, everyone will say, "It didn't take long to start a friendship with Richie Hall." Richie has a very friendly, and yet professional, demeanour. When you shake his hand for the first time, and see his very friendly smile, you can't help but start up a conversation. Once that discussion begins, you find out quickly that you aren't talking to just another player on the roster—you are conversing with a great person who cares about getting to know you, and your family.

I played free safety in Saskatchewan, and Richie Hall was a halfback, so we would be playing side by side. It is always important in any job to get to know the person you work with; however, I knew immediately that there was a sincerity to Richie that transcended the game. He wanted to get better at his craft every day, and he sincerely wanted to help his teammates get there as well.

At the start of training camp in Saskatoon in 1989, Richie and I decided we would try to get an edge on the opponent. On day one of training camp we created a pre-practice ritual that we would do every single day. It was a sit-up routine that you had to do in pairs; it was intense but didn't take all that long. No, it wasn't earth shattering, it was simply a sit-up routine, but for me it was all psychological and brought us even closer as teammates. First, we were working together every day before we even got on the field for stretch, so it meant we both had to get ready earlier, and would often walk out on the field together. Second, I had always believed in the premise that if you want to win, and be great, you can never get outworked. There may be better athletes on the field; there may be faster and stronger players out there , all of which is out of your control. What you can control is your work ethic, and I used to think that there was no way that any other player in the league was doing an intense sit-up workout prior to every practice, like Richie and I were doing. The sit-ups may or may not have led to more interceptions, or the two of us making more plays to help our team win. However, in my mind it gave us an edge and an even higher level of trust, and as the saying goes, if you believe it to be so, you can achieve it.

The 1989 season was a roller coaster of emotion. We had a very good team, but it wasn't the most talented in the league. In Kent Austin and Tom Burgess we had the quarterbacks that could take us to the Grey Cup, but it would have to be a team effort. The 1989 Riders were not going to get there simply because we were great players; we were going to have to become a great team. Richie was a galvanizing force in the room, and working side by side with him early in the year gave me a great appreciation for the coach he would later become.

As the free safety I was responsible for getting the signal from the defensive coaches on the sideline and then calling the defensive secondary's coverage in the huddle. Then, when the opponent's offense broke the huddle, I needed to know all the changes and checks that needed to be made, and relay those checks to the rest of the defense. Richie was like having a coach right beside me in the huddle to not only confirm, or at times, correct, the calls that were being made, but also to suggest a better alternative. Richie knew the defense inside and out, but also scouted the opponent like a coach, so he wasn't shy to suggest that maybe we should change the coach's call, and pretend we didn't see it from the sideline. In fact in the 1989 Grey Cup, in the then-Sky Dome in Toronto, versus the Hamilton Ti-Cats, Richie and I discussed a couple of the coach's calls during the game. He was a coach in the huddle and when he had a feeling at that moment and suggested I change the call, I trusted his judgment. I had done it many times before when Richie asked, and I had tremendous respect for my sit-up partner and teammate. He wasn't afraid to make a gutsy call when the game was on the line. He wasn't guessing— he never did—this instinct was based on studying the opponent and our preparation.

For me personally the 1989 season ran the full gamut of emotion, from a terrible selfish mistake I made in a game versus the BC Lions on September 30 late in the regular season, to hoisting the Grey Cup in November. Throughout that season, I had become close to Richie and this helped me to grow as a player and a person, and I did it, because to Richie, the guy beside him in the locker room is a person first and a teammate, or an athlete, second. He was sincere and honest, and he was always there to support you or to give you a push if he felt it was needed.

I remember covering Richie as a TSN analyst when he was a head coach in Edmonton and hearing rumblings that he was going to be "too nice a guy to be a head coach." I tried to explain on the air that the players he is coaching shouldn't ever mistake his smile and non-abrasive approach as soft. Richie was a competitor, and he expected the same from those around him. He had his own style of getting the best out of players, which at times could have been misunderstood, but he was all business when he was preparing for a game or when he crossed the stripe. He rarely showed his emotions, or at least he rarely showed that he was angry or mad. In fact, I used to laugh that when he did get pissed off, which was rare, he would always keep just enough discipline to refrain from cursing. Most grown men when angry on a football field let loose with the curse words, but for Richie it was always "frick", or "shoot," or "dang." In fact to this day I don't think I have ever heard Richie Hall curse.

Richie's first year of coaching in the CFL was my last year as a player in Saskatchewan, and when I heard he was making the transition I initially thought that a situation like that may be uncomfortable. It wasn't, because Richie made sure it wasn't. There was a new coach-player line that we both had to respect, but he trusted my opinion, and I believed in his philosophy, and we always had an excellent working relationship.

Richie isn't just a former teammate; he is and always will be a great friend. He has been an opponent I admired, a teammate I leaned on, and a coach I have respected as an analyst. The teams that he has worked for have always had a top-ranked defence, which is why he is considered one of the great minds in the game today. However, as good as he is as a coach, he is an even better person.

PRELUDE

Leiper's Fork, Tennessee—fast forward— to Langenburg, Saskatchewan

"Smoke and Mirrors" refers to Richie's coaching philosophy. Every athlete and team has strengths and weaknesses. The goal of coaching is to accentuate those strengths and disguise the weaknesses to gain a competitive edge.

In theory, having superior talent in football should always win and often does, but developing and executing a good game plan can quite often be the great equalizer. Great coaching alone will never win championships, but effective coaching that excels with smoke and mirrors is the recipe for upsets and levelling the playing field.

In Richie's three decades in the CFL he has seen and experienced his share of upsets and overachieving teams. Consistently getting his defenses to be in the top third in the league is one of his hallmarks. If one could find the proper metric to measure overachieving success by getting the most out of your teams, Richie Hall teams would have consistently been near or at the top of getting the most out of your players. This isn't just my bias, but the bias of people in the know. Sometimes "just" making the playoffs and being eliminated early is a huge achievement in itself, especially for a team on paper that many predicted would be near the bottom of the standings. Many of the teams Richie has been part of have been highly entertaining overachievers.

Long-time teammate and TSN analyst Glen Suitor echoed this sentiment: "Richie Hall defences are usually at or near the top of defensive stats. Somehow he has coached his teams for over 20 years and has achieved a respect few others have achieved. I have interviewed a lot of coaches and offensive coordinators in my TSN tenure, and a reoccurring theme if you are an opposing offence is, you know you're in for a battle to score on a Richie Hall-led defense."

Peter King is *Sports Illustrated/SI's* premier NFL writer with his weekly multi-page column (very few writers get a multi-page column in any publication) and the insider of NBC's "Football Night in America," which is the feature Sunday evening game of the week. In 2014 Peter and his wife did a Western Canada tour of the West Division for SI's daily online blog. In each city, when he interviewed coaches, general managers, and players, he'd ask who were the best at what they did in the CFL. While being interviewed on Roughrider radio he said:

This Richie Hall. I kept hearing his name when I'd ask who some of the best defensive coordinators are in this league. If there is a defensive genius, the "G" word, in the CFL on the defensive side of the ball, I kept hearing his name. Richie Hall defenses are consistently among the toughest to score against, and it's been this way for over twenty years. I also heard that he is among the top humanitarians in the CFL, too. His name came up in each CFL city we visited. People speak of him with huge respect both on and off the field. He's the kind of person I was hoping to hear about as I asked questions.

This was in July 2014 while I was sitting in my little writer's cabin just south of Nashville in Leiper's Fork, Tennessee, listening to my Riders on the net. I could get most of their games through ESPN, ESPN3, NBC Sports, and a few other streams from around the world, including New Zealand. But I'd listen to the pre-game shows on CKRM online before every game. As King was talking I started writing as quickly as I could because Richie and I were in the preliminary stages of talking about a book. If Peter King used the "G" word, this was like getting knighted by the royalty of pro football insiders.

Of all people steering away from the "G" word it would be the self-effacing, humble by nature, never count your chickens before they hatch, Richie Hall. The "G" word can be thrown around rather loosely in the sports world, but nonetheless Peter King didn't refer to any other CFL'ers as genius as I re-read his 2014 daily blog. Regardless, Mr. Hall has the respect of his peers, the people that know the game inside and out. Whether he is a genius or not—Mr. Hall is good at what he does.

Richie, whom I am taller than by one inch, and I have known each other since the fall of 1988. We have maintained a friendship ever since, a friendship I treasure that goes much beyond our mutual love for football. We share our desire to be humanitarians, a similar faith, philosophizing about the deep issues of life, literally crying together after romantic heartbreaks, seeing the joy in my friend winning those three Grey Cups, and watching him evolve into one of the greatest coaches in pro football history (he'll probably get annoyed with me for typing that—but it is true). On each occasion he won a Grey Cup, he bought me a program and autographed it with a personal message. Of all my sports memorabilia, I treasure those programs the most. Okay, a close second after some curling trophies and medals my teams have earned over the years.

I am a notorious, some say anal, journal note taker. Often with Richie I'll jot notes as he chats, or later that evening pull out my journal and record his life and sports insights. I have filled up napkins with notes in Vancouver, Calgary, Edmonton, Regina, Winnipeg, Hamilton, Toronto, Colorado Springs, Fort Qu' Appelle, Yorkton, Saskatoon, Dafoe, Wainwright, St. Vital, Marsden, Chauvin, and some other little burgs I am sure I forgot about. Early into the 2000s I started to seriously think about a book with Richie, and how it would have some serious merit. In almost every chapter of this book I referred to my journals from over the years…and those napkins.

And then, my primary job in 2015–16 was to put this book together with added interviews from friends, family, colleagues, and Richie himself. My life has been enormously enriched writing and researching *Smoke and Mirrors*. Richie Hall has a story to tell, a philosophy of life and coaching that could enrich the serious football fan and the non-sports fan who simply wants to enlarge their soul. This book is not so much autobiographical (yet it is), as much as two friends who have shared their hearts over the years, with me observing the life lessons for three decades and recording his stories and life lessons for the world to read and be inspired.

Richie Hall is an inspiring man both on and off the field. He is known by his friends and colleagues as a huge overachiever, who inspires those around him to defy the odds, take some calculated risks and live life to the fullest. My favorite quirky stat about Richie Hall is he has never been on a football team in the NCAA or CFL in 35 years to finish first. Never! Yet, three Grey Cup championships! Is this some sort of record in the annals of football history at the highest levels? This was one of those rare research occasions Google failed to find the answer. If this is not a record, he would definitely be in the top one percentile, if there is a top ten for this kind of quirky, yet significant, achievement.

As one studies the teams he has been part of, his teams' improvement levels remind me of former MLB player and manager Billy Martin's managerial career. Yes, battlin' Billy Martin, a persona almost the opposite of Richie Hall.

Both were hugely respected by the players who played under their leadership and respected by their coaching peers. Every team Martin managed in Texas, Detroit, Oakland, Minnesota, and New York improved each season, and if there was a dip, it tended to be minor at best. Martin was known for turning losing teams into contenders—another manager/coach who excelled with smoke and mirrors. Both men did the bulk of their coaching in rebuilding or re-tooling circumstances. And both men were part of championship teams on multiple occasions. They were brilliant men who learned the tools of their trade.

Once again, Richie would probably not agree with my next assessment, but to use a Hollywood icon to compare, he is one of the Yodas of pro sports. The analogy may be more apropos as one goes down this trail. Yoda spent much of his life out in the outposts of his universe in Dagobah. I'm not saying Regina and Winnipeg are outposts, but for many sports fans beyond the Canadian borders, the perception of the Canadian prairies is like Dagobah. But is that a bad thing? Think of all the sports players and coaches who got their start, and often made their mark, on the great plains of North America: Phil Jackson of NBA fame; almost 25 percent of the NHL Hall of Fame; Bud Grant, a member of both the CFL and Pro Football Halls of Fame (NFL); Roger Maris, who some still believe is the one-year home run king; the bulk of world-class curlers who essentially gave the Olympics the newest oldest winter sport. And iconic CFL stars like Lancaster, Reed, Campbell, Clements, James, Mini Mack Herron, Stegall, Ploen, the Lincoln Locomotive Leo Lewis, Bill Baker the Undertaker, Elgaard, Austin, Walby, and Dressler, to give the short list.

Never finished first—can you believe that? But three rings and a ton of playoff wins. Smoke and mirrors. There are a lot of factors that go into winning a championship or at least contending, one of which is coaching. As Richie often says:

The best any team can hope for is to have a chance. That's my goal as a coach. There are no guarantees in this game or life, but all we can do is work hard to at least put ourselves into a position to have a chance.

FIRST QUARTER

IT ALL BEGINS

SECTION ONE

★ ★ ★ ★ ★

CHAPTER 1

57 Days in '89

"I can't believe it!!!"

Those were Richie Hall's words as Dave Ridgway's 1989 Grey Cup game-winning field goal went right down the middle of the uprights.

If you were a die-hard Saskatchewan Roughrider fan in the 1980s, 1989 will go down as one of your favourite life memories ever, not just as a fan, but ranking up there with having a child or accomplishing something you have dreamt about or worked for years to accomplish. Hyperbole maybe, but probably not if you are an honest Saskatchewan Roughrider fan!

If you were a CFL fan during this era you'll probably smile and say, "It was about time some good fortune came the way of Rider Nation." If you are a Hamilton Tiger Cat fan you might say, "It was payback from our Grey Cup win seventeen years earlier over the Riders on a last-second Ian Sunter field goal, but it was a heck of a game with Tony Champion making one of the greatest catches ever to tie the game at forty with barely a minute to play." If you are an Edmonton Eskimos fan, you'll remember your greatest regular season ever (16–2) snatched away in the Western Final at Commonwealth Stadium with a near dominant Roughrider performance from the second quarter on.

Over the years both Richie and I have heard from serious to casual fan alike that the 1989 Grey Cup game was a yellow highlight moment in most people's sports psyches. In Canadian sports history it ranks up there with the 1972 Canada-Russia series as to where were you when that Game 8 Paul Henderson goal was scored in Moscow (Grade 9 French class in Langenburg, Saskatchewan), or, "Where were you when the Golden Goal was scored by Sidney Crosby when the Canadian Olympic men's hockey team finally captured Olympic Gold in 2002 in Salt Lake City, Utah, after a 50-year wait? (Calgary, Alberta, with the Brown family)." And, for the record, I was at my home with a handful of close Rider fans in the metropolis of Ribstone, Alberta, with my pregnant wife while she was feeling internal kicks from my son who would be born a couple months later. Quite ironic actually, as that 1989 game is simply referred to as "The Kick"! So it was natural that we named my son Reed after the most famous Roughrider of them all. And yes, Reed is a Rider fan!

But…the story of the '89 Grey Cup championship had a tipping point. Like a Shakespearean play, tragedy or near-tragedy preceded a glorious ending. September 30, 1989, was one of the strangest endings to a football game—ever! No hyperbole intended. This was bizarre!

One image I will never forget is #7, Richie Hall, throwing his hands up in disbelief about what just happened and was about to happen. Mr. Hall was the closest player from either team from what just happened. He was an eyewitness. The playoffs, almost guaranteed at this juncture of the season, were now in some serious doubt. Forget the Grey Cup dreaming, the playoffs were in jeopardy. I have asked him on a few occasions what he thought or said during that moment.

His answer, "I can't believe it!"

What we are about to describe is so horrible. Being on the losing end of it—as a fan, I had to grab my coat, put on my walking shoes and go for a very long walk to process what just happened, and how another promising Roughrider season was on the verge of collapse. I was not the only one who either sat by the television set totally gobsmacked, or went for a long walk or drive to clear my soul of the devastation. I was quite surprised by how many people said that game shook their loyalty to the core. Maybe we were Canada and football's equivalent of the Chicago Cubs—lovable, suffering, heartbreaking losers when it came to championships, yet playing such an entertaining style of football for the most part. Teasing us like the best-looking, charming, suave girl or guy in college (Rider Nation covers the genders), but reality being what reality is—a million-to-one shot! Since my degree is in theology, maybe my cries were more like prayers, which God actually considered. Maybe the whole of Rider Nation was crying out to God and He felt a tinge of mercy to throw down to the central part of the Canadian prairies. Regardless of the mysteries behind the scenes, September 30, 1989, was a day to never forget.

But 57 days later…57 glorious days later, the Roughriders pulled off one of the greatest comebacks and dramatic finishes in any championship game or sport anywhere on this planet.

But first, what happened on September 30, 1989? This promising Rider team was off to their best start since the Ronnie and George era over a decade earlier, at 4–1. Then the injuries started, then the wheels came off for a bit, and the team suffered through a four-game losing streak, losing close ball games. But the Roughriders started to turn it around, playing very good football, and headed into that September 30 matchup at 6–6, in the driver's seat in third place and the final playoff spot, with their sights set on the second-place Calgary Stampeders, and a possible home semi-final date versus those Stampeders. Two weeks earlier they defeated the 9–1 Edmonton Eskimos who were on a dominant seven-game winning streak, and were setting two CFL defensive records. At this ten-game juncture the Eskimos had allowed the fewest points ever and were on pace to allow the fewest yards ever defensively. The Riders put up 45 points against this daunting Eskimo juggernaut. Many of the CFL pundits were saying these were clearly the two best teams in the CFL, and if the Riders could stay healthy, watch out.

Now, consider this scenario as they were to face off against the Matt Dunigan-led BC Lions. The Lions were chasing the Riders for the last playoff spot, gaining some momentum after a brutal 0–5 start to the season. The Leos were now at 4–8 coming into Taylor Field. This was not your typical two-point game in the standings. If the Riders win and go to 7–6 and drop the Lions to 4–9, they aren't just three games ahead of the Lions, but four games ahead with five games to play because of the tiebreaker having won two out of three versus BC. But if BC wins, going to 5–8 and dropping the Riders to 6–7, they are only a game back, but they now have the tiebreaker if they finish even at the end of the season. The reality is if the Riders win, they are only one Roughrider win away from the playoffs or one Lions loss away from the playoffs, with a month to go in the season. This is huge!

So…with absolutely no time left on the clock, but time for one last-gasp play, and the Riders up 30–25, the Lions went into "Hail Mary" mode. They were at midfield and needed a touchdown to win. All the Riders had to do—which they had done dozens and dozens of times in their history in this situation—was to drop back their DBs (defensive backs) and linebackers, and keep the Lions receivers in front of them. Let them catch the ball or be in a position to simply knock it down. This is as long a shot for a victory as there is in football at any level, especially the pro level.

Hall of Fame quarterback Matthew Dunigan dropped back to pass and threw the football about as far as he could throw it. He threw it to the Lions' receiver, David Williams, around the Rider 15-yard line. Glen Suitor, whom David Archer of the former Sacramento Gold Miners and Edmonton Eskimos once said was the best safety he had ever faced even after his seven seasons in the NFL, was right beside the Lions receiver. Richie was the next-closest Rider DB. All they had to do was let the receiver catch the ball, tackle him, and the game would be over and they would be only one game away from the playoffs. This was beyond routine. Suitor saw his man about to catch the ball and hit him almost as far as Elphinstone Street, knocking the receiver before the ball reached him. Everyone watching the game knew it was a clear pass interference penalty. There was no booing or grumbling from the fans toward the officials. The silence in Taylor Field, Regina, Saskatchewan, was deafening, except for a very small contingent of BC Lions fans.

Richie just threw his hands in the air and said, "I can't believe it!"

The Lions had one more play with no time left on the clock. Dunigan dropped back again and threw it into the end zone. This time the Rider DB, Albert Brown, was clearly beaten, so Brown did what any desperate DB would do and committed a "good" pass interference penalty. Richie looked up from across the field where he was covering another Lion and stared in disbelief.

All Richie could say from the opposite side of the end zone was, "I can't believe it!"

The officials placed the ball on the one-yard line. This was the third play where there was no time left on the clock. Taylor Field was in a state of utter shock. The teams lined up knowing the next play would probably be a quarterback sneak, which Dunigan favoured with his strong offensive line. No secrets, the teams lined up mano to mano. No time left on the clock!

The Lions snapped the ball; Dunigan did what Dunigan does so well, and plunged straight ahead for the go-ahead touchdown and the win. But…he fumbles the ball. Rider fans almost let out a collective sigh of relief. But Dunigan, alert to what is happening, falls on the ball as it crosses the goal line. The Lions win 32–30 and pull within a game of the Riders, and the potential tiebreaker is theirs as well.

The only words in Richie's head are:

"I can't believe it!"

The odds actually favoured the Lions down the stretch. The Riders' final three of five regular season games were on the road, with the additional quirk of having to play the second-place Stampeders in three of those five games and the CFL-leading Eskimos in the other, who would eventually finish with the CFL's first-ever 16-win season at 16–2. The next week would be against the very tough Calgary Stampeders squad, coming off arguably the most devastating loss in Roughrider history. This loss shook the team and shook them hard enough that head coach John Gregory actually brought in a psychologist, who stayed with the team over the next 57 days—some would say a significant part of the turnaround.

What happens next is one of the most inspiring stories not only in CFL history, but in sports period. There is a whole book that could cover the next 57 days, but we'll fast forward.

In a couple of Roughrider radio interviews with John Gregory from the late 1990s and 2015, he talked about that September 30 hit in 1989:

Yes, we were in shock. We all felt for Glen Suitor. He was a great ball player, an all-star. In the preceding weeks I was telling Suitor to get more aggressive and to lay some serious licks on receivers he was covering. Not to hurt anyone, but to send a message, because Glen was capable of big hits and he was our safety patrolling the middle of the field. He laid a pretty good hit on that Lion receiver, but in that situation of course needed to wait a half second, let him catch the ball and deliver the hit. It's so easy to criticize what he did on that play, but to his defense he was reacting and it was a split second.

This could have destroyed our team. We gave the game away. I have never seen anything like this—ever. But the way the team responded was amazing. This galvanized us like nothing else. We knew we had the team to make a serious run, but the psyche was fragile, very fragile. Finger-pointing could have gone crazy both at players and coaches. To Suitor's credit he took full responsibility, and was almost flawless for the rest of the season. That says a lot about his competitiveness and character.

The rest of October and November we stopped calling ourselves the Roughriders and called ourselves the 89ers. Our psychologist we hired also encouraged the players to tape up their ring fingers to remind them of what the goal was. Did everyone take this seriously? Of course not, but somehow that game and the internal galvanizing we had to do came together. That team played incredible football the rest of the way. We went 6–2 counting the playoffs, with that one loss being a total nothing game for us and Edmonton in our final regular season game, as we did finally clinch that playoff spot the week before.

As Richie emphasized, the team became battle hardened and didn't care what environment they played in, home or away, playing in six road games in those final eight games counting the playoffs.

What every CFL fan knows about 1989 is that 57 days later the 89ers (a.k.a. Roughriders) won the most thrilling Grey Cup game ever: 43-40 on a Dave Ridgway (Robokicker) 35-yard field goal with two seconds left on the clock. The turnaround was complete. Bob Poley from Hudson Bay, Saskatchewan, snapped the ball, Glen Suitor was the holder, and Robokicker did what Robokicker almost always did.

Glen Suitor rebounded from adversity like few people Richie had ever witnessed. Richie observed up close and personal how Suitor made huge contributions down the stretch. That play could have toned down Glen's aggressive style of play, maybe for the rest of his career. Over the next five games he had five interceptions, returning one for a touchdown, and played as aggressively as he ever had, but within the agenda of the team. But over the next few days, the team clearly helped Glen realize they had his back regardless. Ironically, or Hollywood-ishly, Suitor not only held the ball on that second-last play of the Grey Cup, he then was the last man to touch the ball and carry it out of bounds as the clock in SkyDome wound down and made it official:

September 30 transcended the game for me in a big way. To this date it is the biggest life lesson ever for me. I strongly considered an early retirement from football. I never slept for even one second that night. I was physically ill. I had let my teammates down in the worst way. I absolutely dreaded facing my teammates the next day.

I had got into a battle with David Williams of the Lions for the entire game. Then I committed that fateful pass interference penalty. I was determined to take him out of the game from the opening kickoff. Not to physically hurt him, but to get in his head. Williams and I had an ongoing battle that whole night. No matter how much you study or prepare for a game, there will be times you have to fight off personal agendas that can creep into a game. I made a horrible, selfish decision. For a split second I let my guard down, I let my personal agenda become bigger than the team. I won't justify away what happened. I can't.

I have been asked was that the turning point for our team, as we really did come together even more after that game. Maybe it was a factor, or maybe even the tipping point, but to say that was the reason we won the Grey Cup is too much for me. So many factors go into a championship team. The next week was an interesting week for me. Along with Head Coach John Gregory's encouragement, I faced the music with the media as best as I could. I did every request. Really, three-quarters of the fans were supportive. My teammates and coaches were unbelievable. Gregory was quick to tell me I was still his safety. I sat next to Richie in the locker room during the season, and he reinforced to me it was "just one play." Players like Ray Elgaard, Kent Austin, Dave Ridgway, Bob Poley, Bobby Jurasin all said or did things to show me they had my back. It was so humbling. Jurasin gave me this book of quotes that he liked which was all about courage, fighting adversity, how to overcome failure. I read it. Richie was Richie. We made a pact at the beginning of the season that before practice or a game we'd be beside each other and hold each other's legs during the sit-up routine. Richie told me, "Let's keep doing our thing, nothing changes." Little things like that rebuild your confidence. I admired Richie and always had looked up to him as one of the best players in the league, definitely one of the smartest I could learn from in so many different ways. That meant a lot to me.

Honestly, I vowed for the rest of my life I wouldn't make a selfish decision that would affect my teammates or colleagues like that night at Taylor Field. It was as if I had clarity like never before. I promised myself I would play the rest of my career at full speed with little regard for my own well-being. I'd play every play like it was my last. I know we often as athletes say this, but from that point on, I really believed it and played that way. September 30, 1989, transcended my whole life, it was that life-changing.

After the on-field celebrations I found a private spot away in the locker room, away from everyone and everything, and literally cried like a baby. Gratefulness, support, love, or knowing how much we as teammates cared deeply for each other, second chances, being part of such a special family of teammates. I was overwhelmed with so many emotions.

Another Roughrider who was only yards away when Suitor laid that hit on Williams was 16-year veteran Dan Rashovich, a gritty Canadian-born linebacker, special teams dynamo. Dan and Glen had been college teammates at Simon Fraser so knew each other well and what each other brought to the field. They had nothing but respect for each other. Dan was also on the field for The Kick. I was able to track Dan down at Richie's 25th annual Red Cross fundraiser in Yorkton, Saskatchewan, during a horrible armyworm epidemic. Dan joined me on a golf cart between shots to share his thoughts of those 57 days in September. The golf greens looked like there were little waves, as thousands upon thousands of these armyworms invaded southeastern Saskatchewan. We laughed as Dan had to putt over these prairie hazards. Maybe it was serendipity as this was a golf day we'd never forget, as September 30 still felt like yesterday to Dan. As Dan started to talk about the 57 days in 1989, his eyes lit up. He told his foursome to skip his shots (it was a best ball tournament); it was like he never forgot even the smallest detail. September 30 was a tipping point, a galvanization of the '89 Saskatchewan Roughriders. In Dan Rashovich's words:

Of course I remember that play like it was yesterday. I was on the field. I remember looking back and seeing the ball thinking that we will let them catch the ball and tackle the Lions receiver or break it up. Richie and Glen had him surrounded.

Instead, Glen hit the receiver well before the ball got there. Unbelievable! It's like Richie didn't know what to say. There was absolutely no time left on the clock. Next play because of the penalty, still no time on the clock and Albert Brown takes a PI in the end zone. Crazy! Then Dunigan gets the ball on the one-yard line and I am right there. I see he fumbles the snap and regains the ball. I was so close to potentially getting that ball as a fumble and us winning the game. That was a real downer. Heartbreak! We were playing a safe prevent defense on Suitor and all we had to do is let them catch it and it's done. The playoffs pretty much guaranteed, and now we were in a precarious situation.

For me, I was obviously in shock; it was like you wondered what happened because the game was supposed to be over. Well the game is never over! Whether you are up or down in regards to the score, especially in the CFL. For me, I have always known this because of some other past experiences. One time when I was with the Argos, a couple years before I got to Saskatchewan we scored 21 points in 90 seconds and won the game.

Back to September 30. This is a team game, and you win and lose as a team. I was never upset at Glen for that, or Albert; things happen and the most important thing is to be resilient mentally and physically. I knew these guys came to play and were hurting. I remember the fans being so upset and wanting Glen's scalp. He was a man about it and faced the music. He went on to have a great season and was a huge part of us winning the Cup. He had a great game in the Western Final against Edmonton as well, with all the safety blitzes we ran. The scheme we ran against Edmonton in the West Final is again a team thing. Everybody had to do their job. It just so happened that certain people were let go to be free on the blitzes while others were covering or rushing. The big turning point play of that game was the hit by Eddie Lowe on Tracy Ham, then the recovery by Albright and the coverage by our LBs and secondary. Ham had to pump and pull the ball down that created a split second for Eddie to hit Ham. It was a thing of beauty. Watching Albright rumble sixty or seventy yards into the end zone. Wow! Man, I was on the field for that play, too.

It was a crazy season with that play against BC, knocking off the 16–2 Eskimos tight at Commonwealth, all the injuries, the four-game losing streak, etc. It was after that September 30 game that we began wearing the tape on our ring finger for where the Grey Cup ring would ultimately be ours. Definitely tested us as a team and brought us together. And, just for the record I was also on the field blocking for Suitor and Ridgway on that winning Grey Cup field goal in Toronto. I remember thinking, "Don't miss your block. Do whatever it takes to give them time." Actually, I wasn't too worried; I was just reminding myself to do what I knew I could do. I knew I could beat my man long enough for The Kick.

Richie will never forget those 57 days in 1989. Going from such a promising start to a new season, the four-game slide, the apparent recovery, then the bottom feeling like it fell out in late September, and then the gutsy turnaround, and arguably the most sensational Grey Cup in history (and the CFL has had its share).

Richie says:

*It was like the old ABC **Wide World of Sports**, "The agony of defeat and the thrill of victory."*

September 30 was my lowest moment or feeling ever as an athlete. Who would have known only fifty-seven days later I would experience what is still the biggest thrill I have ever had in sports.

When The Kick went through the uprights at SkyDome in Toronto on November 26, 1989, all I could think and say was…

I can't believe it!

CHAPTER 2

1989 Part Deux!

(The Rodney Dangerfield League of Pro Sports!)

"The year that changed the world!"
- *Time* magazine, June 18, 2009

(20-year retrospective on our fast-paced changing planet)

"I can't believe it!"

In reviewing 1989, one huge thought hit us: 1989 was a linchpin or tipping-point year like few others in world history. This is not an overstatement.

Consider the following:

- Communism officially tumbles:
  - Poland declares independence through the efforts of Solidarity in April.
  - Hungary becomes independent in May.
  - East Germany—the infamous wall comes down in November.
  - Czechoslovakia becomes independent, also in November.
  - Bulgaria breaks free of Communism in November and December.
  - Romania, known as one of the harshest regimes, has a successful coup in December.
  - Russia becomes independent in early 1990, but the seeds were planted in 1989; all but the paperwork was completed in 1989.

- Nelson Mandela begins talks to end apartheid in South Africa.
- The Cambodia–Vietnam war ends and an amazing economic transformation begins to uplift millions.
- The Ayatollah Khomeini dies, beginning a shift toward freedom in Iran.
- The Tiananmen Square protests happen in China, planting the seeds for major shifts in economic and foreign relations policies.
- The building blocks of the world wide web (HTML) developed by a scientist from the UK.
- GPS launched (on a serious side this is significant militarily— and hopefully on a humorous side—men no longer have to ask for directions).
- The Dalai Lama wins the Nobel Peace Prize.
- Two significant films are released that are part of popular culture: *Field of Dreams* and *You've Got Mail*.
- Salman Rushdie's controversial novel, *The Satanic Verses*, which upset a major part of the Muslim world, is published.
- And maybe this was prophetic: George Bush Sr. begins his presidency with these words, "And, my first act as president is a prayer. I ask you to bow your heads." (For the record we are non-partisan; many "prophetic utterances" have been uttered unawares…)
- And on the lighter side, yet significant, the Saskatchewan Roughriders win what TSN, Sportsnet, CBC, and the Canadian Press still call the greatest Grey Cup game, if not the most exciting final in any sports in Canadian history, as the Riders beat the Tabbies 43–40!

"I can't believe it!"

Richie's phrase seems to capture so much of the essence of the Saskatchewan Roughriders, whether good, bad, or horrific! For Richie Hall, Saskatchewan and the Canadian Football League were made for each other on so many levels: undersized, a smaller market when put up against that behemoth league just south of the border, yet highly entertaining, cerebral, underestimated, and understated.

"The CFL is GOOD!" The level of football is not that far off of the league to the south, if not for all its glitz, glamour, and hype. Highly entertaining, athletes with smarts and speed, and coaches who understand the game on both sides of the border, yet it is so humbly Canadian and understated at its core.

These next three or four paragraphs will be the only self-justification paragraphs in this whole tome. I'm just setting a stage. Richie felt slightly uncomfortable with this upcoming paragraph, yet understood completely my reasoning to type away.

"The CFL is GOOD!" according to Peter King, the prime football writer for *Sports Illustrated/SI* who came to Canada for a working vacation in the summer of 2014. He wrote a daily blog for the digital edition of SI as he and his wife travelled through the West Division of the CFL. One of his conclusions was the CFL is sometimes viewed by some as second rate because the pay scale of the players and coaches don't match the huge seven figure paycheques of the majority of players and coaches in the NFL. "Don't be fooled by the paycheques. People in football know there is virtually no difference in talent level with the CFL. The pay scale and the hype of the NFL throws people off." King said on a CKRM radio interview from Regina.

King went on to say, "People in football know that the CFL is a very thin line of talent away from the NFL, and in many cases equal in individual talent. The games and the rules have nuanced differences where some players could only play in the NFL and not the CFL and excel, but it goes the other way too, where some players could play in the CFL and excel but not in the NFL. I've been watching and researching this Roughrider defense. This is one heck of a defence. They almost set a record for points against last year. This Richie Hall must be one heck of a great defensive football coach."

Terry Jones of the *Edmonton Sun*, a football writer who is in two professional sport Hall of Fame writer's categories (NHL and CFL), once referred to the CFL as similar to professional baseball in Japan. Jones explained, "The CFL is better than AAA but not quite MLB. The Japanese league often competes with the MLB and has always held their own." Jones went on to talk about how the CFL and NFL often need different players in terms of size and speed at varying positions. The CFL is a highly skilled thinking man's game, whereas the NFL is highly skilled but often can get away with brute force.

And maybe the best quote of all time in putting the CFL into perspective is from Bud Grant, who coached the Winnipeg Blue Bombers to four Grey Cup titles and took an expansion franchise, the Minnesota Vikings, to four Super Bowls, winding up in both the CFL and NFL Halls of Fame. Grant is in his early 80s and still follows the two leagues. He was once asked by a reporter in the US, "What is the most exciting division in pro football?" Without missing a beat, Grant said, "The West Division of the CFL is the most exciting division in pro football year in and year out." Grant added, "You never said the best, but the most exciting in pro football." He never changed his answer.

In what many feel is typical Canadian downplaying fashion, we far too often under promote a fabulous product with over a century of history. Currently the CFL is ninth in overall average attendance per game for any pro sports league in the world. Higher than all South American soccer leagues. Greater than Spanish and Italian premier soccer leagues. Higher than all rugby leagues and all but one cricket league (India). The NFL average attendance is almost double that of any other pro sports league on the planet at 68,000. In some years CFL average attendance sneaks up to as high as fourth or fifth in the world. That's how close numbers two through ten are in any given season. There is no sports league that has the television, corporate, and marketing magnitude of our southern rival league. It's time to celebrate that the CFL is a consistent 'Top Ten' professional sports league. As we get off our CFL soap box, the CFL is situated in the second lowest population country after Australia and their Aussie Rules Football League, and those attendance figures between these two exciting leagues tend to fluctuate.

The bottom line is the NFL is the premier football league on the planet. That is without dispute. But the CFL is a high-quality product that is much better than the minor leagues, to use the baseball and hockey vernacular. Michelangelo, Leonardo, Rembrandt, and Van Gogh are maybe the NFL of artists, but Monet, Renoir, Picasso, and Vermeer weren't too shabby either.

The CFL is full of colorful history and charismatic personalities. We'll let you guess or Google if you aren't aware of the following: The Mud Bowl; The 13th Man; The Gizmo; The Kick; Moon to Germany, as the joke went—the longest forward pass in history; The Undertaker; Dirty 30; The China Clipper; The Ronnie and George Show; Argossssssssss; Oskie wee wee; The American Division; The Big Owe; The Atlantic Schooners; Taylor Field; The Grey Cup!

And of course this was the short list. A very short list.

The Roughriders and Richie seem to go together, yet we feel as though "we" have loaned him to our archrivals that we meet every Labour Day, and then return the favour for their "Banjo Bowl." But November 26, 1989, may have been the tipping point in Richie's career, and I don't believe this is overstating it; consider how one of the most popular players in CFL and Rider history was part of that historic team. Only the second Grey Cup win in Rider history, and Richie was a significant part of that championship team. He goes on to be the only Rider player/coach with his name on Canada's Holy Grail three times. The year 1989 changes things on the world scale, but also for Richie. He now has Grey Cup on his resume. He has shelf life as he approaches a decade in the league. His reputation as a playmaker, good teammate, and thinker keeps growing.

People are beginning to notice coach potential. Maybe Richie doesn't fully believe this yet, but others do. His old high school coach and mentor Mr. Steve Hisamoto in Denver is not shocked in the least that Richie became a coach. Just for the record, Richie is very polite and respectful and still calls Steve "Mr. Hisamoto". Dwane Kelley and Junior (Jowel) Briscoe, his Colorado State Rams teammates, could see it coming. Both Dwane and Junior say Richie has that ability to take a complicated concept, simplify it, and then explain it to others on a level they'll understand. Ronnie Hopkins, one of Richie's best friends and a teammate when Richie played for Calgary in the early 1980s, says he could see the coaching brain in Richie right from the get-go.

From that 1989 team, John Gregory, the head coach, goes into retirement a few years later. Then for fun he gets an opportunity to coach an Arena Football League (AFL) team in Des Moines, in his home state of Iowa, the Iowa Barnstormers. Who is the quarterback he mentors for a couple of seasons, but future NFL Hall of Famer Kurt Warner.

Glen Suitor, who laid the PI hit on that fateful September 30 game versus BC, goes on to become arguably the best TSN colour man in all of football. On a side note, while living in the US for three years I'd get my American curling teammates to watch the CFL. Suitor impressed them all, blowing them away with his style and brainy way of explaining the game and the nuances.

Quarterback Kent Austin went on to win another Grey Cup in BC, but also became a coaching fixture in the NCAA and CFL. The Riders have only retired eight jersey numbers; two of the 89ers, Roger Aldag and Dave Ridgway, are among them. Canadian receiver Ray Elgaard, who retired as the all-time CFL catches and pass receiving yardage leader (the record has since been broken), was a key cog during his stellar career. Don Narcisse was also on that team and still holds the CFL record for consecutive games with a reception. Tom Burgess, the 1A backup quarterback who played a major role in beating the 16–2 Edmonton Eskimos in the 1989 Western Final, went on to Winnipeg and helped them win their last Grey Cup almost a quarter century ago.

Bobby Jurasin, the Roughrider sack leader and one of the most popular Riders ever, coached at Northern Michigan, a Div. II contender in the NCAA. Jurasin was the defensive line and strength coach at Northern Michigan for a number of years. He was always a crowd favourite with his trademark green and white bandana, which you can still spot here and there at Roughrider games across the country. One early Sunday morning I was attending a church service in Nashville close to Tennessee State, which produced arguably the strongest armed quarterback ever in Roughrider history, Joe "747" Adams. Near the beginning of the service, the minister Reverend Royal Byers, did two things. He is a good friend of mine who follows both the NFL and the CFL. Royal is a brilliant, funny man at an all-African-American church. Before asking us to turn around and introduce ourselves to a couple of people, he pointed me out and said, "I'd like to introduce my Canadian friend who joins us a couple times a year when he is down here for a writing project. Another bonus of him being with us today is he brings a lot of colour to the congregation." As I was the only Caucasian, Royal laughed and laughed, as did his congregation (for the record one of the warmest, friendliest churches one could ever visit). Then he asked us to turn around and introduce ourselves to three or four people.

Then I turned around and saw one of the biggest men I have ever met. We shook hands and he seemed quite shy at first. I asked what he did in Nashville, and he said he had just transferred down from Northern Michigan to play football at Tennessee State in Div. I. He said his defensive line coach gave him the nicest recommendations. So I blurted out, "Bobby Jurasin!" I immediately saw the biggest smile in Nashville.

He asked, "You know who Bobby Jurasin is? How do you know who he is? He's my favourite coach I have ever had at any level. I have learned more from him than maybe any coach in any sport I have ever played. Do you know he was an all-star up in the Canadian Football League, playing for a team called the Saskatchewan Roughriders? We all started watching the CFL because of him. What a great league and fun to watch. He challenged me, inspired me, and pulled as many strings as he could to get me to Div. I football. He is the coolest man. He challenges you but he is very kind and caring."

This huge, gracious man almost fell over when I said I was from Saskatchewan and they were my favourite sports team—period. And that one of my good friends named Richie Hall was Jurasin's teammate. He gave me the biggest bear hug I may ever have received in church or out of church. Then he said, "I just arrived here and don't know anyone yet, really. I promised my mama I'd go to church and here I am, and the first person I talk to knows of my favourite coach and has watched him play. What are my chances of meeting you, because you're a visitor and we both sat in the same section of church? This just warms my heart that I made the right decision because to be honest I was a little afraid not knowing anyone."

Richie says that was a special team in so many ways. The team had unbelievable chemistry and a locker room full of self-starting leaders. He is not surprised by how many of them continue to lead lives that are impactful in ways both in and out of football.

Richie doesn't bring up 1989 a lot, but he is always more than willing to talk about that team and that year. It's almost sacred to him, and he doesn't have to bring it up too often because people around him bring it up repeatedly. It was his first championship in football at any level. As he says often:

You don't always get rewarded for all the hard work and commitment with a championship. Championships validate, I get that, but all the heart lessons along the way are invaluable, whether you win a championship or not. I am grateful for the doors that have opened because of championships to make a difference; these are something I'll never take for granted. And, for what it's worth, so many of my 1989 teammates feel the same.

And I learned early on and am reminded of this truth often: if I or my teammates, coaches, players, and management stop working hard and doing all the little things that make a difference on and off the field, none of those championships would have ever happened.

1989 was an amazing year for the world and for the Roughriders; it's almost uncanny that we were part of 1989, too. It's so much like the long history of the Roughriders. Just keep showing up, keep plugging away, never give up, get your heart broken [he smiled], but who knows?! I can't explain destiny or what it really is, but 1989 was special on so many levels. If I can use the metaphor, all those things that happened for good on a world scale were laid by a foundation of good people around the world doing many little things right and for a good cause, or a cause greater than themselves. On a small scale, I understand this, but the lessons of that 1989 Grey Cup team paralleled the events of the world on a smaller scale. I couldn't be more thrilled than to win my first championship in football in 1989. What a year!

I still can't believe it!

CHAPTER 3

An Old Soul in a Young Body

This is more than a mere football book, although you will be entertained with many gridiron stories. Just as Richie Hall is more than just a football guy, this tome is primarily about life, using football as the prime metaphor.

The life lessons and principles we will share throughout the book are life essentials that can easily be transferred into other arenas of life, whether or not they involve sports. As long-time Calgary schoolteacher Lloyd Brown said after bringing Richie in to do some motivational speaking at Montgomery Junior High School:

The things Richie talks about in living your life to make a difference and following your dreams are good for anyone to listen to, whether they like football or not. I had students listen to Richie who have no clue about football who were clearly encouraged, and inspired to rethink their futures. I loved seeing a small handful of students roll their eyes that we were bringing a football player into their classroom, and then watching those same students hanging on his every word, and couldn't wait to go up afterwards and meet Richie.

Richie has played and coached for a variety of coaches over his career. He played for seven head coaches in his nine-year CFL career, three different head coaches at Colorado State, two more in high school, and various volunteer coaches as he grew up playing Pop Warner football as a kid. Richie has been an assistant coach in the CFL under eight more head coaches. In his almost 40 years of organized football, Richie has played or coached with just over 20 different head coaches. He has pretty much seen them all as far as philosophy and style: the good, the bad, and the sometimes ornery.

Get this! Every single coach he played for wanted this pint-sized, determined little bundle of dynamite and smarts in their arsenal. The only professional football coach to give Richie his "walking papers" was the then-winningest head coach in CFL history, Don Matthews. Matthews would have liked to have kept Richie around a little longer, but was astute enough to realize that he was reaching the end of his playing days.

As painful as the initial release felt, Richie knew over the next few months that Matthews was simply doing his job. Richie also knew that if he were in Matthews's place, he probably would have done the same thing. Matthews said, "Letting go of Richie was one of the hardest decisions I've ever had to make as a head coach. He's such a good person, but as a team we were moving in a new direction. He made my job real tough because of the kind of training camp he had. He's still a player."

Richie eventually accepted Matthews's decision:

I accepted his decision. I have no bones to pick with Don. Not that I liked it, but I felt good that I had left it all on the field and made his decision to let me go really tough on him. I've always told the players at training camp that your job is to play your hearts out and make our decisions as coaches as tough as you possibly can on who to keep and who not to keep.

Why this tome? Why Richie? First, Richie has a wealth of experience from 30 years in the CFL alone, the number of people he has played and coached with, and his reputation. His finest record may be the following:

No other assistant coach in the history of pro football has served under seven straight head coaches on one team, other than Oakland Raider Hall of Famer Fred Biletnikoff, and never got fired, but rehired by each new regime. Richie holds the record because he has coached longer and Biletnikoff has now since retired. Let this one sink in! What is it about Richie Hall that coaches of all kinds want him, his persona, his smarts, and his ability around?

Next, I am a writer and a student of people, and what people do that causes them to be "difference makers" in their spheres of influence intrigues me. This story isn't all about success, although by most standards of that hard-to-define word, Richie is successful. Richie was a playmaker and is a life difference maker. We can learn much from his life. Listen to what these following three life difference makers have to say about people like Richie:

Don't only practise your art, but force your way into its secrets, for it and knowledge can raise men to the Divine.

- Ludwig von Beethoven

One gets to know God and the way life works best, through their passions.

- Pope John Paul II

If one is master of one thing and understands it well, one has at the same time, insight into and understanding of many things.

- Vincent van Gogh

Richie would come under the category of an old soul. He seeks to master the craft of his chosen profession, and because of this has learned life lessons like Beethoven, Van Gogh, and John Paul II write about. There is an earthy wisdom that flows out of Richie. The idea that he is an old soul is reinforced by many of his close inner circle friends. His sister, Janice Watley, said something to the effect that he came out of the womb an old soul, always thinking, wondering, and pondering, saying things that made sense. Richie would never call himself wise and would be in his "aw shucks" mode as we snuck this sentence by him before officially going to publication. I have heard Richie say on many occasions:

I love the opportunity to challenge others to live up to their full potential, but at the same time I continually challenge myself as well. The learning never stops. I feel I am always in a continual learning mode myself. I learn so much in seeking to inspire other people and preparing workshops for speaking opportunities.

So why is Richie still in demand after all these years, entering his fourth decade in the CFL? Good looks and charisma only last so long in Canada's prairie "show me" provinces. There is an obvious substance to Mr. Hall, a man who is a person of conviction, a practitioner of what he speaks about, and a person who strives for perfection knowing he'll never get there himself. We can all identify with Richie in many ways because of his sincerity in being real and authentic, his underdog, undersized chances of making it in primarily a big person's profession. How many non-kickers have played and started for nine full professional seasons in pro football at only 5'6" and 165 lbs in the last 30 years? Not very many. He makes Doug Flutie look tall.

Richie is a classic case study for wisdom's life lessons and how to be a practitioner. Not to overstate, but he is one of sports' Beethovens or Van Goghs in the nuanced lessons he has learned at a deep level trying to master his craft. He is an observer of people by nature, a philosopher at heart—wanting to know how things work and why. He endeavours to live out what he learns, to try to pass these lessons on to the players he is responsible for as they perform on the field. He talks about these life lessons in his motivational talks to schools, businesses, civic groups, youth groups, men's retreats, women's seminars, churches, and sports teams. Like so much of the Canadian prairies, his talents are somewhat hidden to the rest of the country and beyond. He has so much to offer and has a relatable way of communicating these lessons in a fresh manner.

This is not a biography per se, but you will get to know Richie and his heart through his anecdotes, insights, and stories. Each chapter is a theme or life lesson that can easily be transferred into one's life. Many of the chapters are from speeches he has prepared and talks he has given over the last 30 years. He has spoken in over 300 communities on a wide range of motivational and inspirational topics. I once heard Richie give a brilliant talk on racism in Calgary. I heard him give a talk to high school students in rural Chauvin, Alberta, on following your dreams. While visiting in Regina he gave a talk on overcoming and embracing adversity. And, to top it off, he gave an inspiring sermon to a full church in Neilburg, Saskatchewan.

He was a player participant in the long-running Team Health program, run through the Roughriders that went to schools throughout the province speaking about making positive life choices and the destructiveness of substance abuse. Team Health and this type of program, which has been expanded over the years, is well into its third decade and has been carried on by many Roughrider players and coaches. Other teams such as the Calgary Stampeders, along with some NFL organizations, have adopted and modified this incredible program as well.

I first heard Richie speak at an Athletes in Action week-long event for junior high and high school students in the Wainwright, Alberta, area in 1989. Other communities in the school division such as Paradise Valley, Irma, Chauvin, and Edgerton also took part. Over 25 years later, these communities still talk about the positive impact of bringing in seven CFL players. He presented himself in his typical, down-to-earth, relatable way. He went out of his way to be approachable and humorous in the life lessons he was asked to present. The response from the students, teachers, and parents was incredibly positive, to say the least. I could see why he was asked on many occasions to make a repeat appearance. The church I pastored in this region brought him in four more times over the next few years.

What I like about Richie's approach is how he stays current with his stories and comes across as a cutting-edge, contemporary communicator. Much of his ability to relate so well with his audiences is from his social work background, which is one of his passions. Richie is a certified social worker who graduated from Colorado State, and at times has been employed as a social worker/counsellor. This is part of the reason he desires to inspire and challenge people to live up to their potential.

Richie Hall is a devoted, committed Christian. He will be the first person to tell you he is not perfect and has as many human struggles, fears, and insecurities as the rest of us. He has firm spiritual convictions or beliefs he uses to guide his life. Richie is not a polished classroom professor, but he has a gift for communicating concepts and breaking them down in easy-to-understand, practical ways. Although he shuns being the centre of attention at a social gathering, he is an extremely social person. Richie is not some complex, eccentric, quirky intellectual. He is a down-to-earth, well-read, approachable, neighbourly type. He likes to describe himself as a simple man, but as I have learned over the years, not simplistic. From my observations of knowing him since 1988, he is one of those rare souls who consistently practices the fundamental principles that give a person a chance of making a difference in other people's lives and in and around his vocation. He is definitely an old soul in a young body because of the way he has chosen to live. Too old to play in football terms, where a pro athlete's years are measured like dog years.

The initial reason for this book was that we felt the world needs a personal growth or inspirational leadership book with a twist, and a Canadian-based one, which is often rare. Yes, we are using an American born and raised subject, with a little Okinawa thrown in there, but Richie is an American or an International, as the CFL would call him. A landed immigrant married to the love of his life, Helen, who is a Regina woman. And maybe Richie is more Canadian than many of his Canadian neighbours for his better-than-average understanding of the sport of curling. Currently he is a Winnipeg Blue Bomber who still resides in Regina, the city he has called home more than any other community in his entire life. He has become a part of the fabric of not only Saskatchewan but of Western Canada.

Richie Hall's CFL experience is a bit of a snapshot of pure Canadiana: small in stature, in a resilient, sometimes perceived as underdog league that keeps on ticking and entertaining while being resourceful with what they have. The CFL is considered the furthest thing from a second-class professional league by those who are involved with high-level football. High-quality individuals generally run the football operations, from players to coaches to owners. Like any professional sports leagues, the odd rogue and hypermanic person gets involved, but these things have a tendency of sorting themselves out, like the Toronto Maple Leafs for much of the last half century at one end of the scale, and the St. Louis Cardinals or New England Patriots at the other end. The CFL has had the Shreveport Pirates and Ottawa Renegades, but these only seem to add to the folklore of the league.

The NFL, the mother of all media-driven leagues, respects the quality of person associated with the CFL, the oldest pro football league on the planet (the CFL officially formed in 1958, but Canadian teams in multiple leagues have competed for the Grey Cup going as far back as 1909). Hall of Fame NFL coaches such as Bill Walsh of the San Francisco 49ers fame, the Green Bay Packers' Vince Lombardi, Marv Levy of the Kansas City Chiefs and Buffalo Bills, and Bud Grant of the Minnesota Vikings often praised the virtues of the CFL and tried to raid their top players. We Canadians sometimes feel like the little brother or sister living in the shadows of the older and more populated neighbour to the south. Canadian football fans or casual sports fans often feel this way, and Richie being undersized, yet not under talented for his vocation, had to battle this misguided perception his whole life.

Richie is like the boy next door who has made the big time because of his humility and work ethic, along with the lessons he has learned and assimilated on his journey. His ongoing story reminds us that as Canadians, or underdogs in general, we can learn some pertinent life lessons from people living in our own backyards. We can use a Saskatchewan born and raised icon who has worldwide admiration and respect: Mr. Hockey himself, the pride of Floral, Saskatchewan, old Mr. Elbows, #9 of Detroit Red Wing fame, Gordie Howe. Howe showed that greatness and being a worldwide role model for so many can come from a lightly populated region of Canada. Even a casual sports fan in Florida or New Mexico, or up in the Arctic Circle region of Finland, would know who we are taking about right now.

Richie is an inspiration, showing us that it doesn't matter how big we are or where we are from; what matters is that we use our God-given talents, skills, and passions to the maximum. If we commit to learning all we can and apply those lessons with all our heart, who knows the difference we can make with our lives regardless of our sphere of influence, as Gordie Howe often said and Richie practices. This Gordie Howe nugget has impacted this writer for the last 50 years or so: "There's a reason God gave us two ears, two eyes, and only one mouth. That's why I recommend that we listen and observe twice as much as we talk." Richie is worth that kind of double take because he can tend to be on the unassuming side of life's ledger. This is part of his charm and influence.

There is a happily married couple living on Vancouver Island who came and listened to Richie speak in Chauvin, Alberta, back in that Grey Cup season of

1989. Richie talked about the hope in his soul trying to honour Christ with his daily choices. This spoke deeply to this couple of a dozen years. After his presentation they worked their courage up to introduce themselves. Richie had no idea their marriage was in a precarious position, on the verge of blowing apart. Richie shared his heart with them for almost an hour. As they put it:

We were blown away by his humility and approachableness. We quickly forgot about his celebrity as he made it comfortable for us to open our hearts up to him. We wanted to know more about this God he was talking about. He never preached at us, not even close, but shared with us how putting Christ first, which he explained was trying to follow His teachings and following what we already knew was right in our hearts, could make a difference in our lives and marriage. He encouraged us to consistently open our hearts to God and His strength, and things could improve. He never promised pie in the sky, but emphasized the importance of simply making daily loving choices that Christ taught. It wasn't complicated but it was powerful as we could see he believed what he said.

We both committed our hearts to follow Christ that night. Honestly we felt a peace we had never felt at this depth before. Hope! We decided we would go for some counselling, found a church we felt comfortable at, found some other people we trusted who also believed in a serious manner, and in time our marriage turned around. Going to hear Richie speak that night was our last attempt of trying to turn things around.

Over the years Wayne, Ann Tribe and Richie would touch base. They both seemed blown away by the strength and direction God could give a person, or a couple when they both committed to following a practical spiritual path. The spiritual foundation Richie has built over the years has been his inner hope and compass. He has found, the deeper he goes into his craft, that what works on the football field more often than not parallels what he has learned about faith. As Richie says:

Everything of significance I have learned that works on the football field, marriage, business, everything, has a spiritual foundation or root. Sure, things like a good work ethic, commitment, and practice can be found in spiritual principles, but then it goes deeper. How relationships are built on a team deepen as one commits to applying Jesus' teachings, whether people are aware of this or not. When people realize these things make a difference they usually know where the base is coming from. The stuff that works has a spiritual foundation. So when I see it happening in preparation for a game, then translating on the field, this just reinforces what I believe.

Even when we fail and how we handle failure is best fleshed out with a spiritual foundation as well. We are taught that one learns best when one embraces adversity sees an invisible hand in everything, seeks to learn the lessons, and sees things from a wider perspective. And I have learned when people learn to care for teammates, that this caring attitude, or love as my faith would say, translates on the field in a major way. The more players and coaches care for each other off the field, or behind the scenes, the more they start to pay attention or care about the little things on the field, and those are often the fine-line difference makers in competitive sports.

Richie likes actor Denzel Washington. He was in a movie called *Man on Fire*, playing a former hit man turned bodyguard for a young girl in a rich Mexican family. He is a man in inner crisis and takes a Bible along to read. Part of his job is taking the young girl to a Catholic-run school. Sister Anna is a feisty, lovable nun who introduces herself to Denzel and asks him a simple question upon first meeting. She asks a question Richie could answer with ease. Maybe it's a question we should all ponder from time to time:

Do you see the hand of God in what you do?

CHAPTER 4

"He Who Walks with the Wise Becomes Wise"

Teach-ability, coach-ability is the primary intangible Richie looks for in a player. As Jim Daley said, it's a quality that drew him to re-hire Richie as a defensive coach when he took over the Riders in 1996. Richie looks for this quality, but it's also a quality he possesses both in the game but beyond it as well.

I have heard Richie give many motivational and inspirational presentations over the years. What I have always admired is his ability to stay current with the times in order to relate to his audience. He knows his Bible as one frame of reference, but is definitely not "preachy" in any of his talks. He has a grasp of pop culture and current trends simply because of the players he coaches and the materials he reads. He tries to get a grasp of the audience he is going to speak to, and asks a ton of questions beforehand to better relate and win them over.

As teachable as he hopes his players are, I have seen this very attribute in him since day one. He is a lifelong, curious learner.. I am still amazed at times how he includes me in conversations about football and what I think about it. I have to remind myself he is the expert, but he is curious even from a fan's perspective. I am sure there are times he must inwardly shake his head, but he sure doesn't give one that impression. Long-time Regina friend Cindy Kearse says, "Richie puts you on the same level with him in any conversation. He obviously knows his business of coaching, but he doesn't come across as this arrogant, I've got it together person. He includes you in the conversation and you feel like you are contributing, even though he probably knows in many situations that the person he is talking with doesn't have a clue."

King Solomon said, "He who walks with the wise becomes wise." Richie is a good example of this. He is a treasure to be tapped into. As this story continues, enjoy the stories, but even more take in the life lessons and incorporate them into your life. We aren't promising a Grey Cup ring, or a Super Bowl appearance, or a shot at the Olympics. However, If you take to heart these life lessons, your life can be encouraged and/or your life can take on deeper significance You can make a positive difference in the lives of those around you.

As Vicktor Frankl, the great Austrian psychologist who suffered through and survived Auschwitz, wrote in many of his writings, "What people really want is meaning or significance in life, and this means more than public acclaim. This acclaim or success is the dessert of life, that's all."

There is a natural inclination inside all of us to make a difference with our lives. Most if not all of us have a passionate desire to become competent in our chosen field and to make our lives count within our sphere of influence. Is there a secret to becoming successful? Is there a magic formula, some fast track to accelerating this process? Finding success, or better said wisdom, often feels like searching for the eternal fountain of youth or the Holy Grail.

The quote from King Solomon, the famous King of Israel over 3,000 years ago who so impressed the Queen of Sheba, reminds us that this secret is probably no secret at all, but reminds us that we can all learn truisms to be applied from people who have made their mark with competence. Most of us want to become wiser with our lives and to capitalize on the dreams and talents we possess or are trying to develop further. Studying those who have achieved a certain level of success is a great place to start. Richie often says, "I enjoy tapping into people's minds to see what makes them who they are, and what makes them good at what they do. As Solomon says, 'He who walks with the wise becomes wise.' I don't know how wise I am, but I try and operate this way. None of us has it all together, and we can all learn from each other. Hopefully this makes me a better person, draws me closer to God, and helps me be a better coach and communicator."

By having a mentor, studying people we admire in history, or paying attention to those around us, knowledge can be transferable from person to person. Richie is big on how we can learn from anyone who strives to master their craft. A person we both admire greatly is Boston Celtic and NBA Hall of Famer Bill Russell, who was named the greatest team player of the last century by *Sports Illustrated* and HBO TV. He said many of his mentors for learning creativity and bringing it to the hard court were artists such as Leonardo da Vinci and Michelangelo. Russell was known as one of the major innovators with creating change in pro basketball.

Dr. Reg Bibby of the University of Lethbridge is a multiple bestselling author, sociologist, and follower of cultural and religious trends. The Gallup Poll people call him one of the best researchers in the world, and the best at covering religious trends. Bibby says something Richie has said for years and with which he concurs:

In our culture people would rather learn from people who have achieved in the fields of entertainment and sports, rather than those from the business world, academia, or theologians. Let's be brutally honest here, the average person would rather hear the truisms of the process of success from a Grey Cup champion, an Olympian, an Oscar recipient, or a Grammy winner than a prime minister or a president.

Like Babe Ruth used to say when people asked him why he could justify being paid more than the president of the United States, "I had better years than the presidents, so I deserve to be paid more." No one really disagreed with the Babe. People flocked to hear Ruth and his words of "wisdom," and his words have been credited with inspiring many people to pursue their dreams or to not give up when times of adversity came along. His words were even credited with helping speed up the healing processes for people he visited in hospitals. The Babe may not have been known for his scholastic achievements or being an academic wizard, but his words nonetheless carried an inspirational quality to those who gave him attention. And, in his vocation as a ball player, there isn't a player dead or alive that wouldn't mind a *Field of Dreams* experience with Mr. Ruth to pick his brain on the art of hitting, or playing championship baseball in a team dynamic. Mark McGuire even alluded to wanting to meet Babe Ruth in the next life at his press conference after breaking the single season home run record in 1999. This is not a knock on Ruth's intellectual prowess by any means, but he was considered wise in the ways of baseball and winning championships. This simply reinforces that we are all smart and are privy to learning wisdom; it's simply a matter of discovering how we are smart, and applying ourselves to the truisms we discover. We can learn from so many different sources, but we as a culture are drawn to the world of entertainment.

The wise person in discovering life truisms can be found in any field of endeavour. King Solomon also wrote that we can learn wisdom from many various sources. He challenged us to study the ant, to listen to our parents, to observe the hard-working farmer. The wise can be found in any sphere of life: "He who walks with the wise becomes wise." Thankfully this tome's chief subject is academically sound and proficient at his craft. Richie brings a lot of practical, earthy wisdom both from his personal life and from his involvement with high-level athletics.

Richie is going into his fourth decade as a motivational speaker throughout Canada. He understands the importance of a working knowledge of pop culture. He says his teaching philosophy for relating to professional football players, but also for relating with a public speaking audience or as a social worker, is as Dr. Reg Bibby emphasized:

If you want to relate to an audience big or small, even one on one regardless of age or venue, I have found three areas of life that always draw attention: music, movies, and sports. Really it doesn't matter what you are talking about, be it addictions, a civic banquet, a high school assembly or graduation, or a business setting. These are natural hooks to get the attention of your audience. Obviously, you still must have depth to your presentation, but nearly everyone can relate to music, movies, and sports, and the memories of these areas in pop culture put you and the audience on the same side in identifying with something you all enjoy.

A scene in the Academy Award winning film, *The Gladiator*, supports Richie's philosophy. The unknown gladiator was swaying public sentiment, and the Roman politicians were feeling threatened that their voices weren't being heard. One of the wise old senators said, "If you want to understand the hearts of the people, you won't find it in marble seats of the senate, but in the sands of the arena."

To relate to culture one must be near the heartbeat of pop culture, wherever this may find itself. Richie has been living and breathing in the sands of the arena for his entire adult life. In a sense he has been an underdog gladiator in North America's most popular sport. He is a person who wants to leave his mark on this planet, who has made his living in actual combat in our post-modern arenas or coliseums, and now coaches modern-day gladiators. What adds to his credibility is that he is a social worker by education and trade. One of his strongest desires is to challenge or inspire people to live up to their potential regardless of age. He wants to be a positive influence on as many people as he possibly can. He fully understands that his profession in the public eye can afford him more opportunities than most on a wider scale.

Richie has done something right in his almost 40 years of playing and coaching competitive football. Remember, he is the only known assistant pro coach, other than Fred Biletnikoff of the Oakland Raiders, to have survived seven head coaches of the same professional team in North America's big four team sports of football, baseball, hockey, and basketball. Please stop and soak in that previous sentence for a minute or two!

What's ironic is that Richie's last year in Calgary was Fred's first season in the CFL as an assistant coach with Calgary before he headed back to Oakland where he played in his Hall of Fame NFL career. People often forget that Fred came out of a one-year retirement to play for the Montreal Alouettes before beginning his coaching career. Richie says he used to talk with Biletnikoff a lot about the art of the game, especially between defender and receiver.

It is standard football policy after firing a head coach to bring in a new head coach who usually releases most of his assistants to bring in his own staff and start over. Richie was hired by Ray Jauch, then rehired by Jim Daley, Cal Murphy, Danny Barrett, Kent Austin, Greg Marshall, and Corey Chamblin. This is unheard of in pro sports, period! Jacques Chapdelaine is a long-time CFL offensive coordinator, spending the bulk of his years with the winningest CFL coach of all time, Wally Buono, in Calgary and BC. He enjoyed a lengthy journeyman career as a receiver in the CFL, then went on to help build the uber-successful Laval University football program, and was the head coach in their first Vanier Cup title in only their fourth year of existence. Since that championship no other school in Canada has won more titles. Jacques said this about Richie:

This is unheard of! What does this say about Richie's incredible skills and abilities? No one stays around like he has without your coaching peers knowing how good a teacher and motivator you are. Richie is obviously incredibly good at what he does, and to do this with often a losing team for much of his career is truly remarkable.

Greg Dutchak is a young man Richie has mentored since he was eight years old, from the little hamlet of Rama, Saskatchewan. They met at an autograph session with Greg's parents, Darrell and Monica, in nearby Yorkton. Richie took a liking to Greg and surprised him with a follow-up phone call. This has led to a lifelong relationship. Greg is a very gracious and grateful young man who admires Richie deeply and calls him his mentor, with good reason:

Richie is my mentor for sure. He has surprised me on a few occasions with my hockey and football teams, especially before big games, to encourage me. He is way more than a football player to my family and me. He has made special trips out to our family farm just to visit. That's a good three hours from Regina. He has got my family tickets to games, and always comes over to talk with us. Richie touches people beyond the game, way beyond the game. Honestly I want my character to be like his—humble, grateful, giving, kind-hearted, selfless, approachable, and thoughtful. When people meet Richie or hear him speak, they are affected in such good ways. It's more than wins and losses: that kind of even gets lost a bit, actually a lot You just want to be a better person when you think of him. I know my friends would say the same about Richie.

Allow Mr. Hall to inspire and teach you how to develop an old soul in whatever aged body you may be living in.

Ask yourself the following question as you read Richie's story:

What lessons can I incorporate into my life from the truisms Richie talks about, be it my vocation, personal life, or spiritual journey?

CHAPTER 5

Underdog Meets Pint!

If there was ever a sports marriage made in the heavens, Richie Hall and the province of Saskatchewan is the one. The 5'6" Richie, a.k.a. "Pint" as a player, meets Saskatchewan, the province barely a million people strong population-wise, in the smallest professional sports market in North America. Underdogs in having a century-old pro sports franchise and a defensive back turned defensive coordinator in generally what is considered a big man's game. Richie was the shortest, smallest player in his nine CFL seasons, other than a couple of placekickers. Richie has longevity, 30 years and counting in the CFL, as does the storied Roughrider franchise, which is the oldest professional sports team in North America west of the Mississippi.

Saskatchewan's small population base has always held its own in the world's competitive resource market, albeit many challenging years or seasons. But a bounce-back resiliency is in most of the population's DNA. So it is no secret that Richie became one of the most popular Roughriders and CFL players/ coaches of all time. Smallish, feisty, resourceful, smart, and quick—one could be describing the football man or the province he calls home, even though he is currently coaching the team's fiercest rival next door in Winnipeg. The "aw shucks" nature of a Saskatchewanite and Richie would be a compatibility dream for any online dating site.

Roughrider fans, casual or slightly fanatical, were extremely quick to adopt Richie as one of their own. Saskatchewan, with its known hospitable ways and its down-to-earth persona, was made for a soul like Richie. There is an intense connection and mutual respect for each other. But it is not only Saskatchewan, as CFL fans across the nation embrace him. I lived in Calgary for 22 years, Richie's first CFL home for five seasons. Over 25 years later I have met a number of people who still say he was one of their favourite Stampeders of all time. Former newspaper writer for the *Calgary Herald* Jeff Adams who was on the roster as a running back for the University of Western Ontario Mustangs and is currently the Communications Manager for Samaritan's Purse Canada, says:

Richie was one of my favourite athletes I have ever interviewed. Yes he was short in stature, but my goodness he was built like an athlete. He was so smart as a player and having the speed he had always got the fans out of their seats. I know he has been away from Calgary for a long time, but many of us still see him as a Stampeder.

Jim Hopson, CEO of the Roughriders from 2005–2014, in his book *Running the Riders: My Decade as CEO of Canada's Team* written with *Regina Leader-Post* sports writer Darrell Davis, had this to say about Richie, which captures why the province and those who have followed his career enjoy Richie so much:

Richie is special. He is absolutely what he appears to be—a wonderful human being. While Richie's defenses were criticized at times for being their bend-but-don't-break style, it is virtually impossible to find someone who dislikes him. He is unfailingly humble, polite, respectful, kind, and thoughtful. He is also highly intelligent, knowledgeable, competitive, and tremendously hard-working.

Hopson went on to say that Richie's time as a head coach in Edmonton was not a good evaluation of what he felt Richie could accomplish as a head coach:

Richie's time in Edmonton wasn't successful, with a 16–20 record and one playoff loss in two seasons. But the Eskimos were going through a difficult period as his staff and the organization never seemed to be a cohesive group. In the right environment, I believe Richie could have been successful.

Yes, the marriage of Richie and Saskatchewan seemed to be made in heaven, and those outside of Saskatchewan were happy for this marriage and often admired the union. Terry Jones of the *Edmonton Sun* adds to this admiration society. Jones, a member of the media category of both the Canadian Football Hall of Fame and the Hockey Hall of Fame, and a sure-fire addition to the Canadian Curling Hall of Fame as well, had nothing but admiration for Richie before, during, and after his time in Edmonton. Listening to a sports talk show while driving through Edmonton just after the firing of Richie by the Eskimos,

Jones had the following to say about Richie. I believe I have captured the essence of Terry's words as I had to pull over, grab my journal, and write down his insights:

Was this firing necessary? Good question. I understand it due to the nature of "win now" in pro sports. Do I agree with this mentality? Not always. In all my years of covering sports in Edmonton, I don't know if there was ever a more gut-wrenching firing because Richie is not only one of the nicest men in sports, maybe the nicest I have ever met. But, don't let that niceness fool you as being soft. He is extremely competent in what he does. He made some tough decisions while here, like when he had to let Rick Worman go as his offensive coordinator, and they have a good history of knowing each other. That could not have been easy.

No one in the business will argue this point about his skill level. I just wish the circumstances were different and hope he gets another chance. He'll find a job quite quickly I can assure you of this. Don't be surprised if he winds up back in Saskatchewan.

If there are a couple things I became aware of very early in my Saskatchewan upbringing, one is that the Saskatchewan Roughriders seem to find an uncanny way to emulate the province's ups and downs and its perceived underdog persona. Richie fits in well! Second, and maybe more uncanny, is how this franchise has a weird sense of history, and Richie is such a part of their ongoing history. If a Roughrider fan mentions a certain year or number to another fan, they know what they are talking about. For the uninitiated and for context, indulge us for a couple of paragraphs:

1910 – The year the franchise was born.

1923 – First Grey Cup appearance.

1928–32 – First North American pro franchise to lose five straight championships.

1946 – The official name change from Regina Roughriders to Saskatchewan Roughriders.

1951 – Dobberville!

1956 – The plane crash killing four all-stars flying back from Vancouver after attending a rare CFL all-star game, decimating the core of the team.

1963 – The year the Ronnie and George show was born, and "The Little Miracle of Taylor Field," the greatest CFL playoff comeback of all time versus the Calgary Stampeders, being 26 points down in a two-game, total-point series. Weirdly, Hamilton duplicated this feat versus Toronto in the 1986 two-game, total-point Eastern Final.

1966 – November 26, 1966, first Grey Cup win.

1972 – Tony "friggin" Gabriel I: last-second Grey Cup field goal loss to Hamilton set up by Gabriel after Gabriel catch.

1976 – Tony "friggin" Gabriel II: last-minute Grey Cup loss to Ottawa set up by Gabriel after Gabriel catch (obviously the angel Gabriel is not a Roughrider fan).

1977–87 – The Dark Ages! Eleven years is enough, the longest playoff drought in CFL history. Now get this—only the Riders... Ironically this record losing streak was set up by a phenomenal playoff run from 1962 to 1976, which was then the longest-ever CFL playoff run (15 years, plus 11 straight years in the Western Final, another record).

1989 – **November 26, 1989**, (and Saskatchewan declares November 26 a holiday forever) winning their second Grey Cup in what almost every Canadian media outlet has called the greatest championship in Canadian sports history, 43–40, next-to-last play of the game, The Kick by one David Ridgway.

1997 – Freak appearance in the Grey Cup with a gawd awful 8–10 record...but the province was cranked. The biggest roadblock, though, was a man named Doug Flutie of the Toronto Argonauts, honored as the greatest CFL player of the last millennium, who had a game for the ages. Oh well, April Wine played the halftime show.

2007 – Third Grey Cup victory at SkyDome.

2009 – The 13th man! Grey Cup loss to Montreal. On a personal note, the worst emotional year of this writer's life. Coincidence? I think not!

2013 – Fourth Grey Cup win at Mosaic Stadium at Taylor Field in Regina.

And as many of my Roughrider friends and "enemies" (loosely stated as the Roughriders are often everyone's second team) would say, this is the short list Let's continue the numbers game:

#23 – Ronnie Lancaster

#34 – George Reed

#36 – Robokicker (a.k.a. Dave Ridgway)

#44 – Roger Aldag

And for many, #7, one Richie Hall, the only Roughrider in history with three Grey Cup rings as a player and coach.

Saskatchewan doesn't do things like Wall Street, or Bay Street, or Hollywood. Saskatchewan does things like John Deere, or Dodge City (Saskatchewan has Moose Jaw with a similar colorful history), or *Rocky I, II, III, IV, V, VI*, and *VII* (if you count the 2015 film *Creed*). Saskatchewan and Richie Hall were made-for-each-other underdogs.

If there is ever a player who captured the spirit of Saskatchewan it is Mr. Richie Hall, who has just completed his 31st season in the CFL—nine as a player, 21 as a coach. Twenty-two years in Saskatchewan, plus nine years in Calgary, Edmonton, and Winnipeg. An immigrant, or International as the CFL likes to say, who parallels the makeup of the forming of this unique province. A man who left the province like so many others, but was welcomed back, and has left the province again, yet makes his home in the province.

And, typical of Saskatchewan, Richie has never finished first. Yes, you read that correctly. Richie Hall, in 31 years of professional football in a nine-team league (sometimes eight teams), has NEVER finished first—ever! He has never finished first in pro football or college football, not even at Colorado State in picturesque Fort Collins, Colorado. Yet, like Saskatchewan, Richie makes unique history on the big stage by being the only Saskatchewan Roughrider three-time Grey Cup champion as a player or coach.

Saskatchewan has always relished its role as the underdog province, able to compete on the world stage and compete well, much like 5'6" Richie Hall. It is a place that was once called the world's breadbasket, and for many still is. Rich in resources, and richer in the most precious resources of all, according to most of Canada's prime ministers—its people. Richie is a soul who came to a province "subtly rich" in things that matter—people and values. This may sound over the top, and will to some, but it's as close to regional reality as one may get. But, as Pierre Berton, one of Canada's most famous authors, once said observing this province, "Toronto does the least with the most, but Regina does the most with the least."

Richie personifies Saskatchewan, and maybe Canada, as the little brother to our friend to the south. Saskatchewan is not only farming and resource rich; It has produced the third highest number of NHL players of any province, or region, or country in the rich history of Canada's game. With a population of just over a million compared to Ontario's 13 million, Quebec's 8 million, BC's 4.5 million, and Alberta's 3.5 million, Saskatchewan has produced the second highest amount of pro football players over the course of CFL history. This may change slightly as our friends to the east in Quebec are rapidly catching up with their current explosion of talent. According to *Maclean's* magazine not too long ago, more CEOs, authors, and artists come from this prairie heartland than any other region. This is per capita in some cases and pure numbers in others.

What does this mean? Cool trivia, yes! But, there is also a collective spirit of being a competitive underdog this province loves to embrace. A collective spirit of overcoming odds! A collective spirit of being a proud yet humble underdog! As one of my Saskatchewan oil tycoon friends based in a village—no, it's a hamlet of fewer than 400 people—likes to say, "I love when some of the big city boys in Edmonton, Calgary, or Vancouver underestimate the small-town prairie persona. They think they are dealing with a bunch of country bumpkins. We always get the good business deals when this happens because they tend not to take us too seriously. They almost act shocked that we have the Internet, cable TV, and don't have party telephone lines anymore. Although I am always aware of asking where these big city people are from, because if they have small-town roots, regardless of province, they clue in real quick. Then our 'aw shucks' shtick doesn't go too far." And then he laughs!

Speaking of "aw shucks," I could not believe how many interviewees for this tome used this simple phrase to describe Richie. Similar to the small-town business tycoon in the preceding paragraph, Richie has that "aw shucks" kind of style that cannot be underestimated. His college teammates, along with CFL players and coaches, said repeatedly never underestimate the competitiveness and aggressiveness of Richie Hall.

Roy Shivers, the former GM of the Roughriders during the Danny Barrett era (whom Wally Buono, the CFL's all-time winningest coach, has called the best player personnel man in league history) said this about "aw shucks" Richie: "He does something a lot of other people don't do. He listens, he actually listens. He just soaks everything up. He's so nice, that sometimes it pisses me off."

Here is an inspirational love story of province, football team, its league, and one of its most popular employees.

This *Globe and Mail* snippet, Canada's version of *USA Today* or better said *Washington Post*, may capture the inspirational qualities of Richie best when it reported that Richie Hall as an assistant CFL coach is still in Canada's top ten for a requested speaker on the speaking circuit for people in the entertainment industry. He hasn't played in over 20 years, yet his popularity as a difference maker grows stronger with age. It is still nice to know that a person of humble character and strong values has shelf life in our day and age.

Richie Hall was meant not only for Saskatchewan and the prairies, but is a national treasure to be shared both in Canada and beyond its borders. Being a military child, Richie has never lived in a city, state, or province as long as he has in Saskatchewan. They are meant for each other, meant to share their hearts and what makes them tick with the world.

As Ventson Donelson, former defensive back for almost 10 years under Richie's tutelage in Saskatchewan, says about Richie:

I grew up in Detroit and have settled in Regina. When Al Ford, the Rider GM at the time, signed me, I asked him where in the hell is it? And, 23 years later I'm still here. What is it about Saskatchewan [and he chuckled]? This is my home and this is Richie's home. He is one of the biggest influences for me not only as a player, but as a man. He is a man of deep faith and it doesn't take anyone long to figure this out. He seldom if ever preaches to anyone. He just stays in his lane and lets his light shine. And the influence he has on others is a wonder to behold. Maybe it's the Saskatchewan way; the province and Richie just fit.

SECOND QUARTER

BOMBERVILLE

SECTION TWO

★ ★ ★ ★ ★

CHAPTER 6

Come to Winnipeg and Hang Out

Shane Falco: Hey coach, can I ask you a question?

Jimmy McGinty: Yeah, shoot.

Shane Falco: Why me?

Jimmy McGinty: I look at you and I see two men: the man you are, and the man you ought to be. Someday those two will meet. Should make for a hell of a football player.

- From the 2000 football film, The Replacements

With Keanu Reeves (a.k.a. Shane Falco), the quarterback, and Gene Hackman (a.k.a. Jimmy McGinty), the coach of the fictional Washington Sentinels

There is a gap all coaches in any sport are trying to bridge: observing the talent of their athletes and seeking to bring out that talent on a consistent basis. For three days in the 2015 CFL season, I got to observe up close how professional football coaches seek to do this.

In the three decades I've known Richie, we have had many discussions on leadership, training, and motivating people to bring out their best in whatever sphere of life they are living and working. In August 2015 I approached him about being his shadow for three days as he and his team were preparing for an upcoming game versus the first-place Calgary Stampeders who were about to invade Winnipeg. Mike O'Shea, the head coach of the Winnipeg Blue Bombers, was very gracious and accommodating with my request to join their inner sanctum. For three days I had almost 100 percent permission to follow Richie around from the locker room and coaches' offices to what happens on the field in practice.

A Good Omen?!

The trip didn't quite start out as I intended. I still don't know if I believe in omens and such, but…

My trip started in Yorkton, Saskatchewan, which is about a four-hour drive to Winnipeg. As I'm driving through Manitoba on a very hot August afternoon, I'm reviewing my questions and pondering how I would make the most out of this trip. My car doesn't have cruise control. Take note of this; it's maybe the only vehicle in Canada without cruise. How did this happen? I was living in Vancouver four years earlier and bought my new used car. I just assumed it had cruise control, being the very observant writer that I am. About three weeks after buying the car, I went on a road trip and started looking for the cruise. In Vancouver itself, cruise makes no sense with the horrendous, slow traffic and winding roads and hills. So, I pull over and phone the dealership. The salesman I bought the vehicle from also thought it had cruise. He seemed honest and trustworthy. Honest! He said, "Let me phone you back." A few minutes later he phones and says, "My gosh it doesn't have cruise. What do you want to do?" It was such a good deal, so I said I'll adjust and just find vehicles I can follow to watch my speed. Little did I know I'd be moving back to the prairies where long stretches of highway don't have anything on the road but the odd tractor, dead skunks, and hidden police cars.

Around Neepawa, Manitoba, I get pulled over for being 28 kilometres over the speed limit. Remember I was thinking about the writing project and just wasn't paying attention to speed laws, and no cruise control. This quite attractive policewoman comes to the window. She couldn't have had a nicer disposition, in spite of my breaking the law. I drop my head in my hands onto the steering wheel; she asks for my licence and insurance and says, "So how does this work? You have Tennessee plates, an Alberta driver's licence, a Saskatchewan Roughriders sticker, Saskatchewan address, plus a Tennessee address and an Alberta address. So where do you live?"

I answer, with all due respect, "I don't know anymore."

She starts laughing and says, "What do you do, just tell me what do you do?"

I tell her I'm on a writing project, writing about one of your Blue Bombers, and I'm keeping an eye on my aging parents back in Saskatchewan. I explain to her that I was down in the US (and have a green card), where I was writing on another project, and sharpening skates on the side in a Nashville hockey store.

She just shakes her head and asks me who or what are you writing about? Anyone interesting? And asked if I do a lot of travelling in my vehicle.

I tell her and she laughs, and says, "Well I'm a huge Blue Bombers fan and I like who you're writing about. Of course I know who Richie Hall is. I'm glad he's on our side of the border now."

She goes back to her police car for what seems like forever and I'm thinking my curling money fees for the upcoming season are in jeopardy. Registration was only a few weeks away.

She comes back to my car, hands me my stuff, and says, "This would have been over $400, but I'm gonna let you go. Try and watch your speed a little more closely. Manitoba has the highest fines in Canada right now. How about you put that money into getting a cruise control."

As respectfully as I could I answer, "Yes ma'am, and go Bombers, at least for this weekend."

She smiled and said, "Keep your speed down please. And all the best in writing Richie's story."

Let's just say I was extremely thankful for the free pass from the RCMP (Royal Canadian Mounted Police) and I did keep my speed in check. It felt like I was driving toward a fun and potentially worthwhile trip. I just had a feeling. Maybe the policewoman knew deep down I needed good mojo as I was about to spend time with her Winnipeg Blue Bombers.

Arrival

I arrive at the new and gorgeous Investors Group Field, home of the Bombers. Richie meets me at one of the entrances as he was winding down his day. He said, "Let's go to my office and I'll introduce you to Mike O'Shea and some of the coaches if they are still around, and we'll get you acclimatized to your new home for the next few days."

Mike couldn't have been nicer and more accommodating. He walked with Richie and me to the coaches' lounge, the "let's get away from the chaos" place for all 12 coaches. He told me I was welcome to help myself to all the coffee and beer (yes, a keg in the lounge). He said, "Let me pour you a beer." I felt like I was officially welcomed when he got me that beer. I couldn't turn him down. (I drink about six beers a year. I know, Captain Lightweight…and for the record I never saw a coach indulge the whole time I was there—work first.)

Richie was quick to introduce me to the Blue Bombers coaching staff as they filtered in and out of his office and the coaches' lounge. Over the next few days these were the men I got to observe, and in a handful of circumstances interact with:

- Mike O'Shea, Head coach
- Marcel Bellefeuille, Offensive coordinator
- Bob Wylie, Offensive line
- Paul Charbonneau, Assistant offensive line coach
- Markus Howell, Wide receivers coach
- Gene Dahlquist, Quarterbacks coach
- Buck Pierce, Running backs coach
- Richie Hall, Defensive coordinator
- Barron Miles, Defensive backs coach
- Todd Howard, Defensive line coach
- Greg Knox, Linebackers coach
- Pat Tracey, Special teams coordinator

My arrival was at the end of my trek to Winnipeg and my conversation with one of Neepawa's finest RCMP members. Richie and I chatted some more and headed off for some dinner and conversation. Richie was in the mood for some barbecue ribs, and who was I to argue. We got caught up on life, where we were at in the book process, and then Richie gave me an idea what the next few days would look like.

And as usual we shared much of our hearts and where we were at spiritually and in life. I enjoyed how Richie would relate so much of his world back to spiritual principles or lessons that could draw one closer to God. With Richie it's not a bunch of fluffy truth that tickles the heart, but truth based in God's Word that could be applied in everyday life both on and off the field. So much of his conversation concludes with how these nuggets or truths could be executed right now or when the right situation occurs.

For instance, I asked him about a phrase I saw on his whiteboard. Have I told you about the whiteboards in Richie's offices in Regina, Edmonton, back in Regina, and now Winnipeg? Richie had whiteboards on three out of four walls in his office filled with football plays, reminders, and dozens of motivational words or phrases that he often refers to. What amazed me about this over the years is how these motivational tidbits are part of his everyday conversation. You can tell he thinks about them constantly and ponders how they can affect his life or the lives of his players and fellow coaches. I've been around other coaches, business people, and ministers who do the same (minus the football plays with those XXX's and OOO's), but I often wonder if they are ever integrated into one's life or remembered.

There was this phrase, "unconditional mindset."

We started to chat about what that meant. We have all heard about unconditional love through spiritual books and sermons, but also through many pop culture love songs. I wanted to know how this applies to football and life. Richie had a sip of iced tea, downed a couple of ribs, and started to pontificate:

Well, having an unconditional mindset is about not wavering regardless of the environment or circumstances around you. It is like unconditional love, very much so. I'm trying to communicate to the players and myself that it doesn't matter what life, or what the game is throwing at you, or what the conditions are, we keep doing the right thing regardless. We seek to execute, execute, and execute!

Having an unconditional mindset means at the core that our standards don't change because we encounter opposition or adversity. Our standards do not change!

It means we will try and find a way to execute our game plan, and our overall mission of finding a way to compete and win. XXX's and OOO's are overrated when all is said and done. Yes, the playbooks are critical and so is the Bible. But it comes down to execution of the plan. Really, there are only six to eight fundamental principles in having success on the football field. There are usually only a handful of fundamentals in any endeavour in life one must seek to master.

The Bible is the same way. It's about love and service, humanitarian works, treating each other with respect. I guess it's all about love, and the Bible, as the old Jewish commentators used to say, "is a book about love, and the thickness of it is commentary on how to live it out day by day." A football playbook is very similar. The offensive playbook is about three times thicker than my eighty-page defensive playbook. They are full of schemes, but it comes down to doing whatever it takes to move the ball or to prevent the other team from moving the ball.

I seldom if ever talk about winning, yet that is our mission. Football, like life, is such a process. Step by step you build a life and a team. So an unconditional mindset is making sure your standards don't change. You try and do the right thing or the game plan consistently. Really, it's what being mentally tough is all about. I want our team to develop this mindset because then it means we aren't swayed by our emotions, circumstances, and negative voices. We focus on what we know we need to do regardless.

You want one of my ribs?

And he smiled that famous smile of his, and as usual my soul was filled with a new perspective from a life lesson from the gridiron. Unconditional mindset!

In this section we will walk through the three days I had to observe and quiz Richie on his daily routine. The other coaches couldn't have been more friendly and open when I would ask questions or simply chat.

But before we shut this chapter down—a story.

Markus Howell, Winnipeg born and raised, is the receivers' coach who had a distinguished 11-year CFL career in Winnipeg, Ottawa, and mostly in Calgary, winning a Grey Cup in 2008. He came into Richie's office with a smirk on his face, went to one of the whiteboards, and wrote his name on the board. He turned to Richie and me, and said, "I want to be in the book and I want you to spell my name correctly."

I said if you give me a good story we can arrange for that. The next morning Markus and Paul Charbonneau, the assistant offensive line coach, both came into Richie's office separately, on a mission. First, Paul came in and said they pranked Richie when he first came to the team: "Richie lost a bet when he first came to the team, and we made him strip down and run around the field in shame. It's a true story."

Five minutes later Markus comes into Richie's office saying, does he have a story for the book, he was thinking about it all night: "Richie lost a bet when he first came to the team, and we made him strip down and run around the field in shame. As sure as I'm standing here it's a true story."

Charbonneau comes in from around the corner, laughing his head off and saying, "Whenever there are two or three witnesses it has to be true, right?"

Who was I to argue with Paul, a former offensive lineman? Richie just looks at me and smiles. Locker room humour never ceases, whatever age these athletes or coaches are. Anything to get into a book; I still don't know if the story is fiction or non-fiction, but it was clear these coaches had a good relationship. Richie just brushed it off like a five-yard offside penalty when the game was already in the books. Next…

What an eye-opener to observe the interaction between coaches and players. I was like a sports junkie in a candy store, taking copious notes and having freedom to ask a million questions. Richie was his usual self, elaborating on what took place, and expanding his thoughts, philosophizing on the nuances of coaching and how it all relates to life in general.

So what do Mr. Hall and his fellow coaches do on a typical day or three? To put it bluntly in coach-speak, "Work their tails off." But allow me to elaborate. There is much to unpack.

So we headed off to Mr. Hall's, or Mr. Hospitality's, apartment. We chatted for a bit and got ready for my first full day with the Winnipeg Blue Bombers. I was going to sleep in until at least 7:30, but Richie would be getting up at his usual 3:00 or 4:00 a.m., which has been his pattern throughout his coaching career.

I was going to learn some key fundamental insights about how coaches try to close that gap between talent and consistent execution. I was about to hear the word "overwhelmed" a ton in the next few days and how to take that feeling away. I couldn't wait and would not be disappointed.

What you don't want is players thinking this will require something heroic. You don't want them thinking they have to do more. That's when the pressure can overwhelm them. Rather they should be thinking, we've done this before. All we have to do is execute. They should be calm and confident. If they are, every play becomes a high percentage play.

- Bill Walsh,
former San Francisco 49ers head coach and winner of three Super Bowls

CHAPTER 7

We'll Go Till the Hay Is in the Barn

"It's not achieved until it's understood!"
- Mike O'Shea, head coach of the Winnipeg Blue Bombers

Where have I heard that concept before? Knowing Richie throughout his coaching career, this seems to be his overall mantra as a coach and as a human being. He understands clearly that not everyone gets the concept in the same way. Just as there are approximately 6,500 languages in the world, not counting the various regional nuances, communication just may be the hardest part to master in our time on this planet. I honestly don't know if I have ever met another human being who understands and strives to bring clarity to a conversation as much as he does, be it one-on-one or in the classroom.

If there is an underlying theme to this chapter it is about the art of communication and the myriad ways to achieve clarity. Personally, I have probably learned more about communication from Mr. Hall than from any post-secondary class, work-related seminars, or bestselling books on the subject, and for the record I have learned tons from the above-mentioned resources. But to see an expert in action accelerates the learning process. And, to quote Richie:

I sure don't feel like an expert in communication. It's an ongoing learning curve that will probably take a few lifetimes. Communication is an art and as a communicator I am always learning how to become more effective.

While I was being Richie's shadow for three days, I couldn't shake the memory of reading and watching George Plimpton's *Paper Lion*. Following Richie around the Blue Bombers' week of preparation to face the defending champion Calgary Stampeders was a terrific way to better understand the process of preparation. Plimpton called it *participatory journalism*. I was privileged to have total access to the coaches' meetings, to go on the field to watch the practices, to stand around the water coolers (well, that was more like the buffet tables and photocopier), and to get a feel for what it was like observing a professional football team preparing for its weekly battle.

The only thing I didn't do was suit up like Plimpton and take a few snaps, although I did toss a few balls back to the players from errant passes or kicked balls that came tumbling toward the sidelines. I did learn something, though, from Plimpton's book: he could barely throw the ball 20 yards. I had him beat by at least 20 yards or more. Would that make me a better candidate for pro football? I think not, as there is much more to throwing a ball than having distance. The decision-making with 300-pound bullets (give or take a few pounds) flying around you, from God only knows how many different directions, just floors me. Not to mention how many human beings even in the best of shape could take hit after hit and still keep bouncing back for more. The wear and tear alone makes me want to stay out in the participatory journalism realm.

And then watching Richie operate and him feeling so at ease with my million questions, and patiently answering them all. I'm so glad in hindsight that Richie has a very good internal filter, as I often wondered what he really thought of some of my questions. But it was vintage Richie. The teacher in him was in a constant groove. He explained his philosophies of coaching and how he was always thinking of ways to get his message across, so the players would understand without any confusion. His major desire is that they would get to the point of simply playing the game, reacting to whatever his players were facing, without having to remember, pause, and process.

Richie has three assistants under him that make up the defensive side of the ball. Greg Knox, a long-time CFL player, coaches the linebackers. Todd Howard, who has extensive NFL experience, winning a Super Bowl ring with "the greatest show on turf, St. Louis Rams," is his defensive line coach. Former CFL all-star Barron Miles is the defensive backs coach. All three units meet separately on a daily basis in classrooms next to the locker room. What's primarily involved in these specialized unit meetings is review of past games and looking at videos of upcoming opponents. Obviously technique issues can be tweaked or talked about, but even more so are the philosophies of how they will prepare for an upcoming opponent, and how they can work together as a unit, but also work together with the entire defense. On the offensive side of the ball, the same sort of meetings are taking place with their specific units: offensive line, running backs, receivers, and quarterbacks.

The three defensive units will come together on a regular basis for the overall defensive meetings run primarily by Richie. The goal is that all three units understand their roles and strategy and will connect the dots. Bringing the whole defensive unit together will give the big picture approach of how the defense can work in sync. This is a place where Richie and the coaches explain the game plan, review video where necessary, and quiz the players to gauge their understanding of the upcoming game plan. This was fascinating, as we'll get to shortly.

Meanderings, Meetings, and Possible Memes...

Well, on the official full day one I was still fast asleep and probably only halfway to my early wake-up time. Richie warned me that he'd be leaving his apartment around 3:00 or 3:30 a.m. and heading off to the stadium to get his day started. This isn't just about football, but spending some quiet time with God, walking or running around the football field, processing his life and day, and generally being the first person up in all of the great province of Manitoba, and this was the beginning of harvest season. And, he does this all without coffee!

I woke up, hit the snooze only twice, found out where the nearest Starbucks was, and got me a triple espresso just to keep up with Mr. Hall for the rest of the day. I navigated myself from south St. Vital to the stadium to arrive just before 8:00 a.m. By this time, all the players and coaches had arrived to get a start on their day. I felt like a slacker, although I don't think I was the last one to arrive. That was one of my goals!

I texted Richie out in the team's parking lot and within two minutes he was at the entrance to greet me and get me acclimatized to his office and the surroundings, now full of 70 or more CFL players and coaches. I was like a kid in a football nirvana, be it my team's natural rival or not. I was going to act and look as cool as I could. This should be easy for a born and raised Saskatchewanite, where acting cool is part of that rural makeup. Think of all those cool cowboys on the pro rodeo circuit or those calm, in-control curlers working through some problem solving on the ice. I could be cool, but this was beyond cool.

I was about to observe, talk, and inquire about some inner workings of one of the greatest games on the planet. And I was not about to be disappointed. I loved how the coaches were constantly straining to get their message or game plans across to each other and the players. And the players had a definite eagerness to grasp the plan for the upcoming game. Everything was very businesslike with high focus. There was a definite effort to lighten things up throughout the day in many varying and unique ways, but we'll get to that shortly.

So Richie escorted me through the entrance and down a few flights of stairs to the bowels of the stadium where the team was hunkered down in what seemed like very upscale bunkers. Before we walked to his office to chitchat and have him fill me in on the morning activities, Richie knows me well enough to know that my triple espresso needed some normal caffeine to continue the kick-start. With Tim Horton's being a sponsor, there were a couple of huge urns to stay fuelled.

I have my fresh Timmy's and wander into the Winnipeg Blue Bombers defensive coordinator's office. I sit myself down and am staring at the whiteboard behind his desk, and I start asking Richie about some of the key words he has posted up in the left-hand corner: Eyes, Communication, Tough, Urgency, Proactive Attitude, and of course Unconditional Attitude.

So, Mr. Hall, please elaborate on these key words that have been written down since the season started. And he goes into teacher mode. I start taking notes and I'm getting ready to suit up. I keep forgetting I'm too old, too short, and probably too slow, except on the curling ice where my knees seem to come alive. As Richie talks, I can see this exercise only reinforces to him how important these organic concepts are. They are fundamental to continued growth and success as he coaches. As I keep hearing from the world of football—you can never emphasize the fundamentals enough. And we're talking the less than 1 percent of active football players who are the best of the best. Fundamentally sound technically, but even more importantly, mentally and emotionally.

Eyes – *Make sure you have good eyes. Adjust to things as they break down. Yes, stick to your assignments, but don't be so rigid that you are technically sound but get beat by breakdowns and nuances. Trust what your eyes see and adjust accordingly.*

Communication – *Football is about communication. Talk to your teammates, learn their body language, and learn to understand your teammates' ways of non-language communication. This has to be a constant emphasis, just like in a romantic relationship. Even though in your romantic relationship 300-pound bodies aren't flying at you like missiles...although these emotional missiles* between a man and a woman can bring down a 300-pounder quicker than Mike O'Shea or Reggie White ever could. (I thought this was funny—hope you do too.)

Tough – Don't be out-physical'ed by an opponent. This is a physical game and we can't forget this. But, even more, be tougher mentally. In spite of distractions, the score, or perceptions of an opponent, just do your assignment but with your eyes wide open!

Urgency – Get to the ball! This is called football, and the ball is the scoring mechanism. Sometimes this is easy to lose sight of. This involves wrapping up the ball carrier, helping swarm to your teammates' aid, and taking dead aim at the ball if you have an opportunity. And remember, every play is important. There are only about 150 plays in a game, and your unit plays about a third of them; that's not that many in the big picture.

Proactive Attitude – No excuses! Embrace reality! Dictate! Impose our will! Be aggressive! If you wait for things to happen, especially at this level, you can find yourself two or three touchdowns down before you know it. The game is only 60 minutes long; you only play 18 and hopefully a couple more in the playoffs. Don't wait for things to happen, make them happen. We're professionals. These truisms have to be a constant reminder, all these things have to be. It's funny how we all know what it takes to win, but it's so easy wanting it to just happen. All these things can be said in a million different ways. The more we practice and the more we actively practice these things in practice and in a game, the more they become our corporate DNA and we become a team.

After my mini motivational talk, Richie asked if I wanted some breakfast from the team buffet. If I was going to suit up, I sure needed some food. You name it, it was there eggs, sausage, fruit, cereal, hash browns, and every type of fruit juice, and of course coffee and tea. Never saw a soul drinking tea, but it was there. I was waiting for a free agent British placekicker to wander on by. So I loaded up, took a couple of extra pieces of fruit for later on, and wandered back to Richie's office.

Right after my mini feast, we joined everyone for the opening day team meeting led by the head coach, Mike O'Shea. Personally I like Mike's style. He's a minimalist, but with a message—he always has a message. His meetings, depending on the circumstances, can last from three minutes to maybe 15 minutes at the max. Today was early in the week, so we were in there for maybe three minutes. Mike opened the meeting, had one of the assistant coaches give out the last-minute emphasis for the day, then introduced two new ball players and asked them to say where they were from and Something unique to them outside of the football genre. This usually creates a laugh and hopefully a bonding launch-off point. As an example, if a player said he plays curling in the off-season, the three other curlers in the room will immediately try to track him down and talk shop. Then Mike may have a quick motivational reminder and quickly give out the outline for the morning. Most of the players stay in the theatre style meeting room for their daily special teams meeting for the next half hour or more. Dismissed…

What I found unique about the opening morning team meeting is how Mike included the other coaches in both a serious and in a joking manner. The next morning one of the assistants opened the meeting up with a card trick. This seemed to perk up the team as they were throwing out barbs and trying to figure out the trick. Whether it was Mike or one of the other coaches, they had the freedom to use the language they were comfortable with. Some coaches had the language of colourful metaphors down to a science, while some of the others never even came close to using this form of communication. There was absolutely no judgment or phony trying to fit in. This was a locker room atmosphere with a businesslike approach, but it was all men; the language could be salty, but it was like water off a duck's back. For me it simply brought back a flood of memories growing up in Saskatchewan hockey locker rooms and baseball dugouts. There's a language of locker rooms that brings a certain level of comfort and gets certain players' attention. Don't ask me to explain this fully, it just works, but if I may give this a shot… The locker room is a sacred place, well it usually is, and is a place where one can simply be themselves regardless of language or emotion. The only guidelines seem to be that the team is in this together, and to show respect for each other. The line crossed would be exactly that—when respect is not shown, or the attitude that one doesn't believe in each other is lost. The bonding creates a huge trust both on and off the field. Teasing, joking, and colourful metaphors were all part of the process, but so were encouraging each other, positive realistic feedback, and professionalism. This is a business, a livelihood. Yes it's a game, but everyone is aware that they are one hit away from the dream being over, or a bad losing streak away from being fired. To put it mildly, this is a delicate balance. Building trust and a team safety net alleviates many of the obvious fears or insecurities that come along with pro sports, and helps to stay focused on the next game and striving to win. Fun, trust, encouragement, teasing, and being prepared can all ward off those demons of fear, anxiety, and the feelings of being overwhelmed.

During my week with the Bombers I never saw anyone belittled, although there were a few moments I thought the door was open for this to happen. There seemed to be such an unspoken reality that everyone was human, and humans can get embarrassed really quickly in a sport like football where all your mistakes or apparent mistakes can be seen my millions. There seemed to be an underlying philosophy that everything was about building a team, building constant trust, which meant pulling for each other regardless.

Back to Richie's office. Richie at this time may put some final thoughts and notes down for his upcoming defensive meetings. He's usually more than prepared for this, but maybe Mike O'Shea triggered a thought, or another position coach or player might have said something to Richie that will affect the upcoming meetings.

The day was about to get more interesting as each unit was to have their 30–45 minute meetings, then a similar time frame gathering for the overall units to meet, and then go to the locker room to put on the pads and head off to the practice field.

"The single biggest problem in communication is the illusion that it has taken place."

- George Bernard Shaw

CHAPTER 8

Bridging that Gap

*There's a gap between training and what really happens out there...
My intention is to narrow that gap!*

- Kevin Costner, a Coast Guard instructor in the 2006 film,
The Guardian

Really it comes down to a few fundamentals you need to master. A football playbook is like the Bible; they are big books. The defensive one is about 80 pages and the offensive one about three or four times thicker. It's like our Old Testament and New Testament I guess. Yes, we seek to master what's in those playbooks, but If a player isn't fundamentally sound, you aren't going to be successful anyway. I'm concerned about how players master the playbook and master the fundamentals that lead to executing the schemes.

We chatted about this in Richie's office. This is a conversation we have had over the past number of years, but now it took on new meaning as we were surrounded by his work environment and about to head out to the field for their daily on-field practice. There was a gap about to be filled from classroom to practice field.

Richie was elaborating on the importance of mastering the fundamentals: those few he talked about such as running, blocking, tackling, throwing, kicking, knowing one's angles and position on the field, coverage, routes, and securing the football, to name most of them. He referred to the playbooks and knowing the schemes, the theory of what to do on the field. He couldn't have stressed enough the criticalness of mastering the fundamentals, then taking the schemes and theory to application.

Richie started to use the Bible as a metaphor, or was he using the football as the Bible's metaphor? I think it was both. Regardless, we talked again about Hillel, the second-century Rabbi who talked about the importance of the Torah, the Jewish Old Testament—or the Jewish playbook, to stick with the metaphor. Hillel is quoted in what's know as the Talmud, Jewish commentary books on the Torah, where he said the following:

That which is hateful to do, do not do to another. This is the whole Torah. The rest is commentary—do now and go study.

Hillel is referring to the classic paragraph out of the Old Testament Book of Leviticus that Jesus quoted a number of times when He was asked what the greatest commandment was:

Love the Lord your God with all your heart and with all your soul and with all your spirit and with all your mind. This is the first and greatest commandment. And the second is like it: "Love your neighbor as yourself." All the Law and the Prophets hang on these two commandments.

In other words the Bible is all about learning how to love. The rest of the Bible is commentary on that one major theme. Go and learn it, like a football playbook. Both are thick books that need to be learned and understood. Football is about winning. Mastering the playbook both on and off the field doesn't guarantee success, but if one does not seek to master the playbook there is no guarantee of victory. As Richie repeatedly says, "All we can do is put ourselves into a position to win. There are no guarantees." The playbook is the commentary or theory of how a team tries to put itself into a winning position. The playbook is the strategic side of the game written down; some of it is the techniques explained to better play one's position. Knowing the playbook as theory only and not having the ability to execute is football suicide.

I remember thinking, it's so easy to talk about loving God and loving our neighbor, but so hard to execute. There is a gap so often we as humans must seek to bridge. Football teams plan, study, have classroom sessions, then go to the practice field, get dirty, and simulate a game environment as best as they can. The team as a unit applies the book. The better they apply the book and master its nuances, the greater the chances of winning.

Hold on—this relates even more when it comes to closing the gap. I immediately thought of a conversation with a woman in Tennessee a few years earlier about the nature of authentic faith. As soon as the Tennessee Titans arrived in Nashville, she bought a couple of season tickets. It was one of her first indulgences from getting a paycheque as a model. I was not surprised when she told me this is how she once made a living. She is a very insightful woman on the verge of getting her PhD in clinical psychology. She is also a recovering alcoholic with over a decade of sobriety.

At the time I met her she was working as a waitress to help pay her way through college. I was in Nashville on a writing project and my place of residence for those three weeks was a short walk from her restaurant. The book I was reading for the week was a biography of the famous Hall of Fame football coach, Paul Brown. She started to ask me about the book and we chatted about how Brown was the first coach to take his players into the classroom to master the playbook before they headed on to the field for practice.

This began a friendship I have had with her until this day. I would have meals at her restaurant almost every evening and she'd come over and chat. We discussed my writing, the Paul Brown book I was enjoying, and her classes. She was intrigued and sat down with me as this thought about a football playbook hit a nerve for her. You could see the wheels turning in her mind. Then she threw this Richie-like insight at me:

You know I go to church, but I am having a hard time finding one to join. But I go to AA on a regular basis. I have also been an addiction counsellor. You know what the difference is between most churches and AA? AA is a program of action, where church seems to be primarily a program of information. In AA, if you don't close that gap from theory to practice you die. Why doesn't the church in general see that when you don't apply the spiritual truisms they teach, you die spiritually if you don't apply, and become a less loving person? But if you apply those truisms in your life, your heart is filled with a commitment to love and you grow as a person. I bet my Tennessee Titans don't just study their playbooks; they seek to apply it with their whole hearts, because if they don't, they'll get killed, right!

She smiled and laughed. But there was a Yoda-like wisdom coming from this former Playboy and lingerie model turned psychologist and faith-filled woman. She understood that the Big Book of Alcoholics Anonymous and the Bible are like football playbooks—these are pretty thick books written with the intent that the reader applies. It's the only intent! Man, was I about to get two more full days of reinforcing the importance of application, execution, and closing the gap. As Richie has inferred and said to me over the years:

One only achieves what they emphasize. And we emphasize knowing and applying the playbook to the point where it's in the team DNA. Learning the theory, advancing to understanding, to simply reacting. When this happens on a consistent basis, winning can become a habit. But, and this is a big but—this isn't a one-time thing, it's as the great Vince Lombardi used to say, "Winning isn't a now and then thing. It must become a habit. Winning is an all-the-time thing. Teams must reinforce these things on a constant basis and must practice them on a constant basis."

Now that you have read how pro football players deeply understand the importance of application and read an accidental mini sermon, let's return to a day in the life of Richie Hall as he helps his team prepare for an upcoming opponent, the defending Grey Cup champions. Closing the gap and execution is paramount. The foundation has been set.

The emphasis of application has been laid. Richie had one more emphasis before we headed to some of his defensive unit meetings:

Preparation is fun. I love the problem solving. I enjoy the give and take between coaches and players and trying to figure out a way that's going to help us perform at our best. Discussing the pros and cons of a game plan. Brainstorming ideas with passionate people is invigorating. Of course we don't agree on everything, and I wouldn't expect that. Sometimes it gets quite heated, but when you know everyone has the same purpose in mind, it's so easy to overlook our differences. We have the same underlying passions and desires. Personally I think it only makes us better. I can defer to a better idea. I think all our coaches can. This simply reinforces to me that Football and life are better served when we see it takes a team effort.

We discussed the human element and the possibilities of people coming in with different agendas, and just wanting to be right, or trying to get ahead at the expense of the team's overall picture. Richie said of course that pops up every now and then, but more often than not the coaches keep this in check from his experience over the years:

I have found whenever a team has success, whether winning a championship or in the rebuilding process, the ones who have success are the best ones at putting their egos aside or on the shelf. What I mean by that is when one makes a conscious choice to put the team first, and it is a conscious choice. I have discovered the more one does this, the quicker it becomes part of your makeup as a human being. And believe me, this is powerful in a group effort where everyone or at least the core comes together on this.

I'm not saying this is easy. We all have egos and have this tendency to come across as right. But, what I have learned over the years is the ones who are able to put their egos on the shelf tend to move up the ladder anyway in this business. You can't have team success if you are not a team. I believe this is a deeply seated spiritual paradox. You know that old Biblical line, "The first shall be last and the last shall be first." This adage runs deep throughout all aspects of life. In football, in all team sports, even in individual sports, you need a support system. We need each other to get ahead; no one can do it on their own, and if they think that, they are only fooling themselves. The key is to have people who are willing to stick to the common purpose. At this level you learn real quickly, it's about TEAM!

Richie observes other coaches and has respect for men like Bill Belichick of the New England Patriots, Gregg Popovich of the San Antonio Spurs, and Phil Jackson of Chicago Bulls and Los Angeles Lakers fame, who have all won multiple championships. These three men place high emphasis on team dynamics and sticking to their guns when it comes to keeping their philosophies in place. Phil Jackson went so far as to say:

A team is like a sanctuary and must be treated as such. Guarded to the nth degree and constantly nurtured. It's all about team and I seldom talk about winning. You know, John Wooden of those great UCLA Bruin basketball teams never talked about winning. Well that's what I've heard and read from his former coaches and players. He always talked about the process and fundamentals of winning. The building blocks a team must put in place so that winning can become achievable. This is how I try to operate.

I was about to go to my first CFL defensive meeting before the defense broke down into their three units to further sharpen the game plan and to refocus on their particular fundamentals. The entire defense was at the meeting, including defensive coaches. Head Coach O'Shea pops into all these meetings—he may stay for the entire length, contribute where necessary, or just absorb and observe. I can tell the team is in sync and has been together for well over three months. Everyone seems comfortable with each other, yet there is respect for when the coaches speak. Somehow the coaching staff has developed an atmosphere of learning, of give and take. One of the keys I observed was the respect for the individual that was apparent. Richie did say we try not to belittle anyone in front of each other, yet we will call a spade a spade as we watch a video together, or rehash a previous game or practice. They do not want any stone to be unturned.

Teaser: There was a huge opportunity to belittle a player in a couple of days, but it was interesting to watch how Richie, O'Shea, and the players responded to the huge gaffe that was made. I believe the point was made without destroying this player's psyche. This is such a fine line when you think each coach and player has his job on the line in such a precarious way when the team is struggling to rebuild or reload through a month of mostly losing. We'll get back to this dynamic in the next chapter.

Richie kicked off the meeting by asking what the team's slogan or mantra was for the year. This was the emphasis or philosophy the defensive unit distilled down to what it will take to be successful as a unit. I was surprised at the mojo the players responded with as they shouted out "TSO: TOUGH-STINGY-OPPORTUNISTIC!"

Remember this is pro football. Yet, the next words out of Richie's mouth were:

The ball! The football is the number one thing. We need to get to the ball and we need to be aware of being playmakers as we go after the ball. Make the play, but always be aware of the ball. Yesterday's practice was not good enough. There was good energy, but we weren't on top of it like we know we can be. It's always about execution. We need to be thinking at all times. Execution is about being present every series, every down, every play.

Then to lighten the mood, the defensive line coach, Todd Howard, got up and shared a joke. A little locker room humour that involved women, but it seemed to remind these men that the coaching staff saw them as men. It was tasteful, a tad crude, but it brought the players into listening mode; there's always a method to their madness. Sometimes Richie never knows what the joke may be when a coach says he has one ready for the players. But, they all seem to know there are certain lines not to be crossed. Not to say this is sanitized by any means, but I got the impression that one of the wives or girlfriends could have walked in and thrown a joke back in their faces and got the same response. Although, why would a woman want to join a bunch of testosterone-filled athletes about to put the pads on and get down to business?

Humour bonds men very quickly. Then Richie reminded the players about clarity. This was day three in their overall preparation for the Stampeders. He wanted no grey areas whatsoever, and reinforced if there is any uncertainty at all, please ask questions. He reminded them of the Stampeders' tendencies as an offensive, possessing arguably the best offensive line in the CFL and an extremely smart quarterback in Bo Levi Mitchell. He used the phrase "heavy alert" to be aware of those tendencies, yet to keep their eyes open and react to any modifications in their play calling or things breaking down in the middle of a play. These are smart athletes at this level who have seen almost everything football can throw at them, but the human element is to be comfortable in one's routine or ways of doing things. The polished teams like the current edition of the Stampeders prey on the tendencies of their opposition as well.

Richie in some consultation with his assistants chose eight plays for this meeting to look at what Calgary likes to do on the field. This can vary from meeting to meeting, depending on what needs to be emphasized or re-emphasized. One of the things the defense was looking for was potential soft spots in Calgary's offensive line. There was constant reminding of the little things that could potentially make a difference. Richie would show the video, repeat, talk, and repeat if necessary, until he felt it was time to move on to the next play.

Make them earn it, every yard. Penetration, play football (meaning let your talent and instincts take over), nothing fancy, just do it. Communicate on the field. Make sure you have good eyes. Adjust as things break down. Communicate, communicate, communicate. Impose your will; don't wait for things to happen. We make things happen.

Then the defensive meeting was about to break up, and the players were going to their separate meetings before heading out on the field. Mike O'Shea had a few last-minute words he wanted to reinforce from the meeting. You could tell he was pleased with what the meeting was trying to accomplish. O'Shea simply said, "Okay guys. Be right mentally! No grey areas. Communicate, ask questions."

The meeting was over and the players headed off to their individual units. Richie looked at me and asked if I wanted another coffee before we popped our heads into all three meetings. He asked me what I thought. I was pumped and wished I was 25 years younger, 25 pounds heavier, and had 80 percent of the speed Richie possessed in his prime. Oh yeah, and had the physical talent these athletes had. I liked the business approach once they got rolling. It was quite matter of fact, yet emphasized the emotion and smarts it takes to be successful. There were the reminders of fundamentals, but also nuances were coming out during the video session. He tried to get the players talking as much as he could, and he wanted as many different players as possible to contribute. It did get easier when the lights were turned down and the video came on. One thing hit me as I was pondering the meeting. Richie and Mike left them with a challenge, but also left them with a spirit of hope. You felt they were all in this together. It wasn't about the male ego being right; it was all about what are we going to do to give ourselves the best chance to win.

Stay tuned: the life lessons, metaphors, and insights into what makes Richie tick only get better. This was like watching Leonardo or Michelangelo working on a masterpiece, or that Edmonton Oilers juggernaut led by Gretzky and Sather working their dynasty. Maybe these Blue Bombers weren't on the verge of a dynasty, because let's face it, there are many factors that go into those beautiful anomalies, but watching people like Richie and his colleagues in action was definitely working the process toward a masterpiece.

Mastering the elements that led to success won't ever guarantee success—but unless you seek to master these elements your chances of success decrease dramatically.

- The late George "Sparky" Anderson
World Series-winning manager of both the Cincinnati Reds, the Big Red Machine of the 1970s, and the 1984 Detroit Tigers

CHAPTER 9

Playmakers

Eric Olczyk: How do you keep doing it coach?
Coach George: Stay on the job when you're up
against something bigger than you are?
Guys like you and me, that's all we can do.
We keep showing up.
You clawed your way to victory, Olczyk.
You kept your focus. You hung in there.
You just kept showing up.

- From the 2003 ESPN series, Playmakers

(The coach was going through a personal marriage crisis, plus the ownership group was on the verge of firing him. Olczyk was an aging linebacker who felt he was overmatched by a new star quarterback. Of course the savvy coach and middle linebacker find a way... Olczyk outsmarts the quarterback late in the game and intercepts a key pass because he's a proven playmaker.)

Richie was talking to me before we headed to the three defensive unit morning meetings. I wonder if he still would have been talking if no one was there? He was going on about how his defence needs to be more conscious of being playmakers, creating takeaways, getting to the ball. Yes, making tackles, filling up gaps on running plays, and breaking up passes is critical to a team's success, but making scores or setting your offence up in scoring position takes your team to a whole new level.

This took me back to a couple of conversations we had had in 2007 and 2013 when he was the defensive coordinator of the Roughriders, two of the years they won the Grey Cup. The defenses he was coaching led the league or were in the top third of the league in most of the defensive categories the league could grade. They either led the CFL in turnovers, defensive touchdowns, two and outs, or were near the top of those stats that made a significant difference on the scoreboard.

Richie reminded me that he doesn't pay attention to statistics very much. Oh, he is aware! But, he is like a sabermetrician in the football world. For the uninitiated, sabermetrics is a baseball term for studying relevant statistics that affect the outcome of a game more than putting up mere numbers. Some stats are more important than others. In football, sacks often come across as a defensive lineman's most important metric in terms of making an all-star team or winning an award, yet it may mean very little in the big picture. Yes, sacks are important, but some of the fiercest pass rushers don't always get a lot of sacks because they may be double- or even triple-teamed because of the havoc they create. A less skilled player in this category may get more sacks at the end of a season simply because the more talented player getting double-teamed is creating more one-on-one situations for the other lineman. This is a hard metric to measure, yet the players, coaches, and opposition know what's going on from watching the video or being on the field.

The general metric or measure of rating a defense is yards allowed versus the opposition. Generally this is a valid measurement, but it doesn't take into account garbage yards at the end of game where your team may have clinched the victory early in the fourth quarter, and now the team has gone into a prevent defense, or filled their lineup with backups to get in some necessary playing time. How often have we seen a good defense give up a 60- or 70-yard play late in the game, where they haven't given up a big play all game long? The big play that didn't affect the win or the loss, but was given up by a backup player or a miscommunication with a couple of newbies trying to get in the lineup.

Back to 2007 and 2013. Playmakers, difference makers, were and are what Richie was hoping to see develop under his leadership, along with the head coaches he was with:

It's a mindset! So often players just want to get their job done, which I understand. Make the tackle, knock the pass down, blanket the receiver in coverage, raise your arms to knock down a pass. Good, fundamentally sound football. These things are important, but what separates the difference maker from the merely good is his grasp of the nuances. We sometimes forget the game is about the ball!

It's about scoring. Offences don't just have to do the scoring. There is no law against the defence scoring some points. When you can get a big defensive takeaway to set the offense up, or to actually score a touchdown, it energizes the whole team. I just want to see players become very conscious about being a difference maker. I've seen this become infectious. When you have a couple of players thinking this way and starting to create takeaways and such, often the whole D starts to think this way. I'm not asking players to forget about the basics like making the tackle, but I'm asking them to do a little bit more without abandoning a fundamental. Or, when you see the tackle is going to be made by a teammate and you're close by, go after the ball. It's a mindset.

Remember that 1989 Western Final versus Edmonton?

Of course that was a rhetorical question. I reminded Mr. Hall that that game is embedded in my DNA like few other Roughrider games, or any sports games, period. For me this is probably my favourite Roughrider game of all time. The Eskimos were the dominant team of the previous decade and a half, and the Riders hardly ever won at Commonwealth Stadium during the 1980s. Goodness, hardly any visiting team won at Commonwealth during this dynastic era. It's kind of ironic that the Roughriders' last game of the 1980s in Edmonton would be a victory in a playoff game, in a stadium where they had never won, versus a 16–2 juggernaut.

The 9–9 Roughriders were going up against the first team to ever win 16 games in a CFL regular season. Even the *Edmonton Journal* and *Edmonton Sun* on game day were calling this a "coronation." People forget that the Riders beat the Eskimos three out of five games that season including the exhibition tilt. The Riders faced an unusual amount of injuries after getting off to a terrific start, and by the end of the season the team was returning to health. Key players such as Ray Elgaard, David Albright, and Jeff Fairholm were all recovering. As Richie and I have talked about for years, this was more like a 12 or 13 win kind of team; the record was a bit of a mirage. Maybe it worked in the Riders' favour, in hindsight?

The 16–2 Edmonton Eskimos. It was a defensive play that was the turning point. I don't think anyone from that team would argue the point. Edmonton came out smoking and jumped ahead of us in the first quarter. What were we down? At 10–0 early, moving the ball with Tracy Ham at the controls, quarterbacking for the Eskimos. Near the end of the first quarter, we got a field goal by Robokicker, Mr. Ridgway. About three minutes into the second quarter, the Eskimos are on our twenty-four-yard line, we're down 10–3. We get a huge sack on a first down around our thirty. That was big. Edmonton was in field goal range. We could have been down 13–3, or worse. Then a ten-point swing, really.

On the next play, our all-world linebacker Eddie Lowe blitzes and gets to Tracy Ham and just crushes him, knocking the ball free. [Note: Lowe played for the great Bear Bryant at Alabama, who was once asked about his outstanding linebacker. Bryant said, "He's not just an All-American, he's All-Universe. It's just too bad he's a little undersized for the NFL."] *David Albright, the middle linebacker from Vanderbilt, a rival school in the SEC with Lowe, scoops up the fumble and rumbles down the field eighty yards for the tying touchdown. The game turns on that play. The TSN turning point was an easy one on that Sunday November 19 afternoon in Edmonton.*

We go on to win 32–21. After that 10–0 deficit we outscore them 32–11, and it really gets going after that Eddie Lowe hit and Albright return. Dave could have just fallen on the ball, but we watch him pick it up, making sure it's secure, and he goes for it. That's a playmaker. The game was different from that point on. We started dominating the dominant team, in all three phases. Once that fourth quarter hit, I had no doubt we were going to win. It's maybe the most fun I remember having on the football field. It really is hard to describe, but point being made how a defensive needs to be opportunistic, aggressive, and have a playmaker mindset. People often forget Kent Austin went down early as our starting quarterback and Tom Burgess came on in relief and got us the win. It was such a team effort. But that Eddie Lowe blitz, sack, and caused fumble was the turning point! I don't think there's a person on that team or in Saskatchewan that would argue the point.

Hey, I'm a Bomber now! I don't know if it's healthy being around you getting me to reminisce about my Roughrider moments.

This whole idea of having your players having a playmaker's attitude seems to be the eternal quest of Richie. One of the common phrases you hear sports teams talk about is "imposing your will."

In 2008, the NCAA basketball tournament was won by Kansas, which was coached by Bill Self. In the semis, the Jayhawks beat the University of North Carolina, coached by Roy Williams (note: he has coached UNC to an NCAA championship). After the game, Williams had this to say about how Kansas imposed their will on his team, hoping his team could have done the same: "All the great teams I've been part of come out with great intensity. Kansas just came out and punched us in the mouth."

In the final, Kansas beat Memphis which was coached by the well-known John Calipari. He echoed Williams's comments in his post-game press conference: "Bill had his guys ready to go tonight. If you're not ready to play his teams, you'll get swamped."

This is what Richie wants to see out of his football teams: coming out of the gate with intensity and swamping the opposition right from the get-go. As Richie elaborated:

Yes, the great teams impose their will from start to finish. One thing I struggle with is when people say a team, especially my units, didn't come out ready. They weren't ready to go, they weren't aggressive enough. You know what is usually the case? Teams are too emotional or aggressive, and they start a game too hyped up and try to do things they aren't asked to do or that isn't part of the scheme. It's the opposite of what the average fan or reporter thinks. Controlled intensity, or as John Madden, former Oakland Raiders coach and NFL TV analyst, liked to say, "Controlled fanaticism."

When a team doesn't play with a balanced intensity, or a thinking man's intensity, and starts to do things outside of the game plan, disaster can strike and throw a team off its rhythm. It's usually being thrown off your rhythm that hurts teams. Most high-level athletes want to come out of the gate hard and fast and impose their wills. Reality is, often you have to hold them back—within reason of course. Getting rhythm back and trying to find it is one of the arts of coaching and performing.

Another football truism came out of Richie's mouth, "You gotta play the play." I have heard him mention this number of times over the years:

Everyone has their assignment as the play starts; then the fun begins. Each player has to do his job, yet be aware of how things are developing and react properly. Be aware of the situation, down and distance, the time clock, the score, your personnel, their personnel. This is where the study and preparation comes in, along with years of playing experience. We DON'T want robots out on the field. We want them to react and embrace the nuances that can make for a successful play. The better we practice and prepare, and communicate on the field, the easier it is to adjust and just react.

Barron Miles, the defensive backs coach, also touched on this as we sat in on the morning team meeting earlier when he said:

We can't over-coach. This is a tendency of a lot of coaches at all levels. I learned a long time ago as a player that I can only really have one major thought in my head before a play, maybe a secondary thought, but generally more than one kills your reaction time when things break down. In my rookie season as a DB, I remember being out on the field having all these thoughts running through my head. I got beat so bad on a play that I know I could have made, it was ridiculous. I finally said screw it and just do what I know I can do. A player can't have conflicting thoughts in his head. Hesitancy in this game will kill you.

From that point on, I had that one major thought in my head, and adjusted accordingly. It was so much easier when things broke down. Often I could allow my athleticism to take over, but more often than not I found myself adjusting on the fly because of my preparation and practice. I could react properly without having to over think and try to please my coach. It's not about pleasing my coach anyways; it's about making the play. And of course the paradox is when you make the play, the coach is happy, and as you make more plays, he gives you more freedom because he trusts you more and more.

As Richie would say, when a player plays with this kind of freedom, there is more of a natural flow taking place. Great coaches have a thorough knowledge of their craft, yet seem to be minimalists in communicating their message so players can grasp the game plans and/or schemes. A robot-like player may have a lot of knowledge but usually has a pretty hard time executing consistently because there is that balance between knowledge and athleticism or reaction. A good coach gives the primary message and lets the athletes assimilate it in a way they can perform to the best of their abilities.

Playmakers! You certainly don't want to over-coach them. The coach wants them to get it down in the video and meeting rooms, and on the practice field. And hopefully your playmakers do take their work home with them because the game is a passion. This doesn't mean they shouldn't relax and have some healthy outside interests, but that they do some self-study, and process and ponder what they have been learning and practicing.

Having this chat with Richie set up the upcoming unit defensive meetings we were about to go to. The underlying themes, as I was about to find out, were getting more aggressive, making things happen, and having a playmaker's mindset. Create havoc, be the aggressor. I was about to learn about the importance of the tomahawk chop.

Richie was an outstanding baseball player in his high school days. He knows the importance of batting cleanup—that number four spot in a lineup where a team wants their best RBI (runs batted in) man or woman, someone who can hit for average, with a little bit of power. Generally a team's best RBI player is the cleanup hitter. I once lived in the Lloydminster area of Saskatchewan and Alberta, and played on a semi-competitive slo-pitch team. We did okay, but our Achilles heel was meeting the ultra-competitive teams who were going for provincial titles, like the Provost Shooters.

Provost was a very good sports town just inside the Alberta border. Currently they have two players in the NHL from this town of 1,500 people. They have also produced some of Western Canada's best curlers and ball players. The Shooters were the team to beat in slo-pitch in the 1980s and '90s in this part of Canada. We couldn't beat them. Not for lack of effort or trying, but because they played tournaments every weekend. We were known as the Porter Lake Marshalls and played in two or three tournaments a year with moderate success. We seemed to be the best of the mediocre teams, but we struggled against the Provost Shooters and Wainwright John Deeres of the region (although for the record, the Marshalls' highlight was winning our only tournament versus those John Deeres).

These teams had players who went on to Nationals. I asked one of the Shooters players, their primary pitcher Allan Murray, what he felt made them so successful and tough to beat. He sounded like Mr. Hall:

Everyone on this team wants to bat cleanup. I mean everyone. This is a nice problem to have. And what else is positive, and crucial, is we are fairly good at putting our egos on the shelf. This never happened overnight, but we're there now, and you can see it in the results. The guys have more fun winning and knowing we have a chance every time we play. Everyone wants to take responsibility for our success and we know it's also a team thing, but we all feel we as individuals can make the difference. It's so nice to be on a team where everyone wants to be a playmaker.

In typical Richie fashion, he smiled and laughed and said we better get to our first meeting. I put on my Blue Bomber hoodie. Talk about feeling out of place—initially! But everyone was wearing some kind of Bomber shirt or jacket. When in Rome, or should I say, when in Winnipeg.

CHAPTER 10

Tomahawk Chop

Look at this! Look at this! Look at this!
Do you think they got the message?
I mean the play, is over and three of them
are still doing the tomahawk chop.

- Todd Howard, defensive line coach of the
2015 Winnipeg Blue Bombers

I was walking around with Richie, talking shop and life philosophy as the triggers naturally came along. This launched us into so many conversations from the past, but put us into this current situation. I felt like I was walking around with a football Yoda who constantly got the life lessons of his craft: the art of leadership, the art of living, the art of teamwork, the art of developing a substance-based, spiritual heart.

Class was in session and Richie was more than cooperative. It was fun and educational watching Richie and his colleagues striving to put together a championship-calibre team. As he has said countless times:

It doesn't just happen. There is a process. Even when a team loads up on free agents, they still have to find the chemistry to work together and to manage their egos. Yes, it may happen quicker when the money is at a premium, but you still need the intangibles.

I have had the pleasure of observing and picking Richie's brain and heart for over 25 years. I have seen him operate when a team bottoms out at 3–15. And I have seen him win three Grey Cups and make the playoffs 18 times. The general process I have seen him work and be part of doesn't vary a lot. Some of the tightest coaching staffs I've seen him be a part of have been on teams in the rebuilding mode that missed the playoffs, yet the growth may have been more significant on these teams than on a team that makes it to a Grey Cup. These things are hard to measure if one simply looks at wins and losses. But the players and many die-hard fans see the progress and can appreciate the growth in a team that obviously over-achieves.

The principles and lessons Richie and I talk about, and talked about in depth during my three days undercover with the Blue Bombers, had a quality to them that could be applied or transferred over into so many other aspects of life. As that Vincent van Gogh quote says, "If one is master of one thing and understands one thing well, one has at the same time, insight into and understanding of many things."

We walked down the hallway to my first defensive meeting with the defensive linemen. Todd Howard is the coach in charge of this unit. He is a very animated, engaging, and passionate soul who wants an extremely aggressive, smart, and physically overpowering unit. He worked with Richie for two years in Saskatchewan before joining him in Winnipeg.

I sat in a corner beside Richie and watched Todd go to work. Richie was highly tuned in, mostly listening, but throwing in comments that related to the overall scheme of the defense. Todd picked out about eight to ten video plays to review the work of the line and to make emphasis points for the upcoming game. This has been a fairly solid strength of the current Bomber team.

Three words that came out strong were: tendencies, awareness, and recognition. He wanted the players to know the tendencies of the Stampeders' O-line. The human tendency is for players to stick with their strengths and only to deviate when things break down. But he also emphasized the importance of being aware of the wrinkles the Stampeders have shown in the past or might possibly use in a couple of days. And Richie emphasized one of his mantras that the players trust their eyes to recognize what is happening when the play develops.

Richie told me afterward that Todd is good at creating understanding. He strives to be crystal clear with the schemes he's coaching and to intertwine them with the philosophy of the overall defense. He checks and double-checks to make sure the players understand their roles and the roles of their teammates.

The last item on Todd's list for this meeting was for the lineman to create takeaways. He brought up the "tomahawk chop." This is when a player goes to make a tackle, or make a sack, and brings their arms down on the ball carrier where the ball is located. Sometimes the ball carrier can't hold the ball in his preferred manner and fumbles are easier to create. So Todd emphasized that during the upcoming on-field practice, players should get it into their minds to tomahawk chop on every play, even if the player wasn't close to the ball.

I could hear a few rumblings or jokes from the players, but they knew they needed to create more takeaways. There was no argument from the players as they knew Todd's message was apropos. This is basic defensive football, but the tendency is for players to focus so much on making a good tackle that they often forget about creating extra havoc. He wanted extra havoc to occur. Richie sure didn't argue the point; in fact, he encouraged Todd's emphasis.

Richie would say this was good fundamental football. The tomahawk chop is taught in Pop Warner football and high school football, but in the heat of battle the primary fundamental is to bring down the ball carrier. Both Todd and Richie mentioned that when gang tackling, the extra player coming in should have the tomahawk chop ready to go.

If there was one takeaway the players were not going to forget it was to practice the tomahawk chop until it became a habit. I was ready to start practicing the tomahawk chop as I walked out of the meeting with Richie. We would find out in a few minutes if the players took Todd's message to heart as they were about to hit the practice field. As we'll find out a bit later, I will say a resounding, yes!

As we walked out to go to the DB's meeting, Richie started talking about good fundamental football, and how easy it is to forget the fundamentals or to slack off practicing them. So much of coaching and practicing is centred on being fundamentally sound. They must be stressed constantly, and he talked about how he, as a coach is always trying to find fresh approaches to get the players on board. The players know how important it is to be fundamentally sound, but again the human tendency is to cut corners, or to think they are at a talent level beyond the fundamentals.

As Richie reminded me, good coaching is mostly about reminding the players and teams about the basics. It's all about muscle memory; and without practice or emphasis, the crispness can grow stale on the playing field, and you can get beat by a mental mistake. The successful teams do make fewer mental mistakes than their opponents. Getting overpowered or beaten by a physical mistake is human and can be tolerated to a degree. But a mental mistake can usually be minimized, and this comes with continual practice and reminders of the fundamentals. Nothing frustrates Richie or his colleagues more than mental mistakes that could be avoided. Richie understands the human element as well as anybody, but he also knows in order to be a contender, mental mistakes must be minimized, ideally eliminated, and dealt with appropriately and quickly.

He said something fascinating:

There is such a fine line dealing with mental mistakes. Players usually know when they have committed one. My job is to find that elusive balance of confronting the player, the timing of it, without discouraging him, but challenging him regardless because these generally are the mistakes that cost you football games. They are going to happen, but they must be minimized.

Sometimes I know a certain player will give himself a talking to, and self-correct. If I know that's the case, I'll pull back and look for an opportunity to quickly encourage him when he does something well on the field. But some players you got to get on them right away. But then I have to watch and see if his teammates get on his case first and how he responds. If he responds well, then I don't have to play bad cop. So it's that tension of correcting, encouraging, and hoping the player knows you believe in him. It's all about making our team the best team possible. I like what Corey Chamblin would say in Saskatchewan all the time, "One affects all!" I'm seeing things constantly from a team perspective, so my reaction is how things affect the team. I probably err on the side of confronting a mental mistake quickly, but I really hope the player knows I have his back. I know as a player if I knew my coach had my back, I wanted to self-correct right away and not let a mental mistake happen again.

Then Richie shifted gears as he often does. We talked about fundamentals in the spiritual realm, like prayer. According to some sources there have been more books written on prayer than any other topic universally. The next rival would be romance novels and poems. Yet, as Richie pontificated, prayer is a pretty basic and simple exercise, just as the tomahawk chop should be basic. We can study it, understand its value; but unless we practice prayer consistently, we will stifle our spiritual growth and miss out on opportunities where God wants to get involved because our wills stay closed to his presence getting involved in our lives. Okay, this is a football book primarily, and we'll leave the whole free will and God's sovereignty for a theological volume. But the point is that for a fundamental to be vibrant or useful it must be practiced and emphasized consistently. It's the old "if you don't use it, you lose it" principle.

Now we popped into the DB's meeting room with assistant Barron Miles who worked with Richie for three years in Regina. Barron had a 12-year career with Montreal and BC. He has won four Grey Cups, two as a player and two as a coach. Besides being a nine-time all-star, he holds the CFL record for blocked kicks. As Richie says, "Barron is a cerebral ball player and coach."

Barron is the ultimate minimalist. He knows the game—I mean he really knows the game—but he wants uncluttered players. He was a fundamentally sound football player who knew how to be flexible and to trust his eyes as the plays developed. He's Richie's kind of player and now coach. The more I talked with Barron, the more I realized why Richie wanted to work with him. Richie was also a fundamentally sound DB with the ability to adjust. Barron and Richie understood the value of speed and reaction, key for a DB as much if not more than any other position on the football field. It's almost all about reaction and communication.

Barron opened the meeting with one of his players telling a joke. This didn't always happen, but he does like a loose and free atmosphere within proper limits. This is very much how an effective DB has to play on the field as well. DBs are kind of like goalies in hockey. They tend to be creative freethinkers whose job description includes getting beat. The key to longevity of course is a combination of a short memory and the ability to minimize how often one does get beat. Perfection is the goal but virtually impossible to attain.

Barron is a deeply spiritual man but far from prudish. How can I say this? He allows his players to be human, and he sure doesn't come across as judgmental. The opening joke was premised in sexual innuendo. Some religious folk would act all offended. Barron didn't look particularly amused by the joke, but he let his players be themselves. They obviously knew where Barron's spiritual convictions were centred, and seemed to know how far they could push their jokes or language. Even as the player told the joke, I could see him looking at Barron and Richie from the corner of his eyes, to see if any offence was taken. Barron and Richie understand locker room culture and just let it go, gave a token smile, and moved on. The spirit of the joke was to loosen things up and to bond. Men being men, they laughed, and now realized the next 20 minutes or so were to focus on today's emphasis.

Barron chose 11 clips from the previous day's practice. He showed some plays over and over again a number of times. His emphasis was on communication between his five primary DBs. Sometimes they would add a sixth if the situation called for this. Barron and Richie at times would ask questions to make sure the players understood their responsibilities and how they could best work in sync. The coverage would vary from man to man to zone. The keys they would use were words like Bentley or Porsche, which would indicate what coverage Richie wanted. Richie joked afterwards that teams often use cars and their makes as cues, or women's names. Men tend to like fast cars and women, and remember cues like this. Maybe there was a connection to the opening joke?

Then there was talk of remembering some of the fundamentals that Barron saw were a tad lax the day before. Richie backed him with some of his own observations. They talked about the DBs looking at the receiver's hips, not his eyes. This is football 101 (a.k.a. the fundamentals). The hips are the centre of the body, and will tell a defender quicker than watching his head bobbing or his eyes where he will be going. Reacting to the hips makes the receiver work harder to read his quarterback. If he is going to catch the ball, make it as hard as possible for it to happen.

They talked about staying in the receiver's window, or the area on the field where he was expecting the ball to be thrown. If the DB stayed in the window, chances are the quarterback would check off and throw to someone else, which could create more time for the D-line or linebackers to disrupt or sack the QB. Or, if the QB panicked, he might try to force the ball into that window, which increases the chances of a knockdown or interception.

Both Barron and Richie emphasized, "Don't settle your feet. Make the receiver guess where you are thinking of going for coverage."

And, as we wrapped up, Barron must have said four or five times, "We have to be on the same page in our communication. Be talking out there. Be clear on the coverage. Lock in. Be focused." All those key phrases these players have heard for years, but need to pay attention to, and execute.

I liked Barron's style. He is passionate in creating understanding and not putting too much information into his player's heads. A minimalist, but a minimalist with a vast array of knowledge, or database to draw from. Speed and reaction are critical in defending against a pro football team. If one is bogged down by too many thoughts, the physical reaction is also bogged down.

We never had time to join Greg Knox and his linebackers for their meeting, but he joined Richie and the rest of the defensive coaches along with Coach O'Shea after the morning practice and lunch. Greg is another CFL veteran DB who played seven seasons in Calgary, winning two Grey Cups and two all-star selections. Not bad for an athlete from one of Canada's top NHL producing cities, Peterborough, Ontario.

But I did sit with his wife, Robin, during the game a couple days later. Greg was new to the Bombers, having coached extensively in the CIS, at the University of Toronto, and mostly at McMaster University in Hamilton. Robin flies in for the odd game in Winnipeg, and will re-evaluate where they will live after this season with Winnipeg. Ah, the life of a football coach, or should I say a football coach's wife?

We paused for a quick coffee and got ready to join the team on the field for practice. It was time to take the lessons and reminders of the classroom, and implement them in a dress rehearsal of sorts.

Richie joked and said:

This may get a little boring as we take to the field. It's all about the process of internalizing. There is going to be a lot of repetition. This is where we try and close the gap from theory to action. We videotape the whole practice, and it will be ready for us after lunch when we get together with the defensive coaches. Yesterday the players seemed to just be going through the motions; it will be interesting to see if they crank it up a notch today. I'm thinking they will because that's one of the messages they heard a few times this morning.

Personally, I was "cranked"! I was about to be on the sidelines with a professional football team, watching and observing their preparation. I knew it wasn't full speed or a game, but I was curious as to how the gap was about to close from theory to action. I think the coaches were, too.

"Every decision we make is based on three factors. The team! The team! The team! That's generally when you make the right decisions."

- Rex Ryan, former head coach of the Buffalo Bills and New York Jets and long-time NFL assistant.

CHAPTER 11

Testosterone Ballet

To create a romantic moment on the field, it takes hours and hours of practice and preparation behind the scenes.

- Jerry Rice, NFL Hall of Fame receiver who holds more receiving records than any other player in NFL history

This was fun!

It was a gorgeous, Manitoba harvest fall day. The sun was T-shirt warm. I walked with Richie through the players' tunnel, out onto the field. I felt like James Earl Jones (a.k.a. Terence Mann) in *Field of Dreams* as he was about to walk into the cornfield to meet the baseball ghosts.

I actually took a tentative step on to the playing field. It seemed like sacred turf. But I savoured the walk. I'm sure Richie would have thought I was nuts if he knew what was going through my head. I had walked on Mosaic Stadium at Taylor Field once before, and it was surreal for a Saskatchewan-born and raised, lifelong Roughrider fan. But this was still sacred. It was stadiums and arenas like this where, as a kid, my heroes did battle. Yes, this was brand new, but it was where the fun and inspiration took place. Field of Dreams in the Manitoba capital.

Immediately my mind went to Centennial Park in Langenburg, Saskatchewan, population 1,352 (last Google check before publication). From 1967 to my graduation year in 1976, I estimate my friends and I played a little over 1,000 touch football games, every night from late June until mid October. Sometimes we could squeeze in two or three games during the summer months. It's funny, I remembered a couple games where my cousin Brad came from Winnipeg to join us. I remember pretending that we traded for him from the Peg, and he'd be our speedy import for my Roughrider team.

I thought of my high school football days (nine-man version…small-town population), when we were the Kings of the Mainline Football League. We played such powers as Esterhazy, Moosomin, Broadview, Grenfell, and Whitewood. I always laughed at the name of our league, considering we grew up through the '70s. And, just for the record, we never failed a drug test. And yes, we were Kings; actually we were Golden Eagles in a small pond! We were part of a five-year championship run.

And I thought of all the games in the CFL I have attended over the years in every CFL city but Ottawa and Montreal. All the names that popped into my head: Lancaster, Reed, Bill "The Undertaker" Baker, Brock, Clements, Moon, Germany, Young, Austin, Fairholm, Flutie, Flutie, Joseph, Durant, and defensive backs like Dushinski and Hall… Then names from the Blue Bombers' past that I have read about over the years, such as Gerry James, Leo Lewis, Fritz Hanson, Kenny Ploen, and Bud Grant. The Bombers do have a cool history.

It was nostalgia about to meet a testosterone ballet!

After I walked the field, Richie set me up on the sidelines to watch, observe, take notes, and stay out of the way. The players seemed somewhat curious, and appeared to accept this intruder hanging out with their defensive coordinator. Richie would come over every now and then to ask if I was bored and how I was doing.

This was too much fun. I'd been to a pro practice a few times before, but never this close and with interaction. For Richie this was probably his millionth practice as a coach and player. This was a work day for Richie and an important one in light of the schedule. Yet I could tell this was also a passion for him and pretty much every coach and player.

The on-field practice generally lasts from 90 to 120 minutes depending on circumstances such as long weeks, short weeks, weather, which day of the preparation the time is in, and if certain aspects of any of the three units need to be worked on a tad more. On this day there was some focus on short kickoffs at the tail end of practice.

I wasn't on the field the previous day, but the coaches weren't pleased with the overall effort of yesterday's practice. Not that it was a total waste, but there seemed to be an overall lack of focus. Coach O'Shea said thankfully that was maybe only the second or third time all season this has happened. Richie said much the same a few minutes earlier when walking out to the field. I asked if this was common, and he said all teams go through little ebbs like this, human nature being what it is. It's funny how a couple of key players, if they aren't totally focused, can influence the rest of the players without it even being intentional.

The opening of practice was more about stretching, throwing a few balls, some short sprints, and some obvious teasing among the players and coaches. I counted a tad over 60 players being dressed for practice. In the CFL, teams can dress 44 players for games and two reserves who can only go in case of a game-ending injury. This was not a full-padded practice by any means. After the short time of stretching, the offence and the defence broke up to different ends of the field to walk through their schemes and plays.

On the defensive side the three units broke off into separate areas to work through some basic fundamentals. Richie walked around to all three groups, chatting with certain players and touching base with the other coaches. Some of this chatter was observing and checking on some of the players who had minor injuries and asking how they were feeling. Some of the other talk was about technique and scheme, and some of the talk was just touching base.

This day was day three of the overall week and referred to as "polish day." The players were cleaning up certain emphasis points and getting comfortable enough with the game plan. So far, Richie told me, the focus was much better than the day before. There was a little more sense of urgency on this day. After all, the defending champions were coming to town and were in possession of the league's best win/loss record.

If there was a theme of the day, it was all about understanding and clarity. Richie said:

We are taking the classroom to the field and trying to close that gap from theory to practice. It probably looks boring to an outsider, but this is a process of internalizing. We need lots of repetition, so the players can have that muscle memory necessary to get to that point of reacting rather than consciously thinking.

My goal, as is the other coaches', is to chip away at the learning curve. To minimize that overwhelming feeling that there is a ton of stuff to remember. Hopefully, getting on the practice field will break it down in the player's head and take away the intimidation. Once this kicks in at a certain comfort level, then the game does slow down. One of those interesting paradoxes of sports...the game seems so fast and it is, but when the building blocks fall into line, the game does slow down and the players' reaction time speeds up. Then you can dictate play a lot better than having the opposition take it to you.

Like the late Yogi Berra of New York Yankees fame used to say, "You can't hit and think at the same time." Football players perform better when reaction takes over. The brain is always working of course, but overthinking is the enemy of speed. Repetition is about the only way to close this gap.

Once the defence and offence went through their individual unit practices, the overall units came together and an organized game of offense versus defence started to take place. This seemed to me like a testosterone ballet as the offence faced the defense. Both sides were working on specific plays or schemes. This was not full contact by any means. At times the players almost seemed to walk through their choreographed plays, and at other times the pace was almost game speed. Emphasis was on each player doing what the playbook required. There was constant chatter between the players, but also between the coaches and players. Understanding and clarity!

The defensive linemen were obviously paying attention as they were all tomahawk chopping—every player, all four of them, every play. Richie and Todd Howard were happy. Even when the ball was almost a hash mark away, the four defensive linemen were tomahawk chopping. Later that afternoon in the defensive meeting along with O'Shea the coaches got a good laugh out of the over-emphasis. But the message was getting through to the players: do your job, but go that extra two kilometres, and try to force a turnover. A team achieves what is emphasized.

Even though the attitude of creating takeaways should be ingrained in all the players, this is not always the case. The reason once again is their focus on fulfilling their assignments, which is paramount, but this is going that extra step in teaching teams to win. Not just to play well, or to play to play. This was the message Richie was more than glad to second from Todd Howard. Coach O'Shea was more than pleased.

When Richie was with the Roughriders one of his defensive line coaches was former Edmonton Eskimo Hall of Famer Ron Estay, who was part of that five in a row dynasty coached by the great Hugh Campbell. Ron Estay had this quote on his white board in big bold letters:

We don't practice to practice, we practice to win!

That probably wasn't a Ron Estay original, but it was one of his mantras that Richie was more than happy to reinforce. The tomahawk chop emphasis reflected why professional football players play the game—to win!

Sounds simple, but oftentimes players and teams are just happy to be playing. This is developing a winner's mindset and cultivating this mindset at all times. As Richie often will say:

Learning to win is developing good habits and being conscious of being a difference maker. This isn't something one can turn off and then turn on right away. I find it's got to be there all the time. The great players, and especially the championship teams I have been part of or observed, have this mindset and it prevails through a team. Your core players at the very least have to have this mindset.

When a team has a bad practice day, it can be an indicator that the winning mindset hasn't grabbed hold enough. Attitudes are so infectious, especially from your leaders or core players. The core players set the tone, they really do. And if your best players have this mindset, the winning mindset can become a team thing. Maybe that's why I enjoy this game so much and watching this develop.

One of the things that intrigued me from the offensive side of the ball was watching the three backup quarterbacks. Teams talk about practice reps, and according to the CFL Players Association rules, teams can only practice for a set amount of time, thus limiting the reps for the backups. On every play the three backups would drop back and simulate what they would do in throwing the ball or handing it off, to mimic what the starting quarterback was doing. This was a way to mentally have their heads in the game and to take mental reps.

Richie said that whether this is a quarterback or not, when players do this while they are on the field it does get them in the right frame of mind and has them thinking through the plays. Hopefully this will create muscle memory. And a team certainly doesn't want players just standing around when time is at a premium.

The last phase of this day's practice was the special teams and in particular the onside kickoff. Second year placekicker Lirim Hajrullahu was practicing this by himself earlier when the offense and the defensive were in their separate sections of the field. Lirim has one of the strongest legs in the league. His background growing up was very unique as his family were refugees from Kosovo who settled in St. Catharines, Ontario. He remembers much of the trauma of this journey as a very young boy. I chatted with him a bit when he came over to the sidelines. I asked him who his kicking heroes were. When he said Sebastian Janikowski of the Oakland Raiders was his hero, I wasn't surprised. Janikowski may have the NFL's strongest leg, and has a similar background growing up in Poland and remembering how his family came out of the Iron Curtain in 1989.

Now it was full dress rehearsal for the special teams. The team seemed to have fun with this practice, which went on for almost 15 minutes. Lirim seemed to be on a roll, making his short kicks look almost like short passes for his teammates to run under the ball. He looked really good in practice; now will it work in upcoming games?

Richie came over after this was finished and said practice was over. A few of the players did some more stretching, some threw the ball for a couple minutes, and other players gathered in small groups, seeming to review some of what went on in practice.

Richie's evaluation as we walked off the field was acknowledging at first glance that the intensity level and focus was noticeably better than the previous day. His biggest concern was about execution:

Execution is key to this game as it is to everything in life. It's easy to talk a big game. Execution is the hardest thing in life. Closing that gap from theory to practice. It's like our faith. It's easy to say we are going to practice faith principles, but often when we talk about them, we think we are doing them because we are talking about them, but the real test is beyond church walls out in the real world. Do we love the unlovely? Do we practice generosity, mercy, and the like?

In football we get a test once a week to see if we can take it from the classroom to the practice field to actual games. You find out real quick. It's all about execution. I'm not impressed when a player says all the right things, looks good in practice, but falls apart during games. I don't want a good theorist; I want a playmaker. I'm real impressed when the theory and the practice happens in the actual games.

Then he smiled, "I bet God feels the same about us. Faith without works is dead, but combined with action is powerful...and catchy."

CHAPTER 12

Football IQ

"Educate, teach, and find ways to connect with their hearts and ways of thinking. It's part of why I enjoy this game so much. Developing their Football IQ as Mike O'Shea likes to emphasize. But remember Football IQ is more than just knowledge, but building trust or chemistry as well."

- Richie

My last full day with Richie in Winnipeg was final prep day for Calgary coming to town. We spent about two-thirds of the day at the stadium with the players and coaches. As Richie likes to say, "We were trying to get all the hay in the barn. Once the hay is in the barn, there isn't much more you can do. You prepare the players as best you can and then it's in their hands come game day."

Richie being Richie had already been at the stadium since 5:00 a.m. I rolled out of bed around 7:30 and prepared for my short trek to the stadium. Nothing against Timmy's, as I could sip on the team coffee sponsor all day long, but I needed my Starbucks fix before driving over to the stadium. I picked up an Americano, which got me thinking about "the ratio." With our many chats over the years, the ratio of Canadians (a.k.a. Nationals, formerly non-imports in CFL parlance) and Internationals (a.k.a. Americans, formerly imports) is always in the back of any coach's mind.

At the time of this writing, there is an almost 50-50 split in the CFL roster. Trading an International for a National or vice versa can upset the roster apple cart. Currently a team has to have seven Nationals in the starting 24 offensive and defensive players. Canadian or National depth has always been a key for playoff teams in the CFL. The reality is that there are more International football players to choose from in the football pool of players. The US, of course, is 10 times the size of Canada, and their annual crop of high school players alone compared to Canada is well past that 10:1 ratio. Canadian players that make the CFL are quality athletes, but the depth of the pool is not as deep—thus the constant tension of who starts and how does it affect the ratio.

So I arrived at the stadium with my Americano almost finished, thinking about players' birthplaces. I texted Richie after I parked, and he met me at the entrance. I tossed away my Americano and replaced it with a Timmy's. I was metaphorically getting ready to hang out with coaches who were putting their final touches on the CFL ratio. My java choices seemed apropos for the day.

Richie and I sat in his office before the team meeting with Coach O'Shea to start this final preparation day. We had our usual deep philosophical discussions about life, faith, women, and football. I don't know what triggered the following, but Richie said:

Good coaching is all about getting the team back to the purpose. It's always back to the purpose. And our purpose, like most organizations, businesses, churches, and families, is simple.

Don't be surprised if Mike brings up the term "Football IQ" sometime today. He is constantly trying to leave a nugget or tidbit with the players to get them to think. He wants them to understand what it takes to win. Like we have talked about before, we can all live with physical mistakes out on the field, but it's trying to eliminate, or at the very least minimize, those mental mistakes that shoot a team in the foot.

It's all about our purpose, which is to win football games. We don't play just to play. Every decision we make is intended to make our team better. Every team I've been on that has won a championship or come close strives for this. It's easy to say we put our egos on the shelf, but it really is fun to watch a team improve and have a chance to go deep in the playoffs. They know their purpose and make decisions around that—trying to put ourselves in the best position to try and win.

We are not the opponents; the opposition is the opponent. Sounds simple, doesn't it? Human nature and egos being what they are, it is almost a constant battle to get us to stick with our purpose as a team. If there are morale problems on a team it tends to be when egos get in the way, and someone is trying to further his own agenda at the expense of the team for whatever reason. It could be to get a starting position, or to move up the ladder as a coach, or just to come across that "I am right." I always try and remember that if I put my ego on the shelf, my career being what it is, will have a better chance at longevity, or whatever accolades I get will come naturally without trying to force things. We win as a team, we all know that, but we sometimes try and force things. Forcing things usually, if not always, backfires eventually and usually costs a team in the long run.

And there is such a satisfaction when a team acts like a team and has success. It's very fulfilling. And what's ironic is coaches are constantly looking for players who are willing to put their egos on the shelf, rather than promoting themselves.

This reminded us of the New Zealand All Blacks Rugby team who has won three World Rugby Cups, and has medalled in all but one Cup. Their coach is Steve Hansen who is a big believer in building your team around character players who put their egos on the shelf. In a 2015 interview in preparation for the 2015 Rugby World Cup in England he had this to say, which echoes Richie's words:

For us, we are trying to find people of good character because if they have got good character they will have good character on the track under pressure. Invariably the people who are d---heads off the track are the ones who wilt when they are on it. There are obvious exceptions to that, but most people's off-field character, I reckon, shows up on the field.

Marv Levy, the NFL Hall of Fame coach and two-time Grey Cup winning coach with Montreal, said much the same in his interviews over the years: "I am always looking for character players who put the team first and have some healthy outside interests. I have found over the course of my career that when the pressure is on, these are the players who come through for the team."

We walked over to the movie theatre-style classroom for a 20-minute meeting to start the day. Mike O'Shea got down to business fairly quickly as is his style. He talked about Calgary for a bit, where the Bombers were in the standings, and how the playoff push has to start now, as Labor Day is only a week away, meaning the season is half over.

Then he mentioned Football IQ and launched into a quick lesson. He reminded the players that he didn't want robots on the field, but players who have expanded their minds in understanding the game at a deeper level. To his credit he had the players' attention, as well as the coaches. He mentioned that the more they understand, this creates flexibility on the field. The more they practice their fundamentals and schemes, the more they will understand, and the more they understand, the more chance they have of imposing their wills on the opposition. This will increase their chances to be playmakers, and a team filled with playmakers is pretty tough to beat. He wanted to lead the league in takeaways, and lead the league in preventing takeaways.

Man, I was ready to get the pads on and hit the practice field. Or at least dust off my slider and hit a curling rink, and get a team together to compete for the Brier.

A few weeks later, Richie added to my Football IQ. He said up until this point in the book I have mentioned turnovers. And as even a casual football fan knows, the team with the best turnover ratio in their favour always makes the playoffs and tends to go deep in those playoffs. He said:

This may sound petty, but I don't talk about turnovers; I like to emphasize takeaways. There is a subtle difference. A turnover implies a mistake, which is true, but it sounds too passive. I like takeaways because it implies active aggression. We make it happen—it doesn't just happen. I need players who are thinking like playmakers. We don't just play defense, we think scoring, or setting the offense up to score.

Petty! I thought subtle, significant difference. It's a mindset he is trying to constantly coach. Aggressive football. It's what Eddie Davis was saying earlier, "How people don't always see Richie as aggressive in his philosophy, but he is very aggressive in trying to get all of us thinking takeaway." I must admit I laughed a little on the inside when Richie said he hoped he wasn't being petty with my terminology. Richie is ultrapolite with everyone he meets, but that doesn't mean he won't share his opinions, or emphasize his philosophy when necessary. Richie is a nice guy, with a tremendous amount of respect he shows people, but he has as big a backbone as any competitor I have ever met. That wasn't petty, it was huge!

I went and got another Timmy's from the coaches' office and rejoined Richie for three pop-in meetings within the next hour before taking to the practice field. We went to the defensive line meeting first. We didn't stay all that long as Richie seemed satisfied with the direction and integration from the previous two days. The linemen seemed to understand their assignments for Calgary, and they laughed a bit at their grasping of the tomahawk chop. But they knew it was to be a conscious part in the next day's game in order to take full effect. The line has been getting good pressure on opposing teams, and Richie didn't want to mess with what was working, but simply reinforce what has been working, and to have that takeaway mindset.

I wound up in the defensive backs meeting with Barron Miles. I was intrigued by Barron's emphasis for the day, so never made it to Greg Knox's linebacker meeting with Richie. Richie is a teacher and coaches from a teacher's perspective in the sense that he has three or four points to emphasize, and systematically goes through those points. He is very effective at what he does as he keeps things pertinent and interesting. In my three days with the team he had the players' and coaches' attention. He doesn't over-teach but gets down to business trying to simplify, or better said demystify, his game plan so it comes across as doable for the players.

Barron's strength, as I saw it, was creating chemistry because communication is so critical for the five and sometimes six DBs as they shift from man to man to zone defense, sometimes in a heartbeat. Barron didn't mind me sitting in on his meeting without Richie. I was about to be highly entertained and instructed in building team chemistry. Barron's teaching point was, "Let's be physical, and communicate."

As Richie has said to me for years, "Communication is built on trust, and I really don't care how the trust is built as long as it is genuine and authentic." Well, welcome to Barron Miles's methods.

Before Barron's teaching point that lasted all of 45 seconds, he again let a player tell a joke. It was slightly off-color and there was a teasing aspect toward Barron. It wasn't disrespectful, but I could tell they loved their coach. Some of the players were tentatively looking around to check out Barron's response. He laughed it off to let everyone know we are a team—a family.

Then a part AA, part *Saturday Night Live* show was about to begin. Honestly I think the players thought they were just killing time. There were 12 players in the room. The veterans seemed comfortable with each other, but there were recent additions and practice players to include in the DB family. Barron asked a couple of players to tell a recent joke they had heard to further loosen things up. Then a player said he had a song he'd like to play on his iPod, plugged into a stereo system he just happened to have beside him. I started to get the plan, or thought I was, but Barron had previously selected a couple of players to initiate a song or joke. The song was culturally current and motivational. I didn't know what it was but the players sure did. The song seemed to galvanize them a tad.

Then one of the players asked a new player who had recently arrived to tell a story he thought everyone would enjoy from his journey toward Winnipeg through the college and pro ranks. Barron briefly stepped in saying, "Anything but football." The player seemed somewhat shy at first, not knowing how he'd be received. I saw Barron was about to speak again, when a teammate said, "Just tell the story; we're interested." I was taken back because there was so much teasing going on. The newbie told his story. A couple of teammates said right away, "Man, we need to go out for dinner. What you doing tonight?" You could tell the DBs wanted to create a tight unit, a team within the team.

The meeting continued with this AA style of acceptance and safety, within a serious vein and then a teasing vein. The teasing seemed to indicate a level of acceptance. The male locker room at its finest!

As the meeting wrapped up, I was on the edge of my seat, observing something quite unique and effective. I was sitting in the very back of the room trying to be quiet and respectful. I don't think the players even knew I was there the more they engaged each other. The laughter reached a couple of crescendos when Richie knocked on the door from the linebackers' meeting, asking the players to keep it down. I could tell from the look in Richie's eyes he was okay with what was going on, but aware that the meeting next door may misinterpret what was happening.

As they were getting ready to leave, Barron shared what he was doing the last 20-some minutes. He said,

There was a point to all of this. As a coach I'm trying to build connection. The more you guys are relaxed with each other, the easier it is to trust each other, and the more you trust each other, communication becomes a priority. As you all know, we need to excel at communication as DBs. I want you guys to relax around each other so you'll play with and for each other.

Miles was building chemistry. It was brilliant, and of all the meetings I was in over those three days it's the one that has stuck the deepest for me because like Richie I love to teach, and teach in a classroom kind of setting. Not to over-teach, but to have some informal formality that hopefully is interesting and educational. Barron took it to a whole other angle without violating teaching principles. He knew his audience and what to do to create deeper chemistry. As I watched the DBs over the next couple of months they became a tighter unit and one of the team's best units.

As I pondered Barron's chemistry lesson, it occurred to me that when you date a person you are interested in, you don't take them to a classroom per se. When you're building romantic chemistry, you try to have fun and connect with the other's heart in ways that they'll cherish and remember. Barron was creating relationships of trust that will produce results on the field. It was brilliant! Like I said earlier, this was part AA and part *Saturday Night Live.*

Talking with Richie afterward, and over the next couple of weeks, I saw how Richie is a teacher! This was the message I was getting in my myriad interviews already. But I saw how he hired or suggested people to work with who teach in different ways. Richie wants chemistry, he wants thinking playmakers, and he doesn't care how it's achieved as long as it is achieved:

I like Mike's emphasis of Football IQ. This resonates with me as it always has. You want and need thinking players to be successful. I believe you can teach Football IQ. And there is a ton of different ways to do this. Some players are predisposed toward this, like anything else in life. But what I have seen over the years is you can educate people to think. As a coach we need to fill our players with knowledge, but knowledge alone won't win you ball games. You need chemistry, you need a strong awareness of the game plan, you need awareness on the field to react and not just follow the playbook. Good teaching plus strong chemistry builds not only a holistic athlete but a holistic team.

Football IQ includes trust. We can never forget there is a human element involved in sports. We are relational creatures, so that involves connection, which involves trust. If Barron can create that trust I don't care how he or anyone else does it as long as it's effective. When players have strong morale with each other, they naturally want to learn more—or they pay attention more because their respect for each other goes up. It's human nature. Barron can classroom teach, but I like his ability to be versatile, and always be aware of the necessary balance between knowledge and chemistry.

In 1989 Richie started in the Grey Cup DB backfield along with Glen Suitor, Harry Skipper, Steve Wiggins, and Larry Hogue, who replaced the injured Albert Brown. Looking back that was one solid group of talent. All the players other than Wiggins had six to eight years of CFL experience. They had a strong understanding of opposing offences and how they could work together as a unit.

We had a veteran group who clicked on the field. We had what we are trying to develop in Winnipeg this year. We had a feel for each other and the game. We probably wouldn't have needed a meeting, or very many meetings, like Barron had when you were here in Winnipeg because the trust was already pretty deep. A lot of our on-field communication was non-verbal because we had a corporate understanding.

I equate that to a healthy marriage. In many marriages, if not most, the verbal communication is very strong in the beginning. In healthy marriages I have observed the verbal is still good, but the non-verbal is excellent. There is a feel for each other. You know we joke about being able to finish each other's sentences in a good marriage. And usually that is the woman because they tend to be more verbal. [This is a direct Richie quote and he laughed, but was quick to say, in most cases.] Point being, when a team gains a feel for each other, it has gone from just thinking to reacting, which opens up creativity and mastering the nuances. This is when a team really becomes a team and great things can occur.

I know Barron is trying to accelerate the learning process for this unit. If he can deepen the trust where players are talking on and off the field, it's going to only improve the chemistry. One thing I can say is this unit has improved to one of the best in the league and it's been fun to watch. Feel! When the unit has a feel, you know you are in relatively good shape because then the players are reacting more than thinking, which means they are adjusting on the fly to make more plays.

"There is nothing more beautiful in the arts and sports than when improvisation takes over. When you react, play with feel and don't have to over think. This happens through mastering the technical fundamentals and building trust with your fellow musicians."

- Ron Block

14-time Grammy winner with Alison Krause and Union Station

CHAPTER 13

Don't Muddy the Waters

"Remember you don't handle players. You handle pets. You deal with players. Stand up for your players. Show them you care—on and off the court. Very important! It's not how or what you say, but what they absorb."

- Red Auerbach, former coach and GM of the Boston Celtics dynasty of the later 1950s to early 1970s

Our last day before game day, day three of shadowing Richie around, climaxed with a meeting with the entire defense. After the on-field practice and then lunch, the defense met for a little over an hour. This was final prep day, the last major time the team would meet together until the game the next day. Richie and the coaches wanted to get a feel for the players and whether they understood the game plan. Richie picked out about six plays or schemes the Bomber defence was going to use against specific formations the Stampeders liked to use. This was exam day, so to speak. This is something Richie does at the end of every preparation week for upcoming games.

Richie kicked the meeting off with a mini motivational speech to supplement the Football IQ emphasis of Mike O'Shea. This was definitely in Richie's wheelhouse. He is an accomplished public speaker who speaks from the heart, a prepared heart. He has a terrific way of getting his point across with a sense of urgency and sincerity. It's hard not to get drawn in as he speaks. You get the feeling this is serious material one needs to apply to their life and their game. This is not filler time at all.

Today's seven-minute talk was about leadership: how everyone on the team has a role to play and how to take it seriously. He is trying to create ownership and involvement with everyone. He has that uncanny way of making everyone feel important and that they have a role to play. It's not an act for rah rah-ness, but Richie's deep-seated philosophy comes through loud and clear, in a very interesting, matter-of-fact way. He doesn't talk down to his audience but talks at a level where you feel we are all in this together.

You get the sense from the players that they know Richie has been around. He doesn't advertise this fact, but you know after 30 years in pro football, combined with his time at Colorado State, he knows what it takes both technically and emotionally to win at the highest level. Richie is trying to create a team atmosphere. He doesn't want any passengers, but he wants players and coaches who can't wait to make a difference. Dealing with all different kinds of temperaments, personalities, and cultures is not an easy task, but Richie loves the challenge of trying to bring it all together. This may be his most fulfilling part of the job.

His three-point message went something like this:

If we are going to be a successful defense, a successful team, we need a team full of leaders. Whether you are starting, backing up, or on the practice roster, you are leaders.

Number One: Example

It's not just the words we say that make us a leader. A leader challenges and inspires. As we all know, actions speak louder than words. Look like you care; act like you care. Your body language speaks volumes. Attitudes are infectious. Let your overall demeanour be positive and encouraging. Don't give false platitudes; just be real, and find the good in one another, reinforce the good actions you observe and the positive performances on the field.

Please remember, you can all be examples whether you are on the field or not. A leader is an influence. Pay attention at all times. When you pay attention to the little things off the field, you'll pay attention, and be more conscious of, the little things that make a difference on the field. This will show that you care, and if you care during the preparation during the week, it will show up on the field where you'll care about doing all the little things, beyond just your assignments. We can all do that.

Number Two: Effort

What affects one, affects all of us. In your blocking and tackling, pursue, swarm, gang tackle, and help each other out. This isn't new information for any of you. But these attitudes and actions are contagious. Play with energy and focus.

The game is only sixty minutes long, about a hundred and fifty plays: sixty plays on offense, sixty plays on defense, and thirty special teams plays. For some of you, you will be on the field for ninety out of those hundred and fifty plays. Each play is the most important at that time.

As you know, five or six plays often determine the outcome, but you never know which of those plays may be that determining play. Make them all count. One hundred percent effort on each play, that's all we are asking. Being aware and being prepared for each play. I know it's cliché, but one play at a time. Maximum effort on each play, each series, each quarter, and each game.

Number Three: Communication

Good teams are in constant communication.

Communication is a key in being a good defense, staff, and team. Clarity, knowing your assignments and role, making sure you are on the same page with each other. There is the obvious verbal communication you need to have, but be more aware of the non-verbal, especially when you are on the field. This game is fast and decisions must be made fast. Learn each others' tendencies in as many situations as you can. The better you are at the non-verbal, the tighter and more cohesive you'll be on the field.

Always be paying attention in the video rooms, the practice field, and especially during the games. Look for ways to encourage each other constantly and to support each other. We are a team and good teams communicate. This is not something that comes naturally; communication is an art to be learned. Work at it, make it a priority!

Conclusion

We can lead in these three ways. Be an example, show effort at all times, and communicate, communicate, and communicate. We are all leaders, and the more we take this to heart the stronger our team is going to be. The intangibles are the difference, and if we can excel in our examples, our effort, and our communication we are building a strong foundation to excel as a team. This will get us doing the little things that can make a huge difference.

Once again, I was ready to suit up and make a difference, until I remembered my favourite team was still the Roughriders. Richie had the team's full attention. I could tell Mike O'Shea was pleased, as I am sure Richie was simply reinforcing what the head coach was hoping would go deeper with his team. As Richie says often, some players respond differently to a different voice, or a fresh angle, trying to get the philosophy of the team across. Richie is open to whatever it takes to communicate.

Before Richie got to the main course of this meeting, he emphasized something I have been intrigued with in many of our conversations: the eyes! He went on to say:

I have a handful of "key reminders" for tomorrow. Anticipation is critical. Study and remember the tendencies of Calgary and whom you are facing across the line from you. But…

Believe your eyes and what you are seeing out there. Yes, go with the tendency, but react to what you see. If you see a receiver running his route from the video and he's your man, and he's changing his route, adjust to what he is doing, or communicate to your teammate to switch responsibilities. Find a way to communicate, verbal, non-verbal, whatever it takes. We need to be on the same page.

Know each other's jobs, at least know them enough where you can adjust and be flexible. If something is off, go to that player and get it right. Be clear.

At this point O'Shea interjected briefly to re-emphasize what Richie was saying, "It's not achieved until it's understood. Let's communicate and emphasize communication. We have to be clear and understand what we are doing. Over-communicate if you have to."

Then Sam Hurl, the former University of Calgary Dinos star linebacker who plays middle linebacker, got up with his notepad and sat down beside a teammate. I could see them looking at something Sam wrote down, and his teammate nodded their head, like he understood something they were to adjust to on the field. The teammate gave a thumbs-up, as they didn't want to interrupt what Richie was talking about. Hurl was constantly taking copious notes at every meeting I saw him at. He was one of the few defensive players bringing a notebook to all the meetings.

Richie and I talked about the eyes again after the day was over at the stadium. He believes it's one of the most important attributes a player can possess. Believe what you see happening on the field.. This grows in proportion to how well the player knows and understands his assignments plus how well he knows each teammate's role. The better an athlete reacts to what is actually happening in the heat of a game, the better chance he will be a difference maker on the field.

After Richie's mini motivational message, the fun began. As is his custom, the last all defensive players' meeting before game day is a review of the game plan, which includes, as he calls it, "peer teaching." Richie picks out six to eight plays or schemes the team is going to use the following day. He calls a player to the front of the room, and they have to go to the big white board and explain each player's role on that specific play. The players don't know who is going to be called to the front. Man, I was nervous as I watched the players trying to look cool and not noticeable to Richie. It felt like ninth grade algebra class all over again.

Richie has a way of not embarrassing the players and maintaining their dignity through this process. But this is a necessary process to get a read on whether or not the team is prepared enough. He calls a player to the front and sits back and sees if they can explain the roles of each player and the overall defense. If the player doesn't get it all right away, he gives the green light, where the player can ask for input from the others. At this stage things loosen up a bit because the players are relying on each other, another subtle, yet brilliant way to develop team unity. They are all in this potentially awkward position together. You can see the players pulling for each other. What affects one affects all.

Only once through the six plays Richie presented did a player not have a clue. This is when I really wanted to crawl into a hole, and I wasn't even part of the team. Obviously, I won't mention this player's name, who is a CFL veteran. Eventually Richie gave the green light for the players to help out this ball player. It was easy to see the player was embarrassed that he wasn't properly prepared. After the play was discussed and gone over, the player went and sat down. He sat there paying attention, but not looking around at anybody. I don't think anyone knew what to say to him, and they were thankful it wasn't them caught in this awkward situation. If I was reading the room right, many of the players were disappointed in him, yet understood the awkwardness, but the team wanted to be thoroughly prepared. This could be cause for concern.

I asked Richie about this afterward. He said he was going to let this one go because he knew this player fairly well. He felt that the peer pressure of silence alone would send him a huge message to be better prepared. If it happened again, then he would approach the player one on one. And the question he would ask himself as a coach is, how can he communicate with this player in a more effective manner that would help him understand more clearly what his job is?

At the end of this day Mike O'Shea came into Richie's office and started chatting about the day, and asked Richie how he felt about the team heading into tomorrow's game. Mike was concerned about the one player a couple hours earlier who didn't grasp the play he was asked to explain. He felt "the hay was in the barn," and didn't want to interject new schemes or plays at the last minute as that could do more damage than good at this stage.

Mike said, "It always concerns me when a player doesn't understand it enough. This worries me a bit. In this situation I feel this is way too close to game time to confront the situation. It's always a timing issue. Do I confront or not? I'm sure willing to."

Richie felt in this case from what he knows of this player, he would review his playbook, and his teammates will be talking with him and vice versa. He is a team player and a proven professional. But if this continues of course it must be confronted. This seemed to be an isolated incident. From what I observed through my short time around the team, both Mike and Richie are quick to confront when necessary.

Having the team in a good mental state was paramount. They both talked about the importance of communication and encouragement. Before Mike left I gave him a copy of my bestselling curling sports psychology book co-authored with Olympic medallist Cheryl Bernard (shameless, shameless, shameless plug for me and Amazon), *Between the Sheets*. Mike joked and said he was going to show it to his wife, and how he found a new book about making your marriage better, starting…between the sheets.

As he left I thought about how these last three days were like a mini-practicum in team building and communication. Wouldn't it be interesting if athletes took these principles consistently into their romantic relationships? I immediately thought of a powerful insight from Gary Pomerantz's outstanding book on the Pittsburgh Steeler dynasty of the 1970s, *Their Life's Work*. He shares a story about his interview with J.T. Thomas, the savvy defensive back from those Super Bowl winning teams. Thomas was saying what had changed the most over the years as he attended their various reunions was how many players were working on second and third marriages. Thomas pontificated quite articulately:

Contact sports are the best form of communication. In real life, you've got those masks you put on every day. You forget who you really are. But in contact sports every contact tells who you are. We know through contact if you are scared or timid. Out there on the field it's like you become buck naked. Your teammates constantly affirm you. In the huddle, they'll say, "Way to go T-man. Way to kick his ass!" The different ways they affirm you is awesome. You don't hit a guy in the butt or grab him by the facemask in life to affirm him.

This ended my last day with the Winnipeg Blue Bombers as they all headed home for a good night's sleep to wake up to the Calgary Stampeders.

"It's too close to game day; I don't want to muddy the waters."

- Mike O'Shea

Head Coach of the 2015 Winnipeg Blue Bombers

Not the tallest DB at Colorado State University. (Courtesy of Colorado State University)

Happy Birthday Glenn Sutior, day before '89 Grey Cup game. Gotta love that pole. Dave Ridgway provided a helping hand..
(Courtesy of Royal Studios)

1989 Grey Cup player into — boy what a feeling.
(Courtesy of Royal Studios)

1989 Grey Cup Champions (Courtesy of Royal Studios)

Me, Uncle Skipp, Daddy, Cheryl (wife), Mrs. Uhl (mother in-law) Mommy, Aunt Doris. 1989 Grey Cup Champions (Courtest of Royal Studios)

Last year as a player in '91, with Mommy and Daddy. (Courtesy of Royal Studios)

Family at SkyDome 2007 Grey Cup vs Winnipeg + Winnipeg fan Helen Kiezik,far left. Yes Winnipeg was #2 on that day.

2007 Grey Cup Champs DBs, sporting their rings. (Courtesy of Royal Studios)

Ken Miller,Ron Estay,Mike Gibson,Alex Smith,Paul LaPolice, Me, Kent Austin. 2007 Grey Cup Champions Coaches

20th Anniversary Grey Cup Team (Courtesy of Royal Studios)

Coming off the edge to sack BC's Matt Dunnigan. (Courtesy of Royal Studios)

I was also a punt returner at Calgary. (Courtesy of Calgary Stampeders)

Richie talking to team after game. (Courtesy of Dale MacMillan)

I look better than I play.

Jr Briscoe, Joe Porter, Me," before "Sheila". Insert period after "Creepers".

Kelly Martin. I can't believe she got me to run miles with her at CSU.

Most influential person outside of my family, Mr. Hisamoto (teacher, baseball coach, good friend).

I even curl, with Guy (author), his daughter Anah (next to me), and Carol Weller (next to Guy). Curling isn't easy and you do work hard, it's but fun.

Richie Hall/Red Cross Golf Classic committee. #7 Joanne McClenaghan ,chairperson who had the vision.

HALFTIME

THE ECLECTIC WAYS OF MR. HALL

SECTION THREE

★ ★ ★ ★ ★

CHAPTER 14

Jazzing It Up!

"Richie is a Maestro when it comes to defensive football. He's the most creative coach I have ever witnessed or played for. His brain was always thinking football 24/7. And if he didn't appear to be, those thoughts were always bubbling under the surface. Incredibly smart and creative."

Do you think his creativity stems from how he has mastered the fundamentals of his craft?

"I think it does… The more you know your craft the more freed up you are to be creative."

- Eddie Davis, 15-year CFL veteran and Hall of Famer. One of the best shutdown defensive backs in CFL history.

Eddie Davis played for and was coached by Richie for eight of his 15 CFL seasons. Richie often called Eddie an extra coach on the field because of his smarts and his desire to study and apply. Eddie was given a tremendous amount of freedom along with Omar Morgan to improvise and call their own coverage within the schemes Richie game planned for. One of Richie's core philosophies is to empower players to think on their own and to improvise within the system. But in order to give players that freedom the fundamentals must be in place.

How does a coach or leader give up control to allow his players the freedom to do this? Like most football coaches, Richie is a stickler for mastering the fundamentals. In conversation with Eddie we chatted about jazz musicians and how they master their craft. Eddie is from St. Louis originally, which is in the blues and jazz region of North America. Jazz musicians especially have to master the fundamentals of their craft. When the fundamentals are mastered, one's mind is then made clear to improvise and to bring all those nuances into their songs. Jazz musicians are known as the great improvisers.

Football players, similar to a competent musician, must consistently work on the fundamentals. Musicians work daily on their runs, scores, and finger work, as an example. Defensive football players work on their footwork, tackling, running, stripping the ball, receiving, stretching, and video study, to name some of the core fundamentals. When players are fundamentally sound, their minds are freed to observe and react on the field when plays occur. The more fundamentally sound one is, the more one's creativity is freed up to react and make plays that often look routine or at times spectacular.

Ron Block has been a musician in Alison Krause's band Union Station for almost 20 years. At the time of this publication, Krause has won more Grammys (27) than any other living artist and is second only to the late Hungarian-born conductor Georg Solti (31). Ron and Richie both volunteered to be part of a Teen Challenge Curling Charity event in Calgary in 2008. Their approach to their crafts are quite similar. During this event Ron shared with us how important mastering one's fundamentals are:

Great musicians, artists, and athletes all know the importance of fundamentals. I know I have to work on them every day. The more in tune I am with the fundamentals, I see the correlation to creativity. Your mind is freed up to create and go with the flow. I can only imagine how that is for an athlete as well.

A couple of years ago I went to a Nashville Predators' hockey game with Ron and his wife, Sandra. Much of our talk on the way to the game and at the game had to do with mastering the fundamentals. I asked Ron if he was a hockey fan.

Not really, but I love to watch high-performance people perform any task because it is so inspiring. I just appreciate talent that is developed using their skills. And believe me it is a reminder to me, to keep working on my fundamentals. Oftentimes when I watch a game or go to a concert, I naturally think of the fundamentals these artists or athletes must be practicing daily.

Richie's defenses generally are in the top third statistically in the CFL. His emphasis on the fundamentals is key, finding the right players to play their positions is another key, but the biggest intangible is finding players he can empower to stay within the system yet maximize their creativity on the field. As Davis says,

Richie studies the game inside and out. He observes and experiments. One of his mentors was Gary Etcheverry, who was the Rider defensive coordinator when Richie looked after the DBs in 2000. Richie saw how his schemes were so successful, and over the years he used some of Etcheverry's stuff, but continually tweaked it to adapt to his players and changing offenses.

A lot of times in the off-season we'd get together and Richie would run things by me. And he'd keep thinking and sometimes talk himself out of his thoughts before he got to try them out because he knew they wouldn't work. He knows the game. Honestly, I think he's the most underrated defensive mind in pro football. His teams are almost always in the top third defensively, year in and year out, and if they're not the team is a work in progress.

This is where the nuances of the game take over, and a player can step out of a rigid style of play to become a playmaker, like a jazz musician truly becomes an entertainer when they go from the rigid score to colouring it up from the paper to the audience's soul and make a piece come alive.

On the football field there may be nothing more dangerous in a team's arsenal than a fundamentally sound player whose creativity is unleashed. Richie wants a player to get to the stage where mentally they understand the concepts of the team's philosophies or schemes so well that they can either add to the strategies or cut corners to accelerate a play. But understanding schemes and being physically in shape are keys: mastering the fundamentals.

Richie has had so many influences in his life. Not all of them have been direct. His brother, Michael, played for the great Eddie Robinson, at Grambling State in Louisiana. When Robinson retired he was the winningest coach in NCAA Division I football. He is currently #2. Over the years Michael and Richie have of course talked about Robinson's philosophies and ideas.

Michael said:

Robinson used to make us run plays over and over and over and over again till we could do them in our sleep. He didn't have a huge playbook on either side of the ball, but we could execute what we knew like few other teams. It's no wonder he sent so many players to the pros, both CFL and NFL. At one time Grambling was in the top five NCAA schools in producing pro football players. His players were fundamentally sound and exciting to watch.

There's that link between mastering the fundamentals and creativity once again.

One of Richie's oldest and dearest friends from his days at Colorado State is Kelly Martin, who grew up in Ann Arbor, Michigan. Kelly grew up in the same neighbourhood as Jim and John Harbaugh, who are the only brothers to have ever coached against each other in a Super Bowl, in 2013. She played with them as kids. Hearing about the Harbaughs subliminally would trigger Richie to pay attention to their ways of doing things. Not that Richie is a copycat; he's more of a complier who adds his twists by studying his players and the opposition.

Richie is always observing and asking questions, receiving indirect influences but also direct influences from other sports that all emphasize the importance of fundamentals and creativity.

As we go through this manuscript, much of the underlying theme of Richie Hall and his philosophy is mastering the fundamentals and taking players from thinking to reacting in the midst of a game. Richie is a teacher at heart, and the principles we are going to talk and write about capture the heart of a master teacher.

The principles of teaching and communicating Richie talks about, as you will see, will be applicable to many areas of life. As we have read and re-read this manuscript, we get comments that his teaching principles are obviously good for coaches, but also for school teachers, parents, anyone in the people industries, such as social work and psychology, business leaders, etc.

CHAPTER 15

The Boston Way!

The Boston Bruins are my favorite NHL team. It comes from my dad being based in Maine in the military as a kid. We lived pretty much on the US/Canada border.

I like Boston's history of the Bruins, but then you have Ted Williams with the Red Sox and players like Bill Russell with the Celtics.

- Richie

I was once privy to sitting down with Richie Hall and Tim Thomas, the two-time Vezina trophy winning Boston Bruins' goalie. Richie has been a lifelong Boston Bruins fan. When his father was in the military, they were once based in the New England states and Richie started to follow the Bruins. Richie and Tim actually have a lot in common from their professions. DEFENSE!

Tim and Richie started talking about styles or philosophies. I was privy to the conversation and almost starting pinching myself as they started to chat. They clicked immediately.

Tim has often said:

I think every goalie has to find their own style. I don't think my style is the perfect style by any means, but it works for me. You've got to take the tools that you have and make it work. I'm kind of like the redneck of goaltending that duct tapes everything together. You give a redneck a job, and they're going to use whatever is available to do the job.

When it comes to mastering the fundamentals, Richie, like Tim Thomas, is open to being unorthodox in his approach as long as the fundamentals are sound. Sticking with hockey and throwing a little baseball and basketball into the mix, Richie resonates with "the Boston way."

Kevin Constantine, former San Jose Sharks coach as well as long-time assistant for various NHL teams, nursed the San Jose Sharks to the largest one-season turnaround in overall points in NHL history. He liked to say, "When the traditional methods or styles don't work, try the non-traditional."

P.K. Wrigley of the famous Wrigley Gum Empire and former owner of the Chicago Cubs said something very similar, "When the orthodox doesn't work, try the unorthodox."

Tim never really had a lot of formal high-tech coaching. Of course he had coaches in minor hockey, high school, and college trying to coach him as best as they could, but in most cases these coaches weren't goalie experts, often by their own admission.

Tim has been knocked over his career about his flip-flop or unorthodox style. He doesn't fit the technically sound directions of USA Hockey and what they teach at their schools or workshops. It's too bad; because of this, Tim doesn't really like to teach kids the technical parts of the game at his hockey schools. He feels like he would be going against what they have already been taught in some ways. He prefers working more with advanced goalies and working on the nuances beyond the basic techniques. He often feels he is at odds with what groups like USA Hockey are teaching. Yet Tim has the equivalent of a PhD in goaltending.

Tim has learned most of his goalie philosophy through watching NHL-level goalies while growing up, and mostly by trial and error at each level he has played. He watched the other goalies at whatever level he played and assimilated whatever workable advice his coaches did offer, but he usually knew deep down, regardless of his age, that he knew what they were saying wasn't up to snuff and that he probably knew more than them.

In our conversations with Tim on his coaching—or lack thereof—he wasn't knocking his coaches from over the years, but it was the reality for goalies of his era. Most coaches were volunteers and could coach the non-goalies because that was usually the positions his coaches played when they were younger. Tim would say they tried, but more often than not he would know from playing the position whether what they were saying worked on the ice or limited Tim's ability to stop the puck.

Tim is a cerebral man and generally processes information from his experiences. When something on the ice works, Tim's philosophy is to incorporate what he is learning, master it, and throw out the things that hinder his style. Tim's instincts are so strong because his work ethic is so strong. Like a jazz musician, the more he practices the good stuff, the more this aids his instincts for the position and increases his learning curve. Mastering one fundamental makes it easier to discover another one.

Tim is as fundamentally sound a goalie as there has ever been in the game. So-called hockey pundits often confuse a playing style as a fundamental. Tim articulates like few athletes the distinction between proper fundamentals and one's individual style. The preferred goaltending style of the last 20–25 years has been the butterfly style Quebec goalies brought to the game beginning with Patrick Roy. Roy brought the flavour of the month, or generation, to the NHL. Tim is a throwback in the sense that he does whatever it takes to stop a puck. Flexibility and lightning-fast reflexes like his will trump certain styles every time.

One of the things that drew me to study and observe Tim is his unorthodox goaltending style. His style may have a few hitches in it but not many discernible flaws. When one studies the great athletes of their sports, very few of the best of the best have what could be termed classic technically perfect styles.

I'll admit I do play differently. I am unorthodox or unconventional to the preferred styles most goalies currently play. This doesn't mean I am not fundamentally sound, but from a technical perspective or style I am different. I like to think of it as thinking outside the box and being creative. It's all about stopping the puck. I am puck focused and will do whatever it takes to stop the puck.

I've called myself a redneck goalie, meaning I will use whatever talents I have been given and whatever methods in my arsenal to get the job done. It's all about creativity and trying to out-think the opposition. Some players have more tools than I do from a physical perspective, but none of us is perfect in every aspect.

Richie is much the same in his playing and coaching style. Undersized as a player, coaching defences on a longer and wider field than what he grew up with in the US, he has learned to adapt and out-think his opponents. Eddie Davis nailed it when he said:

Richie has sometimes been accused of not being aggressive enough. I understand the label but don't get it. It's not true. Too many people define aggressive from a straight physical perspective. Richie's defenses are physical enough but he out-thinks the opposition and tries to get his players to do the same. Mental aggression. If there is a weakness, you can be sure Richie will find a way to attack it and attack it quickly.

Maybe it is a Boston thing when it comes to fundamentals, creativity, and high performance?

Arguably the greatest hitter in baseball was Ted Williams of the Boston Red Sox, who pointed out on many occasions that it's okay to have a hitch but not a flaw in a baseball swing. We'll expand what Williams meant shortly because his baseball explanation explains Richie's coaching style from a philosophical point of view.

Ted Williams would have admired fellow Red Sox Kevin Youkilis, who won two World Series as a member of the Red Sox in the 2000s. He has a batting stance that has been called a lot of derogatory things, from ugly to grotesque. but never classic or sweet, yet Youkilis is considered the best moneyball (a.k.a. sabermetrics) player of the most recent decade because of his larger-than-life numbers for getting on base with his .382 on-base percentage.

Then there is Bill Russell, whom many basketball historians refer to as the greatest basketball player of all time, other than "maybe" Michael Jordan. Russell led the Boston Celtics to 11 NBA championships in 13 years. He was not known for his sexy offensive numbers but is still unmatched for his defensive prowess and rebounding skills. His style of defensive basketball was considered unorthodox for his time, swatting the ball away from shooters, yet he revolutionized the way defensive basketball is now played:

The idea is not to block every shot. The idea is to make your opponent believe that you might block every shot.

- Bill Russell

Bill Russell is arguably the best athlete to ever play in Boston in a city full of sports legends. The short list is Bill Russell (Celtics), Larry Bird (Celtics), Ted Williams (Red Sox), Tom Brady (Patriots), and Bobby Orr (Bruins).

When I first flew out to meet Tim Thomas in late January 2012 from Vancouver (ironic, eh), I made sure I flew out of nearby Bellingham, Washington, as I didn't know if the nice folk at Vancouver International would allow me on a flight to visit a Boston Bruin after what transpired only seven months earlier. Tim and I would spend four days together on this trip to explore his mental approach to hockey and sports. When I flew in I thought I was meeting Tim at the airport, but I was picked up by his good friends Anthony and Molly who whisked me down to the TD Boston Gardens for a game versus the Ottawa Senators. I thought the game was the next night—blame the time change or my blond roots. So we get to the game about 45 minutes before the puck dropped. As I settled into my seat I felt like I was in a sacred building seeing all those Boston Celtics championship banners along with the handful of Bruins banners, plus all the retired numbers from both teams.

Staring me in the face was Bill Russell's famous #6. I had read a couple of Russell's books, and a handful of books on that Celtics dynasty, plus a lot of historic renderings of the Boston Celtics dynasty led by Russell. I admired him not only as an athlete, but as a citizen of the world with his social conscience—reminded me of Richie. I couldn't help but sense the irony of what I was feeling. The greatest defensive basketball player ever played in Boston, and the best NHL goalie of the last five years played half his games under Russell's banner, and led his Bruins team with one of the greatest playoff defensive displays ever, regardless of sport. That's not just me typing, but ESPN seemed to agree with my assessment by awarding Tim the ESPY for best playoff performer of 2011 regardless of sport, with Tim being the first NHL'er to win the award.

Tim was more of a Russell disciple than he even imagined. As discussed, Tim is not a conventional goalie by the preferred styles of general managers in pro hockey, the butterfly style. Not that Tim can't play a format of that style, but his is almost a hybrid of styles; his unorthodox, aggressive, challenge-the-shooter style gets in shooters' heads before they even shoot the puck, à la Bill Russell!

Back to Ted Williams, baseball's last .400 hitter. He wrote a classic book titled *The Science of Hitting* with John Underwood in 1970 with updated versions in 1971 and 1986, a resource that is still used today by batting coaches of all levels. Williams's big emphasis was "hit according to your style":

Hitting a baseball—I've said it a thousand times—is fifty percent from the neck up, and the more we talk about it the more you'll see why that is so. The other fifty percent is hitting according to your style. Except when something is radically wrong, you won't find me doing much to alter a player's style. Chances are you won't even hear me talking about it. Everybody talks fundamentals—arms, feet, legs, etc.—but I seldom do. I like to demonstrate the necessary ingredients of a good swing, because there is logic in using them in the optimum way, but there is a dozen deviations from the norm: the size of the bat can make a difference, choking up can make a difference, moving away from the plate, moving closer— things dependent on an individual and his makeup.

Show me ten great hitters and I'll show you ten different styles... Don't worry if you hitch a little. Everybody says it's awful, but Foxx hitched, Greenberg hitched. I dropped down a little, as a cocking action, but the important thing is not to drop your hands too much because you'll have to bring them back up and that costs time and can disturb your rhythm.

Williams goes on to instruct that the ultimate fundamental in hitting a baseball is the last couple of feet before one hits the ball. You want to develop a square swing and follow-through, but the message is not to mess with a person's peculiarities, because everyone's body shape, size, temperament, and personality is so different.

Williams says there is nothing wrong with having a hitch in your swing; what you do not want is a flaw. A flaw is a swing with obvious hindrances from the set-up to being square as one swings through the ball.

Tim is more like a jazz musician in style than a classical technically perfect singer. Like a jazz performer he has mastered the fundamentals of his craft, which allows him to improvise when the lights turn on and the crowds are huge.

One could not improvise like a Richie Hall or a Tim Thomas unless one had mastered a certain minimum level of the fundamentals. His compete level was there. At the same time, when I spoke to Tim, Claude Julien, his coach in Boston, said, "My job is to make it easier on you as best I can by getting a good structure in front of you so you don't have to guess. You need to know how the players in front of you will react, which will help your style, too." Julien nailed it when he said, "You can get goalies that are technically sound, but they can't stop a puck."

Richie concurs with his philosophy. Creative, fundamentally sound players are what he is looking for within the team structure. When you have enough of these players in a 12-player unit, then the infrastructure is strong, and it feeds off of each individual ball player. It's why Eddie Davis said that from 2005 to 2008 the Riders had arguably the best defence in the CFL. The building blocks began in 2001 as Richie became the defensive coordinator, as the Riders started to rebuild after three miserable seasons.

I have interviewed and studied over 500 high-performance athletes, coaches, and scouts from pro, college, and high school football, golf, softball, baseball, volleyball, basketball, soccer, synchronized swimming, swimming, track, tennis, curling, and of course hockey.

What separates the great athlete or coach from the rest is that simple statement from Claude Julien. The billion dollar question is how can certain sports organizations certify coaches who focus primarily on the technical only while ignoring the ability to get the job done, regardless of what it looks like? This is not throwing the baby out with the bathwater here, because Richie would be the first to say that seeking to master the technical is critical for any athlete, but not at the detriment of performing a task that is required consistently. Too many coaches and scouts it seems would rather tolerate a player looking good while failing consistently than sign a player who may look a little unorthodox by certain sporting standards yet consistently does the task required.

Would these "technical only" certified coaches or scouts throw Rod Carew, Ichiro, or Pete Rose, some of the greatest hitters ever in the Major Leagues, or Sadaharu Oh, the greatest home run hitter in Japanese baseball, out of their respective Halls of Fame? Would the NFL throw out unorthodox passers like Fran Tarkenton or Steve Young out of their Hall of Fame? How about Super Bowl winning quarterback Joe Theismann, or Doug Flutie, who is in two major football Halls of Fame, the CFL and NCAA? The PGA is filled with unorthodox Hall of Famers like Arnold Palmer and Jack Nicklaus. How about the NHL Hall of Fame throwing out Mr. Gretzky, The Great One, who didn't dazzle the hockey world with his physical prowess, lightning-fast skating ability, or 100 mph slap shot?

As Richie emphasizes, these Hall of Famers had what many technically gifted athletes in their sport didn't have: the ability to use their smarts in above-average ways. Mental aggression! These athletes all had the ability to adjust to their apparent technical hitches and understood their disciplines at a level beyond mere technical perfection. And in a paradoxical way they mastered the technical aspects of their disciplines in unorthodox ways to get the job done.

A quarterback's job is to complete passes and move the chains. A defence's job is to stop the opposition's offenses and get the ball back so their offense can move the chains. A batter's job is to hit for average and get on base. A hockey forward's job is to score goals or set them up, and a goalie's job is to stop the puck and eliminate bad rebounds as best he can.

Tim cited former Hart Trophy winner Martin St. Louis as another example of being unorthodox. They were teammates at the University of Vermont, taking this overachieving team to the Frozen Four. St. Louis recently retired from the NHL after a 17-year career mostly with the Tampa Bay Lightning. St. Louis was also a smurf at only 5'8" (most people would say on skates not in street shoes), also winning a Hart trophy as the NHL's MVP. St. Louis feels that too many players in the NHL are squelching their creativity by trying to be too careful and to not make mistakes. They don't want to disappoint their coaches or GMs and be sent down.

St. Louis was a good example of someone who has found a way to stay creative. He tries to work on one new move a year and perfect it. What he does is stay after practice and work on his new move until it becomes second nature. He practices to the point where it just becomes part of his game. St. Louis is an example of someone working on a fundamental until it becomes part of his hockey DNA.

We asked Tim what makes him successful as a goalie. He just kind of looked at us, smirked, and said, "I watch the puck. I'm puck focused." Tim is by his own admission a very unorthodox, hybrid athlete. He thrives on having his mind freed up to be creative. This serves him well. This is not unusual when talking with world-class athletes. For Tim, thinking too much about mechanics while playing would be paralysis by analysis. Improvisers like Tim thrive on creativity, but if he becomes too reflective about the technical process, this will undermine his natural talents and instincts. Tim could lose the mojo or creative flow, so to speak.

Mike Babock, formerly of the Detroit Red Wings and the current head coach of the Toronto Maple Leafs, is considered one of the brightest minds in the NHL today. This Saskatoon, Saskatchewan, native and Saskatchewan Roughrider fan is the only coach in hockey history to have led teams to a Stanley Cup, World Championship, Olympic Gold, and World Junior title. And you can throw in a CIS championship, Canadian University championship, by leading the University of Lethbridge Pronghorns to their only collegiate title.

Babcock wrote a coaching motivational book, *Leave No Doubt*, in 2012 using the 2010 Canadian Olympic team as his template for coaching. He mixes in all his other levels of coaching as well to complement this nugget of a book. Babcock said the one commonality of all his Olympic players was that they were "super-learners." He believed that probably every Olympic hockey player, regardless of their nation, was the same. Whether this is true or not, Babcock would have loved a Eddie Davis or Richie Hall on his team.

A super-learner according to Babcock was a player who was incredibly teachable or coachable. Yes, they have a certain minimum level of talent to get to the NHL or the Olympics, but these types of players have a holistic approach to their profession. They are technically sound. But they also cultivate their mental game, emotional game, and inspirational game. Because they are super-learners, these Olympian-level athletes can adjust to their human flaws by compensating mentally, emotionally, and spiritually. They seek to get the most out of their God-given ability by whatever means it takes.

One week I was questioning Richie about his thoughts on angles, something Tim Thomas also excelled in. I loved his initial response, "It's something about the game I love, and so many of my thoughts go to angles and how to master them." Two of his closest friends and fellow Colorado State Rams, Jowel Briscoe and Joe Porter, both said it was a treat to watch Richie play college ball, and how he probably knew angles better than anyone on the team. Part of this was his size and the ability to tackle players almost twice his size, but also the ability to cut down offensive yards in his ability to get to the ball carrier or receiver quickly.

Two of the best Hall of Famers in their respective sports concur. Just read what Jerry West and Wayne Gretzky have to say about the importance of learning angles and thinking in terms of seeing the game as angles:

"It is a game of angles, and angles fascinate me, even obsess me."

- Jerry West

"People talk about skating, puck handling and shooting, but the whole sport is angles and caroms, forgetting the straight direction the puck is going, calculating where it is to be directed, factoring in all the interruptions. Basically, my whole game is angles."

- Wayne Gretzky

A journeyman is an apprentice who serves under a master craftsman. In sports the term sometimes goes a level deeper, meaning the athlete is a master of the profession or sport in understanding its nuances and multiple philosophies. A journeyman is often an athlete who is technically competent but unable to excel, or has not been given the opportunity for various reasons, usually injury or an unorthodox style, à la Richie Hall. Richie says:

I have learned over the years that the wisest people in pro sports that one can learn from aren't always the name players. It's those journeyman guys who have stuck around in the minors or have become role players on big league teams. These are the athletes who should get their honorary PhDs in their sports. You can't find a better intangible for a team.

They are the guys who usually don't have the God-given talent to make the big time or they have the talent but were in the wrong place at the wrong time. Athletes such as Tim Thomas. I enjoyed getting inside his brain. People like Tim get the most out of their talent. A journeyman who became a superstar. It's amazing that five or six of the top defensive players or coaches in their sports came from Boston. Bill Belichick, Carlton Fisk, Bobby Orr, Bill Russell, and Tim Thomas. There's something about the Boston way.

CHAPTER 16

Granite to Gridiron: Embracing the Prairies

Curling may be the most deceptively difficult sport I have ever tried.

The late George Plimpton, former *Sports Illustrated* writer and author of many sports books such as *Paper Lion*, about his experience being allowed to try out for the Detroit Lions for a book project (which turned into a movie).

Why a chapter built around curling? Simple, really! Richie has either played or coached in the world's curling hotbed region—the Canadian prairies. More Canadian champions and World champions come from this region than anywhere else on the planet, and currently those numbers aren't even close. Consider that he started his playing career in Calgary before heading to Saskatchewan, and has coached in Regina, Edmonton, and Winnipeg, the four prairie cities of the CFL. One can't get more prairie than those four cities. Just think of the short list of curling Hall of Famers:

- The Ron Northcott team and multiple world champions, and the Cheryl Bernard team of Olympic medalists, based out of Calgary.

- Team Kevin Martin, multiple Olympic medalists, world champion, and #1 money winner of all time, plus the Ferbey Four, who dominated the early 2000s.

- Arguably the greatest curling team of all time was Regina's Richardsons, the only four-time World curling champions, and the Sandra Schmirler World and Olympic champions, who most curling insiders would say is the greatest women's team of all time.
- Then there is Winnipeg, home of countless World champs and Olympic medalists: Ken Watson, Don Duguid, Jeff Stoughton, Kerry Burtnyk, Connie Laliberte, and Jennifer Jones, and that's the short list.

Richie is not the first American CFL'er to take to curling. The late Ron Lancaster was very good friends with the Ernie Richardson team in Regina. Stories around Regina tell of Lancaster making trips down to Regina curling clubs to watch the best in action—always learning and studying. Lancaster often played the game in the off-season. Curling is a touch game and quarterbacking is a finesse position in a borderline violent sport.

Jackie Parker was named the top CFL player of the first 50 years of Canadian football. From Mississippi originally, Parker was fascinated by the granite game. He often played two or three times a week in those frigid Edmonton winters. In an old *Star Weekly* magazine from the 1960s there is a Parker story of him skipping a team to a bonspiel win in Sarnia, Ontario. Parker said this was one of the top highlights of his sports career—period.

Bud Grant, whose statue stands out in front of the new Investors Group Field in Winnipeg, writes in his autobiography, *I Did It My Way*, that he learned how to curl during his time with the Bombers even though he came from curling country in Superior, Wisconsin, which was the home of the first-ever US world curling champions skipped by Bud Somerville. Grant played in regular league play in Winnipeg.

Gerry James, born in Regina, a two-time winner of the top Canadian award in the CFL with the Blue Bombers, also curled, but at a highly competitive level. After football he played on a team in Yorkton, Saskatchewan, which came within one shot of going to curling's biggest showcase, the Brier. James was Canada's last two-sport professional athlete as he spent over half a decade with the Toronto Maple Leafs while playing for the Bombers in Winnipeg.

Richie watches curling on a fairly regular basis. He has met and participated in local sports and charity events with the first women's Olympic gold medal team from the 1998 Nagano, Japan, Winter Olympics, skipped by the late Sandra Schmirler of Regina. He once curled in a Teen Challenge, a drug and alcohol rehab centre fundraiser in Calgary. He phones me out of the blue every now and then, asking me things like:

- What in the world was he thinking on that shot in the sixth end?

- Wasn't that a beautiful angle raise for two by the Swedish skip?
- Why didn't he play the take-out on that shot about 15 minutes ago?
- So, if they win this one, does this keep them alive for a playoff spot?
- I love how these teams have all their weights down for the various touch shots…
- So, I guess they didn't play the shot on that piece of ice because of the ice conditions, right?

These are just some of the discussions we have had over the years about curling.

When I was in Winnipeg on my three-day, "a day in the life of" trek, the topic of getting down early in a football game came up when one of the coaches walked into his office, and asked what does a team do to get back in it. Richie looked at me and said:

Well, you know what it's like in a curling game. A team gets down but they chip away a little bit at a time and have to be patient. You don't try to get it all back at once. You see it in curling where a team gets a point or two back, and before you know it momentum sometimes shifts and the comeback is on.

On the flip side, when your team is up, just like in curling you can't let the other team get momentum. Maybe they score a point or two, but you have to amp it up and get those points back when the opportunity arises to try and kill their momentum.

I was quite flattered that Richie included the football coach and me in the conversation. This is typical Richie Hall: he tries to speak the language of his audience. This was a classic sports example, but I have seen it also in school and church settings where he speaks. He finds common speaking points to make his point and to help the listener understand. He is always, and I mean always, looking for communication connecting points. The fact that he does this endears him to his audience and causes them to pay attention, whether that is one person or a hall full of people.

Richie and I have had many conversations about curling. Sometimes I know he is relating to me through one of my favorite sports, but at other times he has phoned simply to ask, what is going on with the decision-making on the ice.

Richie is entering his 32nd year in pro football: 32 years of being in the arena; 32 years of observing and studying competitive sports, period. What works? What doesn't work? The lessons apply to almost any sphere of life. He sees the parallel lessons from other sports and life disciplines constantly. Kelly Martin is a lifelong friend whom Richie met at Colorado State. Kelly ran track and often coerced Richie into running long distances with her during their college days. She says, "One thing I love about Richie is how he takes everyday examples from football or whatever interests another person, and he'll ferret out the life lesson, and usually find a spiritual nugget in that lesson. His mind is so geared that way. He sees truth in everything. It's a great way to think and such an inspiration for us, his friends."

And, to use Richie's favorite Vincent van Gogh quote again:

If one is master of one thing and understands one thing well, one has at the same time, insight into and understanding of many things.

Richie is a lot like Van Gogh in this aspect of life. He understands his sport as well as anyone in football, and he sees the parallel in all of life's other disciplines. So, in my friendship with Richie over the years we have talked curling and those lessons have skipped over to football and life in general. I must admit in my own public speaking, whether in church or another setting, I try to be like Richie and often have used his insights in my presentations.

Back in 2008 we were part of that Teen Challenge fundraiser in Calgary at the Calgary Curling Club. The fun one-day bonspiel filled the entries up quickly. Richie understands the sport but had never played it before. The night before, he asked me to take him down to the rink and give him a crash course on delivering a rock and sweeping. He wanted to have a comfort level at a sport he had never tried. It didn't take him long to learn the very rudimentary basics of delivering a curling rock. His style was like any newbie's would have been, but surprisingly he had a knack for draw weight. No real surprise to me as Richie is an athlete, and of course caught on quicker than the average student.

This wasn't a big-time bonspiel, but humans being humans, everyone wanted to do well. Richie was on my family team and played lead, or threw the first stones. He probably got 75 percent of his rocks in play the next day. But what floored me is how he got the footwork down for sweeping along with using maximum power. He was like a machine and we almost wore him out, and he never took a break. We played four 4-end games, which is the equivalent of two full-time club games. If you had walked into the rink and watched Richie for the first time sweeping, you'd think he had been playing the sport for years. My daughter, Anah, was the other front-end player who did most of the lion's share of sweeping with Richie. The two of them worked so well in sync you'd have thought this was a higher-end event. It was interesting to watch the two of them as Richie was constantly encouraging and communicating with

Anah as to how they could better work well together. This illustrated so clearly Richie's sports IQ for figuring out how to maximize his skill set while working effectively with a teammate. At the end of the day he was dripping wet with sweat with a huge smile, though exhausted, on his face. He helped our team make it to the event final. It came down to the very last rock and about two inches to decide the final outcome. When we lost, on I must say a very well-executed, difficult shot, I thought the look of disappointment on his face was similar to losing a CFL playoff game. Okay, slight exaggeration, but you could tell he was hoping for the win. But his lifetime record is well over 70 percent.

The next day talking with Richie was funny. Here is a man who is generally in pretty good shape even though his playing days are over. He was sore, telling us he had used muscles he had hardly ever used before because of how sweeping works. He could have become a walking advertisement for the aerobic benefits of curling.

Part of why Richie watches curling is the decision-making and the dialogue on TV broadcasts is unique to curling, unlike almost any other televised sport. The players are mic'ed so the viewer can listen in to the strategy and process of making decisions. This is a coach's dream. Not only is there the decision-making, but the team dynamics are front and centre, and the communication skills and breakdowns are there for the world to see. What's also unique to this is you have the differences between men and women and how they process a competitive sport. Obviously there are similarities, but there are differences to observe and glean some lessons from. Richie has a holistic view toward life anyway, so watching curling even subliminally or casually affects Richie's thought processes.

Richie gets the nuances of sports so quickly. Some of the things about curling he clued into are the overall environment of the venue and the mindset of the individual athletes. During the last Olympics he called and started pumping me full of questions. He wanted to know why a certain team favoured what seemed like an easier shot for a slightly more difficult one. As we talked he clued into how the one team didn't know how the ice would react to what on paper seemed like the easier call, but the Plan B did make sense because the team knew the condition of the ice for that call. Even though it didn't look like they were playing the percentages they in fact were. Similar to windy conditions in a city like Winnipeg or Regina where a 45-yard field goal seems like the logical choice—unless it's against the wind, when in fact the wind conditions dictate a punt to pin your opponent back might be the better call in the big picture, especially knowing that in two minutes the quarter will be over and the wind will be in your team's favor. And also knowing your punt coverage unit is more likely to cover a punt successfully than a missed field goal unit with bigger, slower men on the field. Sometimes it's more about field position than scoring points; just as in curling sometimes giving up a point is better than trying an ill-advised gamble for two or three when the game is still in your control.

Richie is so in tune with the factors of what goes into decision-making. In curling we talked about the score, the end (like an inning in baseball), who has hammer (last rock), how certain players are playing, which players can or cannot throw the high hard rock accurately (fast heavy take out stones), the ice conditions (easily predictable or wonky), the strengths and weaknesses of certain teams, and the like. This of course segued into football really easily with weather conditions, having an experienced quarterback or a rookie backup, or a veteran linebacker versus an undersized replacement, is this primarily a pass-heavy team or a run-heavy team, how does the defence match up against the run or the pass, how well do the specific offences, defences or special teams communicate, and the list goes on.

He liked how some curling teams encouraged struggling players to play a shot they have a higher percentage of making, rather than giving them a shot with a weight and turn they may have been struggling with. In football sometimes just taking short five to six yard gains over a series of plays may get the quarterback or running back into the rhythm of a game for when bigger chances must be taken down the road. Both sports, as with most sports, are about building individual and collective confidence, and getting into a rhythm.

He asked about a team who seemed to be playing conservatively when they normally were more aggressive. The curling strategy was about taking the opponent out of their comfort zone, like a good defense in football tries to do. Often when a team takes their opponent out of their comfort zone, they force them to take more chances to get out of their funk, and in doing so their opponents' collective confidence is shaken, and unforced errors begin to take over.

And then Richie would more often than not bring it into his faith. As he often says, he is a simple man but not simplistic. I believe this is strongly due to the fact that he is a better than average teacher, breaking down complex ideas and making them easier to understand for those under his guidance. He would find the parallels that faith is more than mere theory, but has to be executed under conditions people have either experienced in the past, or to be challenged to expand their comfort zone in following spiritual maxims. He sees the many factors involved in living a life of faith and that sometimes we have opposition from other people or philosophies that influence spiritual harmony.

Richie doesn't want to see people overwhelmed, whether it is on the football field or in living a life of faith. Building blocks, or one step of faith at a time, often create more faith and understanding as one grows. He is extremely cognizant of this reality. He sees how a curling team plays it a shot at a time and an end at a time, and how in football it is one play at a time or one series at a time. Being a pro football player and coach and watching other sports such as curling remind him how the principles for achieving success or growth are one step at a time. Faith, like curling and football, is a life of discipline, practice, execution of fundamentals, and high focus.

He likes the words of Paul in 1 Corinthians 9 (24–27) in this context:

24 *Do you not know that in a race all the runners run, but only one gets the prize? Run in such a way as to get the prize.* **25** *Everyone who competes in the game goes into strict training. They do it to get a crown that will not last, but we do it to get a crown that will last forever.* **26** *Therefore I do not run like someone running aimlessly; I do not fight like a boxer beating the air.* **27** *No, I strike blow to my body and make it my slave so that after I have preached to others, I myself will not be disqualified for the prize.*

CHAPTER 17

Magnetic Kindness
(Reflections from the Inner Circle)

"You gave me the greatest gift of all—you believed in me."
Rodney Copperbottom, to his dad Herb in the 2005 film, *Robots*

As we have already written about, one of Richie's fundamental strengths as a difference maker is that relationships are one of the cornerstones of how he operates in every aspect of his life. It would be safe to say that building relationships isn't just one of Richie's cornerstones, but the cornerstone of his value system and coaching philosophy.

Whether through coaching, marriage, humanitarian endeavours or whatever, Richie gets energized by the relationships he has cultivated, and continues to do so. Relationships are the galvanizing key to his spiritual and personal growth, and his ability to influence others. It has been over 30 years since his college days at Colorado State in Fort Collins, yet his four best friends from those years are still his "go to" people, and all four of them said the same thing in return. This inner circle of college friends is as tight a unit of friendship as I have ever interviewed or experienced. Beyond his college inner circle, Richie includes his brother, sister, and high school phys. ed. teacher and baseball coach.

This is as unique a set-up as I have ever seen in all my years as a counsellor, writer, researcher, and minister. We all crave an inner circle relationship where we can totally be ourselves, knowing our mates have our back regardless of the life circumstances, moods, adversities, and joys life will bring. This group of people truly live out the Biblical mandate found in Romans 12:15:

Rejoice with those who rejoice; weep with those who weep.

Richie's inner circle is based on unconditional love and kindness, in which Richie has been a major catalyst. Kelly Martin is one of those college inner circle people. She met Richie in her first year at Colorado State. Kelly is from Ann Arbor, Michigan, originally, but has stayed in Colorado ever since college to raise her family. She ran track for the school's track team and would often get Richie to train with her.

Richie has been a dear friend to my family and me ever since my first year at Colorado State. He is as true a friend as one could ever find in this lifetime. I know why people are drawn to him. He has a magnetic kindness that is so genuine and sincere. We understand why people were drawn to him, not just us, but why others love to be in his presence. When you're around Richie, he makes you feel like you are the most important person in the room. He's the real deal. Magnetic kindness!

Along with Kelly, Richie gave me a list of his long-time friends and family away from football. He would consider these people his inner circle, and they would as well, as I found out quite quickly. The rest of his inner circle includes Sheila Pomeranz, who lives in Denver; his sister, Janice Watley, who lives in greater Baltimore, Maryland; Michael Hall, his younger brother who served as a policeman for most of his adult life and lives in Denver; and of course his parents, Richard Sr. and Jean. Steve Hisamoto was his high school phys. ed. teacher and baseball coach. Richie says that Steve is easily the most influential man in his life outside of his family and younger friends.

Then there are his three buddies known as "The Creepers". It's not as sordid as it sounds, as we'll explain shortly. Dwane Kelley was a teammate at Colorado State, who was from Columbus, Ohio, but has settled in Dallas, Texas, as a sheriff. Junior (Jowel) Briscoe was his high school friend from Denver and roommate at Colorado State who now lives in Columbus, Ohio. The last member of the Creepers is Joe Porter, who also lives in Columbus and was a roommate at Colorado State.

This inner circle has been through a lot together. They have been to each other's weddings, walked with each other through relationships that didn't work out, divorce in some cases, have been there for their children, attended each other's parent's funerals, have chatted over the phone for hours, or hopped on a plane to just be with each other in a time of need.

The Creepers take annual vacations together and meet all over North America. This has gone on for years. Richie and his friends call and text each other on a regular basis. These annual getaways often include spouses or significant others as they enjoy sharing the other relationships they have cultivated.

The Creepers started as typical college adolescents—the college pranks, late nights, the fun of blowing off steam, and connecting in centuries-old, testosterone ways.

Jowel Briscoe said:

Richie and I met in junior high in Thornton, Colorado, and the other Creepers at Colorado State. These are the longest friendships I have ever had, and Richie is the longest friend I have ever had. Goodness, all the things we have done together over the years. All the sports, the college fun, go-karting, our women struggles [he laughed], helping each other move and move again.

I loved watching him play sports. Smart! World-class speed! I don't know anyone else that knew angles like he did on the football field. He can be so soft-spoken and quiet. Believe me, he knows what he's talking about when it comes to the game and to life.

Joe Porter also played with the CSU Rams with Richie:

Yes, the Creepers. I can tell you what makes him a good coach and a good person, period. He is one smart man. Honestly I don't think he ever made the same mistake twice on the football field. He was so aware of what was happening. You couldn't fool him.

He has such a gentle but firm way about him. We have common beliefs and values. He is very open with us about what we need to hear, not what we want to hear. And it is mutual. I know he coaches this way. Don't be fooled by his quietness or kind disposition; it's based in deep, well-thought-through convictions. I think he thrives in trying to figure out ways to overcome the odds, both during games but in the process of building a championship team. He coaches in a manner people want to be coached by him. You don't have to be around him very long to realize he is a master teacher of the game because he is a perpetual student of the game.

Dwane Kelley is a retired sheriff who now lives in Dallas. Dwane reflects on his friendship with Richie:

Yes, the Creepers, 'cause we'd creep around the dorms. We met at 18 years old and always promised each other we'd take care of each other through life. A lot of people make those promises, but Richie of course carried through. We lost touch about fifteen to sixteen years ago for a spell, and now we have been doing these reunion trips every year since 2000, usually the week before the Martin Luther King Jr. holiday.

When my parents died the Creepers were there. They are my inner circle. At our darkest life moments, we have been there for each other. It just deepens the bonds. We love each other like family. It's a great feeling to know you're loved and it's so genuine. We get each other, we can laugh together. Richie has the biggest heart. He has never been caught up in materialism. He gets it, he helps us get it. When a storm of life hits, he brings calm.

As a coach the biggest thing he brings is his knowledge of people and of life in general. I can only assume the players know he cares about them first as individuals. Of course he knows his X's and O's, and can adjust on the fly with the best of them.

These are just a handful of insights into the soul of Mr. Hall from the people closest to his heart, but in dozens of interviews (me included on this one) Richie has that way of making so many feel they are important to them. If he finds out a friend or acquaintance from his encounters over the years needs some encouragement, he makes an effort to care or support. I was trying to find the right words for this chapter and the distinction between an inner circle friendship, good friend, and acquaintance—maybe village would have been better in Richie's case. But, even in a village that one loves and feels like home, some heart relationships develop tighter bonds than others. There are only so many people one can be completely vulnerable with, and when those relationships are based in strong shared values, their character and kindness spill out to others and we all benefit.

"Sports Illustrated", or Richie Illustrated—Winnipeg, Manitoba

The Bombers started the 2016 season at 1-4. The fans around the Bombers were getting restless. You could feel it! This could be their fifth straight season out of the playoffs. This had never happened before in Blue Bomber history. I had gone to all three of their home games to start the season—all losses, and close frustrating ones. After the fourth loss Richie came out to visit me by the Bud Grant statue in front of the new Investor's Group Field. Richie was obviously bummed out over the loss. Words were hard to find. Two players leaving early walked by and both put their hands on Richie's shoulder. The last thing I wanted to do was give my perspective as a fan. But Richie needed to vent a bit, and we talked about the game and how close the team was. Little things and consistency in the fundamentals seemed to be the theme on his mind, and how he could make a difference with his coaching. And then he asks me, "So, Mr. Scholz, how did it go this week?"

I made a joke, knowing what he was referring to. I'm back in the dating world and Richie is one of the few people to know what's going on in my love life. This beautiful woman (I could post a picture) I was dating for over a year asked for a break, and she gave a timeline of when she'd get back to me about "direction."

I'm prepping for heartbreak. I'm at the stage of life where days normally fly by, but when a woman you care about says she wants a break and will get back to you, those days can seem like months.

So Mr. Magnetic Kindness started to share his heart with me and his perspective on romance and what he understood about my current state. I'm sure if a TSN, Winnipeg Free Press, or CJOB Bomber Radio reporter was close by they would assume we were having this intense discussion about the state of the Bombers. I remember walking back to the parking lot after our chat thinking how wise and caring his words to me were. He never gave guarantees, he never gave me some kind of false hope, but I walked away with such renewed hope in my heart and a little more perspective in how patience is sometimes a virtue. I kind of laughed when he said, "You know absence will either make the heart grow fonder or make it yonder."

I know what it's like to lose a game you really want to win. I know what slumps are, but in Richie's defense, other than money bonspiels in curling (more fun money in reality), my livelihood has never been based on the win/loss column, so I assume there is a tad deeper depth to a loss or the onset of a possible slump in pro football. In interviewing Olympic-calibre athletes shortly after a loss, I shy away from any personal or awkward questions unless that person opens that door. I think most of us understand this. Yet, Richie still expressed sincere concern about my heart. It's pretty nice knowing we are part of the same village!

THIRD QUARTER

MUSINGS FROM THE VALLEY

SECTION FOUR

★ ★ ★ ★ ★

CHAPTER 18

Musings from the Valley—Uno!

"Life is a shipwreck, but we must not forget to sing in the lifeboats."
- Voltaire

It was Super Bowl 50 week and we were having pizza in Fort Qu'Appelle, Saskatchewan, talking about overcoming adversities of life and conquering those human inner demons.

During the off-season Richie and I tried to meet up once every 10 days or so. Sometimes we'd meet at my then-home-base of Yorkton, Saskatchewan; sometimes in Regina, where Richie lives with his beautiful wife Helen; or in the picturesque Qu'Appelle Valley, which was about half way for each of us. Houston Pizza was the rendezvous point with their newish sports bar atmosphere. It was homey and good. Of course Richie was recognized every time we went in there, but to the patrons' defense, they were nothing short of respectful, even when they came up to introduce themselves. It was simply a nice reminder of how deep the Roughrider and CFL roots run throughout the prairies, and how the fans are so appreciative of having a pro football team in their backyard.

These often turned into just let Richie talk sessions. He is a philosopher at heart, and I love to give him a topic and let him run with it. The Australian Open major tennis tournament was wrapping up, and both of us were impressed with Serena Williams's run to the final before being upset by first-time major winner from Germany, Angelique Kerber. And Super Bowl week was upon us, the 17–1 (including playoffs) Carolina Panthers being touted as early favorites. Of course history tells us that an aging, savvy Peyton Manning led the Denver Broncos to a 24–10 victory.

Overcoming adversity seemed to be our topic of the day: conquering inner demons and such.As our trips to the valley continued over the next few weeks, it seemed the main theme was about overcoming and managing adversities of life. Maybe the valley wasn't just a geographical meeting place, but a natural segue into a theme Richie often talks about. Musing from the valley!

I kicked it off by telling Richie I got to the Fort early to conquer a lingering inner demon. Thirty-one years earlier I was skipping a young curling team from Regina in Fort Qu'Appelle, losing a final with me missing a last rock by throwing a draw, or touch shot, through the house. I had since gone through the Fort dozens of times on the way to visit family over those 31 years, and I always wanted to return to that curling club and find redemption.

So I arrived early and went down to the curling club. My goodness, nothing had changed. It all looked like my nightmare from 31 years ago. I asked the president of the club if I could throw rocks on the extra sheet, as the other three were filled with early-morning seniors' league play. He said, "No problem, just cover up the hacks at each end when you throw." My first thought was, Does he recognize me and remember my pain from 31 years ago? I let it go, because redemption was on my mind.

I have a little competitive game I call "1ce!" I throw X-amount of rocks and give them a point value where I have to curl at least 75 percent to claim a win. These little mind games are often tougher to win than the traditional four on four battles. Anyway, it came down to the very last stone to make my 75 percent.

Flashbacks from 31 years ago flooded my soul. I have learned to be fairly calm over the years throwing that last stone, but today I was more nervous than excited. What if I missed again? What if I overthrew it like 31 years ago and it bounced off the back bumper? I had to draw at least full into the eight-foot part of the rings. I took a deep breath, reminded myself the ice was pretty keen, so I kicked out slowly and released the rock. I thought it had a chance. As it crossed the hog line, it started to slow down. I wanted to scream sweep, but I had no sweepers. The rock kept sliding, and slid through the eight-foot, then glided to a sweet halt, landing in the four-foot. I wanted to give a fist pump, but thought the seniors on the next sheet might think me a tad crazy. But the endorphins were jumping, and I was cranked for my next interview with Mr. Hall. Inner demons cast out; I had a little redemption and a hankering for a fresh pizza.

I told Richie my little story of redemption. He seemed intrigued. Intrigued at how the human psyche operates, how we deal with unfulfilled expectations and adversity. We had a long afternoon chat that filled up a number of pages. There was some potpourri close by that seems to mirror the day's interview. We were all over the map, yet we weren't, as you are about to read. Here is the gist.

I asked Richie a series of questions about handling adversity and striving for balance, not just in football, but life in general. He gave at least two converted touchdowns worth of insights and wisdom. These are often the topics he touches on in his inspirational and motivational public speaking.

We started off with a Super Bowl quote from a year earlier that I knew would resonate with Richie.

After our Super Bowl win, I went through a heartbreaking marriage breakup. I talked with our team chaplain and he challenged me to 'surrender and surround.' Surrender myself to a higher cause in my relationship with God, and surround myself with special people that believe in me.

- Russell Wilson, Seattle Seahawk quarterback

Of the many life lessons I have gleaned in my relationship with Richie, the one that may stand out the most is his ability to quiet the negative voices around him. Please note I did not say eliminate, but quiet. Those voices that can lie to us, beat us down, or tell us we aren't worthy. Those voices that can cause us to lean toward fear versus faith, despair versus hope, or isolation versus love.

He has developed this uncanny ability to keep perspective and a healthy grasp of reality. Is he always successful? Of course not, but more than any other human being I have ever met he has this grasp of reality, as reality really is. This is not hyperbole, but admiration. I believe you'd have to be a human without a soul to have 100 percent success in this part of one's life.

Mr. Hall being a man of deep convictions, loyal to a fault, values the building of relationships both on and off the field. To say he feels deeply would be the understatement of this tome. We've had many conversations around "people" in our vocations and personal lives who we were trying to connect with or re-connect with. He has wept with me after he had a romantic break up. I have wept with him after the same. We have cried over football and cried over women.

> *"There is a sacredness in tears. They are not the mark of weakness, but of power. They speak more eloquently than ten thousand tongues. They are the messengers of overwhelming grief, of deep contrition, and of unspeakable love."*

> - Washington Irving, 19th-century American author and historian who wrote classics such as *Sleepy Hollow and Rip Van Winkle*

Richie has developed his inner circle of friends and family from high school onward and this has been an anchor that keeps him in perspective. As he elaborated, "Putting God first is not just words, but how I try to live my life. The truths and principles that Christ taught are what I seek to live by, and I have found over time works. Having close trusted friends, which is really an extension of the body of Christ, keeps me grounded and helps me maintain perspective when things can get a little crazy. Yes, I learned so much from my family and friends, and I owe my mentors a great deal. I am so blessed."

So…some thoughts on pressuring a quarterback as a defensive coordinator, as we segued from a Russell Wilson quote, to a former CFL'er, Joe Theismann, who was interviewed on a TSN CFL telecast in July 2012. Theismann said, "Quarterbacking especially, but this goes for other positions as well, is all about confidence and comfort." We had both watched the recent AFC championship game where the Denver Broncos harassed Tom Brady by hitting him 23 times, the most a quarterback had been hit that often in a playoff game in over a decade in the NFL. And yet Brady persevered and almost put the game into overtime with one last touchdown drive.

Richie said, "We always try and get to the quarterback out of his comfort zone. We want him worried about getting pressured, and being physically punished rather than him thinking about his responsibilities. Obviously, if we can do that, we gain the upper hand."

One of his favourite defences he coached was in the early 2000s when the Roughriders were being rebuilt after an awful 3–15 season. They became known as the Silent Killers. They had T-shirts made up to reinforce how the D was developing. Richie said:

We weren't flashy, we were a bunch of no-names mostly, but we wore teams down. It was like a slow death at end of day the way the D attacked. I loved it; they were quite methodical in the way they played. Nobody really show boated. We had good, solid players like Eddie Davis, Trevis Smith, Fred Perry, and Omar Morgan, who just played sound, mistake-free football—as mistake-free as possible. At the end of a game we'd look and behold how few yards we had given up, or how few TDs were scored, if any. Not a lot of fanfare, but this unit played with emotion, yet they weren't very vocal. Silent, committed, and they played well together. It brought to mind the Miami Dolphins' defense of their 1972 undefeated season: the 'No Name Defense'!

I took a sip of my coffee and thought of another segue: the NFL/CFL comparisons. The Roughriders' assistant GM, Jeremy O'Day, had gone down to Minnesota and Green Bay to learn, observe, and scout when he was new to the job. O'Day said, "It is amazing how small a difference there is between the NFL and CFL."

Richie jumped on this:

You take away their superstars and they have them. Take away an Aaron Rodgers, Peyton Manning, Von Miller, or a Tom Brady. Once you take away three to four superstars on most rosters, the rest of the talent is much the same in both leagues. So much of it comes down to draft position, the investment teams are making with their high dollar bonuses, and/or age, body type for certain positions. And let's be honest, some players develop later than others in the pro game, and it may be too late for them to transfer leagues, or it could be simply a case of poor timing. Poor timing could mean injuries, lack of experience playing a new position and not having the proper time to understand what is necessary, age, or is the player competing against someone that team has made a huge investment in, meaning a high draft choice or veteran.

We chatted about Johnny Holland, who coached for the Riders in 2013, then moved on to BC. Holland was a linebacker who played in Green Bay, and played so well that he was elected to the Packers Hall of Fame. He also coached in Green Bay and Oakland. He is a linebacker coach. He had a CFL connection through Corey Chamblin. Corey invited Holland to come north to stay in the coaching loop in between gigs. Holland loves the CFL, and has coached the last two CFL defensive players of the year in BC. Richie said,

I enjoyed having Johnny on our staff. He was a wealth of knowledge who understood the depth of talent in the CFL. He knows Tony Dungy well and goes on fishing trips with him in the off-season. He has since gone back to the NFL as the linebacker coach of the Cleveland Browns (2016). He has embraced the CFL and enjoys working with the athletes up here. Johnny once said that coming to the CFL has helped him understand how to better prepare defenses for the now pass-happy NFL. The CFL was already a step ahead in some ways, with embracing elements of the run and shoot, zone blitzes, and the like. In many ways the CFL was more west coast with their offenses than what was in the NFL.

Johnny Holland was all about finding that balance of stopping the run and shutting down the passing game, which led me to ask Richie about one of his favourite words.

Once of Richie's favourite words or concepts is balance! I heard him give a talk to some junior high and high school students in Chauvin, Alberta, with Athletes in Action, a few years back, that had us all talking about it afterward, including the other CFL players who were with him. I will always remember hearing Vince Goldsmith and Rick Worman talking about Richie's way of explaining balance through melding together his zodiac sign with scripture and maintaining above-average scripture integrity. It was brilliant.

As Goldsmith said, "We were told to not preach at the student, which is acceptable, but to share our hearts in giving a positive message about decision-making. Richie is aware of pop culture and communicating spiritual values by using the culture's language and interests. Richie is a Libra, which is about balancing the scales, and he talked about how we need to balance our lives physically, emotionally, mentally, and spiritually—meaning our core values. He simplified it in such a way that if one of these four areas is over the top, it will affect the others negatively and we can lose perspective so easily. Half the girls in the audience were probably into their horoscopes anyway, so he immediately caught their attention. He never talked about horoscopes, but gave us all the image of the Libra and how he works at balancing his life. He tastefully said his spiritual values are based on his respect for the Bible and just left it at that."

The high school principal came up to Richie afterward, and gave Richie the biggest compliment about how he appreciated his presentation and how Richie touched on interests that students were in tune with, and how he liked Richie's take on balance.

As I was trying to finish off my lunch—I don't mind cold pizza—Richie elaborated even more on one of his favourite topics:

I guess I am a Libra. Balance is all about the scales. Balance brings perspective along with personal and spiritual growth. I strive for balance in those critical areas of family, work, God, personal growth. When something in my life is out of whack, I know I'm not balancing the scales.

I think about this with my coaching philosophy all the time. I saw it watching the Denver–New England game on Sunday. The Patriots are a huge pass-heavy team, yet they ran it more to try and throw Denver off-balance. We constantly try to make our opposition respect us and to attempt to make a team one-dimensional. Something I have learned over the years is that balance doesn't mean fifty-fifty within the structure of what your team does. Maybe your personal balance to throw off the opposition could be seventy-thirty, or maybe sixty-forty. What works for one team or even for yourself in personal growth is seeking quality or impact. I think there is always that tension of quality versus quantity. But we need to always strive for balance. And balance isn't always mathematical, in all aspects of life. I hope I have made balance part of my lifestyle, and practice balancing the scales everyday because each day is different.

We talked about one of our favourite coaches who coached in the CFL and NFL, pro football Hall of Famer Marv Levy. Levy was big on balance and having healthy interests outside of football, because it was something to take away that anal focus, or take away that pressure when games got tight, or games became do or die in the win/loss column. Levy often talked about this through his career, that the more balanced his players were outside of the game, the better they handled pressure in games that were on the line. He said players who tended to make mistakes or underachieve in critical moments usually were players who didn't work on balancing their whole lives. Levy understood all players will make mistakes or underachieve, but he was talking about the high rate of consistency in those scenarios.

CHAPTER 19

Musings from the Valley—Deux!

"No! World War II was a must win!"
- Marv Levy

Don Matthews had a way of putting things in perspective. When he first came to the Riders after John Gregory was let go, he gave us a pre-game speech. This was his first game with us. We were struggling, and to top it off, the game was at Commonwealth Stadium in Edmonton where we hadn't won in years. Don started talking about pressure:

"Are you guys okay? Are you nervous? Are you scared? Do you feel pressure? This isn't pressure. Going to war, going to Vietnam, that's pressure."

I don't know why but I'll always remember that pre-game speech. Football is not life or death. Remember the **Private Ryan** *movie and how it starts the D-Day invasion. It goes on and on with the bullets flying everywhere and people dying. That's pressure. When I go through adversity I try and regain perspective.*

Speaking of Marv Levy…another segue over an afternoon of interviews in the Qu'Appelle Valley. I don't know if it was because we were in the valley that we got talking about adversity again, or if it was my curling redemption story of facing an inner demon. Nonetheless Richie was on a roll, and these afternoon interviews shed light on so many conversations we had been having since 1988.

We talked about mentors or coaches who have influenced him negatively or positively. We both like baseball and Billy Martin's name came up—Billy Martin of New York Yankee fame, mostly. He once said he had learned more about managing/coaching by observing bad managers because he learned how not to manage or coach.

We mostly talked in general terms, but Richie's insights were worth listening to:

I think what Martin is meaning is we often learn more from failure or losing than being around winning coaches, although I have learned a ton being around championship playoff contender coaches as well. Success sometimes trumps the lessons on successful teams, where you can forget what got you there because winning sometimes covers up a multitude of mistakes. Championship teams tend to be cognizant of those lessons. On a bad team or being around ineffective coaches, yes you can learn how not to do certain things. I can't always tell what I'd like to do as a coach, but I can tell you what I don't want to do.

Even in my marriage with Helen I can't always tell her what I like or prefer to make our marriage work, but it's easy to let her know what I don't like, and vice versa. Any time something fails or you are not successful, you analyze more or pay attention to what might work, or you see what works in other teams and/or relationships. I always try and ask the question of why? Why does something work or not work, especially dealing with people. This helps me re-evaluate various things. What kind of environment do you really want to create? What Martin is talking about is mostly preventative, before disaster strikes.

Billy Martin had most of his success as a player playing for a handful of World Series winners as a second baseman for the Yankees. He was a controversial, yet very successful, manager improving every team he was with in places like Texas, Oakland, Minnesota, Detroit, and back and forth with the Yankees during the tumultuous George Steinbrenner era.

After eight great years with New York as a player he became a journeyman, playing his final five seasons for six different teams, mostly sub-par .500 teams. He played under a number of different managers. Richie could relate in some ways as he has served under a number of different head coaches and coordinators during his playing and coaching career, far more than Billy Martin has, learning from all sorts of personalities.

This led us into some candid conversation about dealing with disappointment, unfulfilled expectations, and failures. What are some of his biggest disappointments in life where he had to work through some serious adversity?

Probably his first major setback was flunking out of Colorado State in his first semester. He was put on academic probation, and had not yet earned an athletic scholarship. He says:

No excuses. I messed up. Sure I was young and away from home for the first time, but I knew better. I had to re-apply myself and take my classes seriously. Education had to be the first priority if I wanted to play football. Without putting my education first there would be no football.

Other moments where I had to deal with setbacks were getting cut by Don Matthews after a pretty good training camp. On July 3, 1992, at 4:29 p.m., I was cut. Not that I remember. This was pretty devastating at first.

I don't talk about it much, but my first marriage ending when I was in my early thirties made me feel like a failure. I now realize that it takes as much work and commitment in a romantic relationship as it does in the classroom, or as playing or coaching on a football team.

I try to look at the big picture in adverse times. I have had a pretty good life overall. Thirty-one years in pro football. I never could have dreamed this is going to play out like it did. I have always tried to take the high road, integrity, trusting a God who is good. This is life. I have had it pretty well, haven't I?

Richie's inner circle friends all touched on his romantic heartbreaks, and how they tried to be there for him, as he was for theirs. They were all ecstatic when he met Helen and she said—Yes!

And of course he talked about his mom.

My mom dying a couple of years ago was very bittersweet. I mean if anyone was ready to go, it was my mom, but still I had to say goodbye to one of my best friends. But, I took a ton of comfort thanking God for all the good years I had with her, but yes I do miss my daily conversations with her. But her love and words will be with me forever.

So, I asked him about head coach Corey Chamblin taking away his play calling responsibilities early in the 2014 season as defensive coordinator of the Roughriders, and what happened in that off-season regarding what his new role would have been going into the 2015 season.

Early in the 2014 season Corey and I exchanged game day roles. Corey assumed responsibilities for calling the defensive plays, and I provided him offensive information from our opponents. The human-side hurt, but it allowed me to take a step back and see things from a different perspective on the field. I still had my regular input. We game planned together, but during the games we essentially switched roles. After a period of time I resumed the play calling, yet with one more change where Corey called the plays in the playoff game.

I always try to look at all the factors. Look at all the intangibles, and try to see things from the other person's side. Seldom if anything is it one thing that causes these things to happen. Yes, it could be one or two major things like philosophical differences, especially in football.

For the record I really like Corey Chamblin and we still chat on a regular basis. Corey felt a change was in order. That's his prerogative as a head coach, I get that. I understand the personal side and the business side to our relationship. I tend not to have any problems separating the two. In this business I have learned you have to respect people's decisions they have to make. Whether it was Don Matthews or Corey, they may make a decision, I might not like it, but I can respect the decision. Goodness, I had the same decisions to make as a head coach in Edmonton. Did I want to let Rick Worman go as my offensive coordinator? That was tough, but we also still talk a few times each year, we're still friends.

Hey, I didn't like Corey's decision, but it was his call. I can accept the decision whether I think it's fair or not. I know in my heart that both Don Matthews and Corey were simply doing what they thought was best. I know it's cliché but almost everyone in sports gets cut or fired somewhere along the way. Even though Corey demoted me, hey, he still wanted me around.

Of course the story continues with the Blue Bombers offering him the defensive coordinator job a few weeks later. Then Richie told me a story from his hero/mentor high school coach Mr. Hisamoto, who benched him during a baseball game. It wasn't personal, but best for the team as he felt Richie wasn't playing well:

He knew how I would react—I wouldn't make a scene—and you know what, it got my attention. Deep down I knew I wasn't playing well. He never had to bench me again. I guess it probably spoke to the other players too, if Mr. Hisamoto would bench me. It taught me that I had to perform at a certain level, no one is entitled to success without hard work and putting forth your best effort. That benching stuck with me for a long time; I guess it still does. The bottom line is that whatever we do for a living, it is a performance-based matter. In Edmonton as an example we didn't win enough football games.

Pro sports are a tough "win now" business. Some teams have a longer leash than others in making changes, and that changes with ownership and front offices. I know this going in as a player and as a coach. Many very good people have been cut or fired for whatever reasons, I'm not the only one. Sometimes even when you feel like you have done your best, it isn't good enough.

One of my favorite songs is by James Ingram, "Just Once," where he sings:

I did my best
but I guess my best wasn't good enough
Cause here we are
Back where we were before

Richie and I got together before a game in Calgary back in 2004, the year the Riders went to the Western Final and got beat in one of those Rider heartbreakers on a missed 18-yard field goal in overtime to the BC Lions in Vancouver. We met at a downtown Starbucks in early October. During this time, both of us were going through a time of self-doubt. In my vocation as a minister I wondered if my time had run its course, being at this church for 11 years. Richie was wondering if his time with the Roughriders had run out, and did they need something else to help them get over the hump?

Danny Barrett was the head coach, and Richie told me he had gone to Danny wondering if it was best for our team for him to step down. Barrett was thinking the same thing. Maybe for all three of us it was our ages as we were all in our 40s, where we just wanted what was best in our work situations. I remember sharing with Richie that we all go through these times and maybe the team was on the verge of a breakthrough. Sometimes those things we teach or emphasize take time to gain traction, yet it looks like we are moving backward.

We both hung in there and both saw things turn around in our vocations. The Riders were easier to measure as in 2004 they had a good October and went to the Western Final. And in this case probably should have won that game and gone on to the Grey Cup, except for that short field goal miss. The way the Riders' October ended, and their run in November continued, just added to the process that built a foundation for 2007. Richie said:

Of course I always want to win, but I don't really care what my role is. I just want to win and contribute. God has been teaching me in this last couple of years it's all about developing an UNCONDITIONAL MINDSET! I simply want what's best for the team, my family, my personal growth. What does getting the credit even mean or validate anyway?

Even though Don Matthews cut me, or Corey Chamblin reduced my role, I'd have no issues playing or coaching with either one of them. They both had to make tough decisions regarding their teams. I strive to accept that it's not about who's right or wrong, but what's best for the team.

I try to keep in mind the God factor. Faith is not always easy. What's really important is the big picture. Do I live by faith or fear? We always have access to both, but what I'm learning is which one dominates my choices regardless of how I feel—unconditional mindset. God has a pretty good track record of always taking care of me.

In dealing with setbacks or adversity Richie has learned how to trust in God and His truisms shared in the Bible. He has learned to choose to take the high road of love versus the self-will road of protectionism and fear. Richie is a seeker of what works regardless of the source, believing that all true truth has its source in God anyway, built on a foundation of unconditional love.

Since we were a stone's throw from a Catholic retreat centre it might be good to quote what St. Augustine shared almost 1,700 years ago, which captures Richie's healthy and holistic view of seeking truth that inspires and directs one's life:

A person who is a good and true Christian should realize that truth belongs to his Lord, wherever it is found, gathering and acknowledging it even in pagan literature.

As we concluded another day in the valley, Richie said this:

This unconditional mindset is constantly making that transition from ego back to God. In situations in my life like with Corey, or getting fired in Edmonton, it's not impossible for me to go back because I haven't burned any bridges. I'm not saying it's easy, but I'm getting more consistent all the time in putting God's ways of doing things ahead of mine. I firmly believe that the more we develop this unconditional mindset the easier it is to deal with adversity. Not easy, but easier!

CHAPTER 20

Musings from the Valley—Trey!

Mr. Hall is a man of metaphors. And, if you follow the CFL, you'll understand the ones he refers to, or has lived through, quite quickly! Even if you don't, the lesson is pretty easy to transfer over to your life situation.

When Richie gives a workshop or motivational talk on adversity, he covers about a dozen points depending on his time frame. For what it's worth I have been to four colleges in my life, mostly in the human services areas like psychology, social work, addictions, and theology. I have heard many good lessons on dealing with adversity, and the talks Richie gives are as good as it gets.

I'll always remember a talk he gave in Calgary in 2010 at an inner city church. The church was relatively new and could fluctuate from a dozen people to 50, but on this Sunday there were well over 100 people from all walks of life. Richie's talk was about overcoming adversity, and the hope faith can give. There was a woman who attended named Deb, who hardly ever darkened the door of a church.

I was consulting this church on developing an additions ministry, and had a coffee with Deb a few days later. She said:

As soon as that football player walked up to the front and began his talk, something told me to listen. Honestly I had this incredible peace or calm come over me. I was filled with such hope and expectation. I watch a little football, but I was a little lost in his football stories. Not lost in interest or the lessons he was sharing, I just didn't always know the people or games he was referring too. But the lessons he talked about were a bridge to my life situation into the lessons he was sharing.

I walked out of there with such hope and perspective, and I have opened myself up to God and Christ like never before. Listening to Richie helped me see a different side of God and His ways. Not a bunch of rules and regulations, but a God who cares and is interested, and cuts me more slack than I cut myself. If he could receive God's grace or forgiveness, why couldn't I?

About a year later I saw Deb, and she brought up about Richie's talk again. She was flourishing in her spiritual and personal growth. She realized that spiritual growth was a journey of ups and downs, and that adversity is a part of life. She said Richie helped her understand from his talk that growth is an ongoing process and adversity is an occupational hazard of being human.

But before we look at those tools to help one manage or overcome adversities in the next chapter, let's look at Richie's most adverse year as a coach, according to the standings. He uses experiences like this as examples, knowing that job loss, relationship breakups, and life-threatening diseases are not games—yet he knows sharing stories from the gridiron can parallel those lessons in many ways. As both Kelly Martin from Colorado, and Cindy Kearse, a good friend of his in Regina (whose daughter Tiffany has done speaking engagements with Richie), have said, "Richie has such a beautiful way to use his experience in football to spark interest in his audiences, and they respond to his stories. Those metaphors stick with you. He finds the tool or the lesson, and makes them transferable to everyday life."

The following is a combination of interviews from the 2010 season, with the two of us looking back on some newspaper and web articles. This was definitely a season in the valley. This was his second and last season as the head coach in Edmonton. His first season was a success for the Eskimos; he led them to the playoffs. This second season as the head man in Edmonton went south really quickly as they started off at 2–9.

The bulk of the thoughts we are going to focus on are from the mid-point of the season, as they stumbled out of the gate at 0–4. Then the injuries started to pile up. It turned out to be one of the worst starts in Richie's CFL tenure. Still is! After game number four, these are some of Richie's words in dealing with the press:

Right now as a football team we're struggling. We're struggling in a few areas and we're getting punched in the mouth without punching back.

And that starts with me. I've got to be better at what I do. And I will be better at what I do! It is what it is. We're 0–4. A lot of people are pissed off and disgusted, and I don't blame them because we feel the same way. This is our livelihood and we're a better team than that. But this is what we have shown. We're 0–4.

It was a butt-kicking, don't sugar-coat it. Maybe we're fooling ourselves when we look at those two games that we had opportunities to win but we didn't win. All of a sudden against Winnipeg the dam broke and we saw the end results.

The way our football team is overall has surprised me. We haven't learned anything because we're falling into that same old trap. We have to be mentally tougher. We have to be physically tougher. When we've had success, whether it was last year or at times this year, it's because we've been aggressive.

If you were brought here to be a receiver, then run and catch the football. Do your job. We have to come to play the game mentally, physically, and emotionally.

It all comes back to that whole attitude…we don't have that tendency to punch them in the mouth. We can't be a counter-puncher because we're getting punched too many times before we throw a punch back. When you don't put up any resistance this is what happens. Yes, football is a thinking man's game, but it's also a physical game at its core.

This is their football team. You want to empower them. We're all part of the problem and we'll all be part of the solution, so you want to keep those communication lines open, as far as what we can do better.

And, Richie being Richie would not let me use injuries as an excuse. We talked about it, but…I still believe they were a major factor. Since I am the primary writer of this tome, please indulge me for a half paragraph. Bill Parcells, the Hall of Fame, two-time Super Bowl winning coach, has said, "There are reasons and there are excuses. In most cases your record is who you are. I firmly believe that, but sometimes injuries pile up, and you do lose a key player or two. A good part of coaching is coaching through the adversity."

Back to the 0–4 press conference, when a reporter asked Richie about job security as a head coach, and whether it keeps him awake at night.

No. Why should I let it? Why worry about things I have no control over? If something happens, the sun will come up tomorrow and we'll get on with life. If nothing happens, the sun will still come up tomorrow, and we'll continue to go on with life. This helps me keep things in perspective.

Then we harkened back and revisited a conversation we had about the season when the two of us got together at The Marriott in Calgary, in August 2010, with his team sitting in last place at 1–6, about to face the first-place Stampeders. I found him quite calm, but we did talk about the team:

Sure, if you look at the standings we have a lot of ground to make up. Adversity with its lessons deepen the lessons we've already learned and can teach us new ones. I want to be cognizant of this. It's easy to talk about overcoming adversity when you're 6–1 and the team is playing well.

He talked about this like it was his Gethsemane in football. Again, a metaphor that he kept in perspective, huge perspective, but as he often does, he found a Biblical parallel to try to relate, too. When things aren't going one's way, he acknowledged how feeling overwhelmed can cause one to lose perspective. He said it was a challenge to get out of this bad start, and being the head coach was, like the old cliché says, lonely at the top. But he saw afresh how one needs to surround himself with a solid support system of faith, family, and friends to maintain perspective.

The 1–6 Eskimos got creamed by Calgary 56–15 that day. Then they rebounded by beating a solid Saskatchewan team 17–14. This was a Roughrider team that went on to play in the Grey Cup later that season. Then Calgary beat them again 52–5, meaning the Stamps had outscored them 108–20. Once the team settled down and got some of their healthy players back, they rebounded and finished the season at 7–11, only one game out of a playoff berth with the BC Lions finishing at 8–10.

He said that season was filled with highs and lows, but mostly lows. He was proud of his team as they finished the season with a 5–2 record in their final seven games. He elaborated:

It's kind of the thrill of victory and the agony of defeat when you talk about our highs and lows. What we did against Saskatchewan in 2010, beating them in Edmonton, and what we didn't do against Calgary was just execution in that middle part of the season. We weren't doing what we were supposed to do that gave us a chance to be successful. We had a team that could still compete against Calgary and Saskatchewan. The game plan for the most part was very similar against both teams during that stretch. As an example, versus Saskatchewan we were in our gaps, we made the tackles; we made the plays when we had the opportunities. When we played Calgary the consistency wasn't even close, so many mental errors. In some ways you agonize as a coach or coaching staff, wondering how you can coach, teach, and motivate better.

When we played the Riders we threw the ball well, we put enough pressure on their quarterback. When we played the Stampeders we gave up big plays right off the get-go. That kind of typified the game for our defence—we gave up big plays in gashes.

When we played the Roughriders we were able to eliminate the big plays by just playing solid, disciplined, fundamental football. Execution!

Did I lose faith? No, I didn't lose faith. Faith to me is about being faithful in the good and the bad times. I understand life and I understand myself fairly well. I was able to sleep when I came home from work. I was able to relax. I try to look at life as being about faith, family, and friends. It does make dealing with negative things a lot easier. Again, taking steps to get back to reality or perspective in the big picture. This wasn't Vietnam or D-Day.

When you work hard and give your all it makes it easier to sleep. Maybe I had to work some things through a little longer, but I slept. Having my faith, family, and friends helped me regain perspective and silence those outside voices.

Let's just say I was very frustrated regarding how our season had gone, especially in a few games regarding not being able to simply execute the fundamentals. Those are things at the pro level you take a ton of pride in, being fundamentally sound.

Maurice Lloyd, the Eskimo middle linebacker, quoted Richie after the Stampeders debacle, saying:

Richie Hall always tells us to take care of things between the ears, start using our brains in making choices. This is a thinking man's game, especially at the professional level. Make better choices.

After the second blowout via the Stampeders, Richie was simply honest with the press:

The last time we were here we got our butts kicked in every aspect of the game. We lost the battles up front. We lost at the skill positions. We lost the heart. We lost everything a team can lose in a football game.

I don't know what to say. Laid a goose egg. Didn't come to compete. Couldn't even execute the fundamentals of football. Couldn't catch. Couldn't block. Couldn't throw. Couldn't tackle. Couldn't cover. There's nothing more. We didn't come out there to compete.

We stunk it up, in every way. We just stunk it up. It was a disappointing effort. It was not going out to compete.

Last week we did a great job against the Roughriders. We played hard. We came to compete. This was a disappointing effort against the Stampeders. It was not going out to compete. A team has to do this every week. A team has to care all of the time. It's not a sometimes thing. It's an all-the-time thing.

It's almost like we never played football before. It's embarrassing. We're not even doing the basic things right. It's everything. It's every position. Until we can do that, we're not going to win any games. Until we can do the basic things right and consistently, we're going to continue to struggle.

Stephen Covey, who wrote *The 7 Habits of Highly Effective People*, calls this the great execution gap:

Execution is the great unaddressed issue in most organizations today. Most leaders would agree that they'd be better off having an average strategy with superb execution than a "superb" strategy with poor execution. Those who execute always have the upper hand.

The year 2010 was a frustrating season for Richie. Those two losses to their archrivals, a few miles down Highway 2, exposed many of the team's weaknesses, and the mental mistakes the team had to clean up. This is the only time he has ever been fired as a coach.

Talking about that season in hindsight, Richie looks back on it with a lot of gratefulness for having the opportunity to be a head coach. He felt the team closed the season with their heads held high, with hope for the future. Being part of a team that easily could have folded their tents when they were 2–9 and instead finished strong down the stretch was somewhat rewarding. The team mirrored much of Richie's "never quit" mindset.

In the next chapter we'll look at the ways Richie deals with adversity to maintain life equilibrium:

Life is filled with peaks and valleys. I try to not to let the highs fool me into thinking life will always be that way, and I try to remind myself that times in the valley aren't the end of the world. I have to admit that what Friedrich Nietzsche said was right, "What doesn't kill you, only makes you stronger." And, as much as any of us don't like it, the lessons in the valley seem to be the ones that you never forget and make you a better human being in so many ways.

CHAPTER 21

Musings from the Valley—Quatre!

Peaks and Valleys!

If there is anything my life in and around football has taught me, it is the game, like life, has peaks and valleys. You can only try and control what you can do on the field, or coach as well as you can. This is a team game. To be successful or fulfilled in life is about team or community. So many things are out of our control. So many factors are involved.
–Richie

Learning to manage or overcome hard times, adverse situations, or setbacks is such a key to developing consistency and maturity in life. Sitting in the valley talking with Richie, we reviewed what he often speaks about, in public speaking and behind closed doors with his colleagues. He strives hard to maintain perspective and balance, so he can be an effective decision maker. What helps?

If we peeked into one of Richie's playbooks—and I have on many occasions—you'd see some sections in the following manner.

Dealing with Inevitable Adversities

#1 Remove emotion

During the course of a game I try and stick to the game plan and its contingencies. In the heat of a game, just as in life, it is so easy to get caught up in life's setbacks.

In a game we have our game plan, and in life I try and use the scriptures as a point of reference and to make choices based in love and truth versus mere emotion. Maybe a better way to say it regarding emotion is to manage emotions, just as we often try to manage games. I try and be dictated by making good decisions and not costing the team by reacting straight out of emotion.

#2 Win and learn versus win or lose

I try to look at a situation and what good we can take out of it. There are always lessons to be learned or relearned. How can I get better, how can our team improve? In football, the reality is that wins don't always tell the tale of a team's growth. Are we improving every week, are we getting consistent? If this is happening, eventually the wins should come. Obviously it doesn't always work that way because you may be a season away. The rewards or wins may not be immediate, but more often than not the wins will start to come, and you begin to win your fair share.

Richie often talks about the seasons leading up to the 2007 Roughriders Grey Cup win. From 1998 to 2001 the team only won 19 games, missing the playoffs each season. In 2000 the team brought in Roy Shivers as the GM, and Shivers brought in Danny Barrett as head coach. The reality was this was a total overhaul to the roster, and there were some growing pains to get back on track. There was constant improvement up until the end of 2006, when they were both released. With the core Shivers brought in, the team started to win and contend and make the playoffs on a regular basis. The Riders under this regime had now made the playoffs five straight seasons, reaching the Western Final on three occasions, but were not able to get over the hump into the Grey Cup.

The win/loss record didn't always reflect the improvements the coaching staff and the die-hard fans could see, but the team had obviously turned a corner. The front office felt that a change at the GM and head coaching spots was in order; there was very little tweaking to the core of the roster. The team that won the 2007 Grey Cup was the core of the Shivers and Barrett era. In 2007 the team brought in Eric Tillman as GM and Kent Austin as head coach. Both men acknowledged that the core of the team that won the '07 Grey Cup was the foundation of that championship.

Richie was asked to stay on as the defensive coordinator under Kent Austin and enjoyed that 2007 season working with him, but felt bad that Roy Shivers and Danny Barrett never were able to win a Grey Cup championship because the team was consistently improving and knocking on the door. From 2000 onward it was such a fulfilling time to watch this group of players grow and jell as a team.

#3 Learn to regroup

So often you hear the phrase in sports, "You have to have a short memory when you get beat or make a mistake." The good quarterbacks I have played with and against don't let the interceptions affect their next series. Danny McManus was one of the best, but as I have been told over the years his main head coach, Ron Lancaster, was the master at having a short memory when he played. When Lancaster retired, he led the CFL in passing yardage, touchdowns, completions, and interceptions, and he may still hold the record for fourth-quarter comebacks. It was up around fifty-four when he retired.

As a DB I had to have a short memory; you can go from the penthouse to the outhouse real quickly. And I had to learn not to dwell on the negative: park it and move on. It's an occupational hazard to get beat, especially in a pass-happy league like the CFL. Sure I would have liked to have eliminated getting beat, but realistically all I could do was minimize and try to learn and apply from the times I was beat. It's like baseball; they have built in failure to their stats, and the best have the higher percentages of success than their peers. Most hitters, if not all, in baseball would die for a .300 average. Less than ten percent of big leaguers at the most ever hit over .300 over the course of a season.

As best as you can, you must maintain perspective and keep perfectionism in its place. You strive for excellence of course, but realize we are all imperfect people.

#4 Life has seasons

Richie and I have talked often about this. We often refer to the book of Ecclesiastes in the Bible where it talks about, "There is a season for everything." The classic 1960s folk rock song "Turn! Turn! Turn!" is based on that scripture. Football has seasons. Every year is a new and fresh start. Even within the season many teams will break the season down into thirds, plus the playoffs, then the off-season that includes the draft, free agency, prospect camps, and mini-camps.

Ray Lewis is the former Baltimore Ravens 12-time pro-bowl linebacker and two-time Super Bowl champion—a sure fire Hall of Famer. In Lewis's book, *I Feel like Going On*, he talks candidly about how he and his teams often feel like they can will their way to win regardless of circumstances. He writes about how that mindset is a healthy one to have, but to temper that with "factors." Football is a huge team game. There are many factors that go into being successful in the win/loss column. Teams need talent; injuries can sometimes take their toll; coaching staff need to connect with the players; there is morale, free agency, and rebuilding; sometimes a freak turnover is the difference. The list could go on, but Lewis talked of these major factors to help see the big picture. Football, like life, has seasons.

Football is a constant reminder to me that life has seasons. We have those peaks and valleys in different components of our lives at the same time. This helps me to maintain perspective. I know there are reasons or excuses for everything in life, and I can be a tad top-heavy in playing down excuses and always looking for reasons, but sometimes there are genuine reasons why things don't work.

In coaching, or even in social work, when a player or client is down and fixates on the negative, I remind them of their successes along the way. I have seen a lot in coaching where a coach will put together a highlight reel for a player, a unit like the DBs, or receivers, or the whole team to let them observe positive plays. Like Lewis says, there are other factors involved. Sometimes in football you just get beat by an opponent making a great play. Everyone out there is trying. Perspective, seasons!

#5 Faith

I believe in God. Regardless of what happens or goes on in my life, I know He is with me. He has always taken care of me in all areas. Relationships, vocation, hard times, even when I have made choices I regret. When I seek to keep God's ways and love first in my life, I sense peace. Even if everything seems to fall apart by my human perspective, something tells me He is always there with His grace. Sure, I have been "tested" in this over the years, but I can honestly say God's track record in my life is consistent, even when I have not been.

I love the scriptures and one of my favourites in this regard is in Psalm 46:1-3,

> *God is our refuge and strength,*
> *A very present help in times of trouble.*
> *Therefore we will not fear, though the earth should change*
> *And though the mountains slip into the heart of the sea;*
> *Though its waters roar and foam,*
> *Though the mountains quake at its swelling pride.*

#6 Don't let the game define you

I try to be a positive person. I also try and not let the ups and downs of life define me. This is easier said than done, but as you mature in life and faith, it becomes easier, if you consciously work at it. I have tried to define myself from God's perspective, and remind myself of who I am in the light of eternity.

It's easy to think of negatives and to dwell on them. I'm not a total failure because I have got fired, or failed in my first year of university, or a failed marriage, or whatever. But, I am also not a football player or coach first. Yes, the rings are pretty cool, the Tom Pate Memorial Award (the CFL's humanitarian of the year award), or even a happy marriage.

I try to take the positive out of the positives, and learn life lessons out of the negative. In most cases I can find positive things or lessons, regardless. Human nature when it has negative hits seems to plant the seeds of doubt or failure, so I go back to that word I love: balance. And being around people that believe in me and I in them always helps, and not that we always have to talk about the setbacks, but it can help.

#7 Time rolls on

When Richie was traded to the Roughriders by Calgary after his first five years as a player, he felt like this was one of the lowest moments in his young adult life. Moving from a city he loved and team that seemed to be maturing, to a team that set a CFL record for being out of the playoffs for 11 straight seasons. Remember the CFL is a nine-team league, and at times has had only eight teams. Never as small as the NHL original six, but still a league where six teams make the playoffs. How would he even have guessed back in 1988 that he would fall in love with this prairie province, live there for well over 25 years, and become the only player/coach in their franchise history to earn three championship rings? "A true Saskatchewan and Canadian legend— forever," as the 112th Saskatoon Men's Curling Bonspiel introduced him as their guest speaker in 2016, as he was entering his second season with the rival Blue Bombers.

We are all aging. Life is about change and adjusting. In life and in football if we stay around long enough we'll be asked to leave at some stage. Not too many get to leave on their own terms, whether this is as a player or coach, or whatever vocation we may be in. Things change, preferences for teams change; it's part of the game and part of life. Even if I wanted to coach forever, that's impossible. All the great spiritual teachers and writers remind us that life is about change, and the sooner we grasp this truism, the easier it is for us to handle.

#8 Quiet time

Gail Mund has run the Roughrider ticket office through the last three Grey Cups and counting. She has been with the Riders longer than Richie and has seen regime after regime, yet Richie was the longest constant by far. They chatted often.

By mere coincidence Gail and I grew up about four houses down from each other on Moltke Avenue, in Langenburg, Saskatchewan. The town bleeds green, and I mean it bleeds Roughrider green. When I can I like to visit with Gail when I pop over to Mosaic Stadium at Taylor Field. One day we got to talking about Richie, and Gail told me this story:

Do you know Richie is always the first person at the stadium? Always. I get here fairly early too, but not that early. There are days he must be here at three or four a.m. I always thought he was consuming himself with the playbook or studying football video. I have seen this habit for years. I don't bother him, although he is always friendly. But you know what he does?

He is in his office listening to his favourite gospel music, and it's good music. I don't know where he finds it all. He has a Bible open and usually some other book. I think it's some devotional or Christian book, and he studies to deepen his faith. I'm sure he probably prays too. And I do know he phones his mom every morning, or I think it's every morning. This doesn't surprise me because he lives it as well as anyone I have ever come across in football or away from football.

Richie has a very consistent quiet time, seeking God's perspective on how to live a life of love and influence in non-preachy ways and how to better his own spiritual and personal growth. He knows the Bible as well as most trained ministers, although he would play that down. Over the years he and I have talked much about spiritual things. If there is a Bible close by and we need to look something up, Richie will find it within seconds. I have seen preachers have a hard time finding the minor prophets of the Old Testament like Obadiah, Jonah, Haggai, or Zephaniah, but not Mr. Hall.

Yes, this is important to me. I see the Bible like a playbook. Constant study and constant tweaking. Not tweaking the Bible of course, but tweaking my life according to my current life situation. And like a playbook, the Bible is at its best when applied or in execution. Just knowing the Bible and not trying to live it doesn't really soften a heart or create a listening audience.

And of course going through the adversities of life the Bible as much as any book gives me almost instant perspective.

#9 Gratitude

Going through hard times or setbacks can play tricks on your mind. But I know getting my perspective back is so important. Maybe the quickest way is by becoming a grateful person, cultivating this as a habit or lifestyle. I know that resentments or bitterness, acted out, can stifle one's spirit or heart. If I choose to be grateful I become a better person, but if I choose to act out in revengeful or resentful ways I grow bitter. The choice comes down to this: am I going to become a better person or a bitter person when I come to these kinds of crossroads? When I am grateful, I find it easier to forgive, even though it may not be reciprocal. I am then reminded that the other person is human and probably struggling with something I am not aware of. This can still hurt, but it gives me perspective again. Hopefully I am able to communicate love to them through it all. It's not easy, but it's good for the heart.

Napoleon said a true leader is a "dealer of hope." Richie seems to cultivate an atmosphere of hope around him. I saw it first-hand spending those three days with him in Winnipeg with the Bombers. He strongly believes a team can't play up to its potential if they are playing afraid, or timidly. Playing afraid increases mistakes; playing with freedom minimizes mistakes and often creates havoc for the other team. As Richie would remind me, this kills creativity and letting it all out. His lifestyle of gratitude filters into how he communicates with the players and fellow coaches. He doesn't sugar-coat reality, but you can see him cultivating an atmosphere of hope—a team that believes in the players and players who believe in the team.

#10 Life is messy

The reality of life is we are human and we are not perfect. We mess it up, even when our intentions are good. Sports reinforces to me that life has obstacles and we have opposition. Your opponent is trying to make your day full of adversity, and sometimes they make your life hell. That's their job. That's our job, too.

It can be easy to get caught up in perfectionist thinking, but I have yet to experience the perfect game or perfect season. I'll bet you that even when a perfect game is pitched in baseball, that pitcher would tell you he never threw one hundred percent perfect pitches. I find it so much more peaceful in my soul whenever I accept that life is messy and so fragile. Life is messy, that's reality!

Hopefully I have a different perspective as a Christian. I can't imagine not having hope regardless of the circumstances. I honestly try and end the day with a smile on my face. I'm not always successful, but I do. I enjoyed playing for Coach Bob Vespaziani in Calgary in 1986 and 1987. This man knew the game and he was so good with people. It's funny how certain statements people say stick with you. Someone else may say it, but it has no impact, but with Coach V he lived it and stressed it, so maybe this is why it stuck. He liked to say, "Better today than yesterday."

I guess my takeaway was that if we are making strides to improve every day, eventually, if not sooner, you will see results, both on the field and in our personal lives. Coach V would talk about how we may be going through a rough patch, or certain players may be in a funk, but if we are alive to live another day, we all have a chance to get better.

Obviously, Richie likes inspirational sports movies. I think it would be a safe venture to say that every high-performance coach and athlete has seen one or all of the *Rocky* movies. Sylvester Stallone was interviewed on *Late Night* with David Letterman as the film was coming out in 2006. The following quote, according to Stallone, captured the essence of the whole *Rocky* series. He said it was not only his favourite quote, but it was the primary life lesson takeaway he hoped many would embrace and live out in their daily lives. Observing and being a friend of Richie's since 1988, I always think of who Richie is and how he lives when I see or hear the following quote:

The world ain't all sunshine and rainbows. It's a very mean and nasty place and I don't care how tough you are, it will beat you to your knees and keep you there permanently if you let it. You, me, or nobody is gonna hit as hard as life. But it ain't about how hard you hit. It's about how hard you can get hit and keep moving forward. How much you can take and keep moving forward. That's how winning is done!

- Rocky Balboa (2006 movie, a.k.a. *Rocky VI)*

FOURTH QUARTER
PRAIRIE LESSONS

SECTION FIVE
★ ★ ★ ★ ★

CHAPTER 22

Calgary

Calgary is where I entered manhood. It's where my journey and introduction to my adopted country began. Little did I know that 30 years later I'd still be part of the CFL. With all due respect to Regina, Edmonton, and Winnipeg, Calgary is still my favorite Canadian city. It reminds me of Denver in so many ways. Both cities have energy and such a positive vibe that I was familiar with. Coming to Calgary was a perfect fit for me as it felt a lot like Denver, where I grew up from junior high throughout high school. It made the transition from CSU easier. Calgary is vibrant, the mountains are close by, and the winters are mild—and you gotta love chinooks.
–Richie

Richie and I first met at a CFL chapel service that I was invited to be the guest speaker at in Edmonton. A couple years later I moved to Calgary to pastor. I was in Calgary from 1992 until 2010. I brought Richie in a number of times to speak at our church and a couple other churches, to do a hospital visit, to do an addictions rehab fundraiser, and to speak at a couple of schools over those 19 years. What I found interesting was his popularity or "name brand" never really waned. He left Calgary in 1988, yet whenever we brought him in it was like Easter or Christmas attendance-wise for churches. Young people who had never seen him play were often mesmerized by Richie as he spoke and interacted with them.

My first time leading a CFL chapel service in Calgary was close to the end of Richie's playing career. It was a Sunday morning before church. I was asked to do the Stampeder chapel inside their locker room. Athletes in Action asked me to do the visiting team first at their hotel, and then whip over to McMahon Stadium shortly after. A good portion of the team showed up. Three things stood out as I shared with my congregation later that morning what I was doing before getting to church:

First, the locker room chapel with the Stampeders was filled with athletes in all form of dress, including just a jersey and jock strap for a couple of them. I am known as a casual pastor, but that was maybe the most casual "congregation" I had spoken to on a Sunday morning.

Second, I stole a page out of the Richie Hall public speaking handbook. Richie uses quotes and stories that will connect with his audience. He tries to bring in "hooks" that will relate. I am a curling fanatic who enjoyed Ken Watson's books from the '50s and '60s. He was the first three-time Brier winning skip from Winnipeg and a sports psychologist-type to boot. There happened to be a player named Ken Watson playing for the Stampeders. I gave the background on Ken Watson the curler. When I mentioned I was going to use a Ken Watson quote from curling that paralleled the theme for the chapel, some of the Americans initially had blank stares, not knowing the difference between a curling broom and a rogue. When I shared the quote, the players really loosened up and started to tease Ken Watson the football player and how maybe he had missed his sport. But this seemed to connect with the Stampeders. Watson, an American, knew little about curling, but he came up to me afterward and asked more about the Canadian curling Ken Watson. He was curious about where to get the books because they are filled with good sports psychology, and he said he got something out of the spiritual application. Little did he know I was inspired by a man he was going to play against on the Roughrider side a few hours later.

Third, after I shared the above two stories with the congregation later that morning, one of the board members said we need to bring Richie in to speak sometime, as he was one of the most popular Stampeders in their history, even though he was now a Roughrider. I found that interesting because the board, many of whom were Stampeder fans, didn't request a Stampeder but a former Stampeder, now a Roughrider. And a couple of the women overhearing our conversation jokingly asked if I ever do another chapel in a CFL locker room, could they come along as my guests.

So after the season was over, we did invite Richie to our church. He drove in from Regina to Calgary to lead a workshop on racism and speak at the Sunday morning service. He was a hit, as usual, and the congregation wanted him back. And he was dressed quite appropriately, knowing this was a tad more formal than a locker room. Richie did leave a part of his heart in Calgary and always enjoyed trips back to his original Canadian home.

Here are seven of the highlight life lessons and memories that have shaped Richie's life from his early CFL days in Calgary.

1. Dreams Do Come True

I was getting the opportunity to play professional football in a highly respected league. When I first entered CSU I simply wanted to fulfill a dream of playing Division I football and to get my degree. Honestly, pro football seemed like Fantasyland. The Stampeders invited me up for a tryout and I could see I matched up well enough to compete, and felt if given the opportunity I could play at this level. I was given the opportunity and was even named an all-star in my first season.

I was playing in a beautiful city that really wasn't that far from Colorado and my family. I had teammates I became close to, especially my lifelong friend Ron Hopkins, another DB. We were both rookie DBs. He still lives in Calgary. In some ways when I think of Calgary I realize nothing is impossible and dreams can come true. I also realized early on, I had to bring it every day if I was to have a long career. These athletes were all playing at this level for a reason. They were good.

2. Loneliness

We often forget that pro athletes are people. Our assumptions can lead us into thinking that because they have a nice paycheque, glamour, and adulation, the human angst that we are all prone to doesn't exist. There is a poignant scene in the Kevin Costner movie *For Love of the Game* where aging pitcher Billy Chapel pitches a perfect game. Chapel celebrates with his team afterward, but there is obviously something missing. He is estranged from his love interest, and after his best friend and teammate drops him off in his hotel room, Chapel sits on his bed and weeps. His body shakes as he weeps. He contacts his former girlfriend and tells her the perfect game was incomplete because he wasn't able to share it with someone he cared for deeply. His heart was lonely and accomplishing the most difficult task a pitcher at any level could accomplish seemed somewhat empty.

Richie has been part of three Grey Cup celebrations. In each one he flew in family and some close friends to be there to celebrate the moment. He understands how his opportunity to accomplish something so big is a team effort of supportive people behind the scenes, who believe in him and have backed him over the course of his life.

Moving to Calgary brought up feelings of loneliness that Richie had never felt this strongly before. Yes, he was making new friends both on and off the field, like fellow DB Ronnie Hopkins. But, for the first time in his life, his family, childhood, and college friends were not a close drive away, but now were an airplane flight away. Richie describes what he felt like in that first season in Calgary:

It was lonely! I had so many mixed feelings. Yes, I was validated as a football player at the professional level. I was meeting new people, and enjoying a new city that was easy to like. But I am a social person who craves deep relationships, and deep relationships take time and effort. I had many established relationships back in Colorado. Even when I first went to CSU, I had a small handful of friends already there. Coming to Calgary I didn't know anyone. It was like starting over and in a foreign country. So these were new feelings for me, but it was also good to get me out of my comfort zone, and forced me to grow up a little more. Really, I was on my own for the first time in my life.

3. God as Friend

Richie is a self-proclaimed "Mama's boy." And proud of it! This is where he began the practice of phoning his mom almost every morning. As long distance rates became unlimited, it evolved into every morning until her passing away only a couple of years ago. Those born before1980 will understand the monetary commitment Richie was making, or his parents were making as he often called collect. During these conversations his mom would remind Richie that he didn't have to call every day, and that God could be his best friend. Now, that can sound so cliché, right? But it's more than cliché, as Richie explains:

Calgary is where God did become my friend and not just an abstract concept. My mom was right. During 1983 I went from being a believer in Christ to a follower of Christ. I grew up in church and enjoyed church immensely. I never tuned into the literal meaning that God could be our friend when the preacher or someone would say that phrase. They were religious words without a deep meaning for me at that time. While living in Calgary, I started to develop on ongoing morning quiet time with God. This eventually became a lifelong habit I enjoy and look forward to. I started to read scripture and inspirational books on a regular basis. I learned how to pray at a friendship level. It wasn't just asking God for things or protection, but talking to Him and learning to listen to His "still small voice…" A whole new dimension of faith started to come alive for me. I really felt like God was my friend and not just an acquaintance or concept. My relationship with God started to take off, and He became a factor in all my decision-making. I can say Christ became my comfort, my life consultant, my friend who had my back, someone who understood me when I felt others didn't.

4. Business World

I was advised early on to get an agent. I did some research and settled on Buzz Green out of Cincinnati. He always treated me with respect and tried to find me a fair deal. He reminded me that I would learn real quickly that pro sports are a business. This is such a fine line because coaches or management understand you need talent first and foremost, but chemistry is critical to building a championship team. But this is a business. Sometimes deals are made for pure financial reasons and not because of the talent involved, or politics, behind-the-scenes reasons that you may or may not be aware of.

A couple of seasons into Richie's time in Calgary, the Stampeders hit a low point financially, where there were rumours the team may have to fold, or restructure and maybe even leave the league for a year or two. It was dire. During the research for this book I had more than a few people bring up a now-famous picture of Richie on the front page of the *Calgary Sun*, sitting in the back of a meeting room, with a tear rolling down his cheek as the team was reporting how they were in trouble and could close up operations.

Glen Suitor said that image stuck in his mind before they were teammates:

My respect for Richie Hall at that point went through the roof. Here was an American playing up here that cared about the state of the CFL. He probably would have gone quickly in a dispersal draft so his job was secure. But I could see he cared and I think he cared about Calgary, a city he grew to love. I thought it would be cool one day if we were teammates. I wanted to play with players who cared, who showed emotion. But it was another reminder of how this sport is a business. Sometimes a cruel business not just for players, but for fans and the cities and regions they play in.

A couple years later Richie was traded to the Roughriders where he becomes Suitor's teammate and they won a Grey Cup together. Richie was not expecting to be traded. He was still young and was a three-time all-star in his first five seasons. But this trade he wasn't crazy about reminded him that pro sports are a business. He was going from a city he loved living in, to little Regina where there were no mountains, but even worse a losing tradition in his mind. The Riders had not been to the playoffs during Richie's tenure in the CFL up to that stage. So for someone growing up south of the border this was like getting traded to a team like the Chicago Cubs or Boston Red Sox, who at that time hadn't won championships since the turn of the century. In Richie's thinking, being traded to Saskatchewan was like football Valhalla.

5. Joy

Yes, I experienced loneliness at a level I never did before, but it was mixed with such joy. I was playing a kid's game for a living on a decent team with good teammates. I was playing good football and understanding the nuances of the CFL better all the time. And I was living in a beautiful city that was getting ready for the Winter Olympics. I was living in a new country and experiencing new cities.

Richie's Colorado support system often came up to visit and watch him perform. Both family and friends came up to Calgary on a fairly regular basis, as Denver was only a short flight away, or a couple days' drive, or one long day, which Richie did on more than a few occasions. This was a fun time for Richie, filled with new relationships and new cities. His favourite road trip was to Ottawa and Hull, beautiful twin cities with great restaurants and atmosphere. Regina was a unique place to play with its passionate fan base and college atmosphere, but he had never heard of Regina prior to joining the CFL, and didn't have a clue how to pronounce Saskatchewan, although he knew the province existed. He always liked playing in Edmonton because of the natural turf at Commonwealth Stadium, yet lost there more frequently than any stadium in the CFL. But this was an adventure. Vancouver, Toronto, and Montreal were all cosmopolitan cities that were fun to visit. He learned quickly that Winnipeg was truly the frozen tundra of the north when that wind started to blow, and Hamilton was a lot like the rust-city of Cleveland, yet both cities loved their football. There was a charm to each of these CFL cities.

Calgary is where he met his first wife Cheryl. Again, this was mixed with loneliness and joy, as the marriage was short-lived. A broken heart will reinforce those lonely feelings. He fell head over heels in love in Calgary. Richie speaks well of Cheryl, as they are on good speaking terms. Cheryl wound up moving to back to Edmonton where her parents live. Over the years, whenever Richie coached or played in Edmonton, they would often have a meal together.

Does Richie have regret over a failed marriage? Of course, yet in all my years of knowing Richie he has never made excuses about a failed marriage, or spoken a bad word about Cheryl. If there is anything Richie learned through his time with Cheryl, it is that marriage truly is a sacred trust, relationships can't be taken for granted, and it does take a high level of commitment. As an outside male friend observing Mr. Hall, he is a romantic at heart, and he shows tremendous compassion to those who have gone through heartbreak, breakups, and/or divorce.

So much of Richie's life was new in Calgary. But it was underscored with a ton of joy and gratefulness. He was becoming not just a good football player, but he was becoming a man.

6. Courage/Fear

Loneliness, the unknown, a new country, a slightly different brand of football, falling in love, the transition into manhood, and a developing friendship with God. Richie says all these transitions could overwhelm a person with some fear. A key word in Richie's vocabulary has always been "challenges."

I have found my faith always grows when I face a challenge. Every challenge seems to be a test of fear or faith. As I take a step of courage or faith, my faith in God, my faith in others, and my faith in myself grows. Every time I responded to a challenge, God became more real in my heart as a relationship. I began to feel His presence and His love for me more and more on an experiential level than merely theoretical. I learned so much about trying to be courageous in my five years in Calgary, both on and off the field, yet what I learned on the field often gave me the burst of courage off the field.

Obviously I had a lot of nervousness in my very first game, an exhibition game against Winnipeg. Was I good enough? Were they going to hold my height against me? Could I perform under pressure, when the lights came on? So many of my doubts were put to rest in that first game. The Bombers had a quarterback named Nickie Hall and he tested me being a rookie. You knew it was going to happen and probably happen a lot. I got a pick and returned it 107 yards for a touchdown. After that touchdown, I knew in my heart I belonged. I always thought it was ironic that my first pick and touchdown came against a player with the same surname.

7. Amazing

Dreams were coming true for Richie. Calgary has always held a special place in his heart. Was it all peaches and cream? No, but it was pretty close in many ways. As he reflects on Calgary he sees his life coming full circle in many ways:

The CFL doesn't have many all-star games, but they did at the end of the 1983 season at BC Place Stadium in Vancouver. I was named to the West Division team. I remember thinking while there, that I flunked out of school at CSU in my first year. I wasn't on scholarship, and almost blew my chance to ever get one as I was trying to make the team as a walk-on. That could have done me in for any shot at a pro career, let alone NCAA career. And there I was playing in the CFL all-star game. I didn't just make a roster, I was a contributor, and knew I could more than hold my own. These were heady times for me and I was grateful.

I more than survived living on my own away from the comfort zone I enjoyed with family and friends in Colorado. If I could stay healthy, I was confident I could have a long career in football. After high school I just wanted a shot to see if I could play DI football, and here I was an all-star in my rookie season. I was on a team that I felt was only going to get better and compete for a ring. This was an exciting time.

I was living in a beautiful city and playing in front of fans that cheered for me, and I enjoyed playing for them and my teammates. I felt like I belonged. I had no idea that 30 years later I would still be a part of the CFL. It all started in Calgary and for this I'll be forever grateful.

CHAPTER 23

Regina I

The number seven has been significant in Richie's life. It's the number he wore at Colorado State and the number he wore for the Saskatchewan Roughriders. When he played in Calgary he wore number 27, making sure he got a seven on the jersey. He was a significant part of the Roughriders' second-ever Grey Cup win at the 77th Grey Cup game in Toronto. His second Grey Cup win with the Riders came in 2007, also in Toronto. Seven has popped up for him many times throughout his career and in life. This is the short list of memorable moments with the number 7.

As we sat down in the 2015 off-season, our conversation evolved into what major lessons he learned and embraced in the cities he coached in or played in. It worked out that he quickly conjured up seven lessons from each stop. We include Regina twice because of his short detour to Edmonton and return to Canada's Queen City.

We'll continue our prairie life-lessons in Regina, and then backtrack to Winnipeg, on to Edmonton, then the second stint in Regina, and the current locale of Winnipeg.

Regina 1988–2008

1. Family

I have learned that family goes beyond blood in many ways. I feel like I am a Saskatchewan person. I'm not from here, but have lived here longer than any other state or province. I feel so fortunate how this province has embraced me. I have grown to understand that Saskatchewan often feels like the underdog compared to provinces with larger population bases. I think the average fan can relate to me in many ways with me being shorter than ninety-nine percent of the league, playing for a franchise that has huge ups and downs, yet somehow I have stayed around through the droughts and the booms, like so many who call Saskatchewan home.

Dave Ridgway wrote about Richie in his bestseller, *Robokicker*, along with co-author David Poulsen. Dave mentions how quickly Saskatchewan embraced Richie as one of their own. Even though he only played for four seasons in Saskatchewan, Ridgway saw how quickly Roughrider fans and the province in general seemed to relate to Richie. It was obviously his size, his humble and gracious nature, and his immediate willingness to make himself accessible toward the fans in giving back. As Ridgway would acknowledge, Richie was adopted from the get-go.

As Richie was embraced by the province, he embraced life in Saskatchewan. Maybe this story illustrates it as good as or better than most. Richie was invited by his long-time friend Heather Hodgson to join her knitting group, Hip2Knit, in 2005, which met on a regular basis. This was the furthest thing from a sports connection, but shows how much of a renaissance man he is. He has a strong creative side that obviously comes out in his coaching and longevity. But something piqued his interest to learn how to knit. It became a fun group to visit and kid around with. As Heather said in her article, "Richie Hall: A Football Yarn," in Regina's *City Life* magazine, "It isn't a book club. It isn't a board meeting. Those who show up have no plans to change the world. They've come to knit—to stitch and bitch." Allison Schmidt, a member of the group, says most people could finish a shawl or a scarf in four sessions. Just Richie and a roomful of women, and a scarf he made for his mom that went well into overtime.

2. Longevity

Being a military kid, Richie moved around a lot until his junior high and high school days in Denver. Born at a military base in San Antonio, Texas, his family moved before any of his early memories, spending time in Okinawa (Japan), Maine, and Wyoming before his parents retired from the military in Colorado.

Regina and Saskatchewan gave him a sense of roots. He never thought this would become his permanent home up until now. He understood the fragile nature of being a football coach and the potential for moving all over the North American map. He has been interviewed by over half the teams in the CFL along with a few bites from NCAA schools in California and Idaho.

Richie really enjoyed living in Calgary for five years and still considers it his favourite Canadian city with its access to the mountains (similar to Colorado), energy, and the many friends he made while there. But for some reason life kept him in Regina and he embraced the city, province, and people.

He often wonders if this was God's plan all along:

The longer I have been around Saskatchewan the deeper the roots go. I met Saskatchewan people all over Canada who have moved to different provinces, and in most cases I have lived longer in Saskatchewan than people who moved right after high school to go to university and get jobs elsewhere, but they usually all feel like they are Saskatchewan through and through because they were raised there.

I'd like to think I've been able to plant a lot of seeds of hope in people's lives through my speaking and involvement. I can see the impact in people's lives is greater the longer I have been around. Longevity builds credibility. And so many seeds have been planted in my life from these opportunities that have come my way. I have been blessed beyond measure being able to give back. I think this is a natural segue into my next life lesson of vulnerability.

3. Vulnerable

You know what I have learned at a much deeper level than I ever expected, looking back on my entire time in Regina and Saskatchewan? Vulnerability.

The longer you live in one place the more vulnerable you become. You become emotionally attached to a place as you develop more and more relationships, and allow yourself to be a part of a greater community, especially with the public speaking I have done, or attached my name to various charity events. The longer you remain in a place the more you can lose, meaning close friendships, a certain amount of security, or comfort. It's easier to get hurt or disappointed, but the upside is you can have so much more lasting influence or impact in people's lives.

This is both in football of course, but much more beyond that, as you lay down roots and get involved. In a sense you take risks and give your heart and soul to a franchise and then to an entire province. The blessings are huge because some of these friendships have impacted me for life and will go on for life. But, I also know transition is never seamless and relationships can sometimes break down.

Even those psychological tests on stress tell you that transition is in the top three or four high stress points. The longer I have lived here the more vulnerable I find myself feeling.

4. Growth/Maturity

After high school Richie moved to Fort Collins to attend Colorado State University. This was his transition from a teenager into a young man. When he moved to Calgary, he was really on his own for the first time in his life, earning a living. He feels this is where he started to become a man. Richie elaborates:

In Saskatchewan I became a seasoned person. The longer you are somewhere the more you have to lose, or think you have to lose. You do put down roots, you do try and get involved and you take all those theories you believe in and see if they work. My faith deepened the longer I stayed here. I have always felt it was my responsibility to give back because God has blessed me so much throughout my life. I'm still coaching a kid's game. I know I am living a dream many people would love to live. It's been an adventure, and I have learned the things I believed in faith-wise do make sense. I am thankful it's more than just theory, but it's more a part of my DNA. I am more committed to Christ than ever.

Richie is the first to acknowledge that he has matured as a soul the longer he has set down roots. His faith, his upbringing, his degree in social work, maybe this all combines where he desires to make a difference with his life. In May 2016 Richie celebrated his 25th Annual Red Cross Charity Golf Tournament in Yorkton, Saskatchewan. This started out as a year-by-year prospect and evolved into a long-term venture that has become a highlight of the year not only for him, but also the Red Cross in Saskatchewan.

The bulk of my writing for this book has been done while living in Yorkton —a total coincidence in relation to the Red Cross charity event. I planned on being close to my aging parents for a month or two, and it turned out to be writing central. I have spent the bulk of my adult life in Calgary plus short stints in Edmonton, Vancouver, and Nashville. While staying in Yorkton I got involved in the curling club and attended sports events around the city. I lost count of how many people mentioned the Red Cross Golf Tournament. In many cases people had no idea I was working on Richie's manuscript. A couple of curler/golfers brought it up after a December curling game. Their response captures so much of what Saskatchewan people feel about Richie:

We've been to a number of Richie's fundraisers. He always brings in a few players and coaches. I like how he makes an effort to talk to everyone, and I mean everyone, and it seems like he remembers people. I like how he makes you feel like you are the most important person he is talking to at the time. He genuinely likes people and his heart is so big. I used to hate Edmonton and Winnipeg teams—

well maybe hate is kind of strong. But I have found over the years that wherever Richie has gone, you almost privately cheer for him. And you hear this from a ton of people. We're Rider fans of course, but I don't know a person in this province who doesn't wish him well wherever he is coaching. He inspires you to be a better person. He doesn't just lend his name to a cause; you can tell he's into it. He gives credibility to the fact that maybe faith is a good thing. He sure doesn't wear it on his sleeve, but we all know he is motivated by his beliefs. It's refreshing for us cynics.

5. Trust

The longer one stays in one place the more vulnerable or under the microscope they become in the entertainment business or a passion like football on the prairies. Every second male in Saskatchewan has played high school football, be it the traditional 12-man version, or Saskatchewan's nine-man and six-man versions of football for the rural communities. And probably half of the girls have been cheerleaders and/or dated a high school football player, and the other half probably wished they had. Well, there is always that small sliver that couldn't care less—but they probably aren't reading this tome anyway. Sounds like Texas or Alabama, but we're talking Saskatchewan! This deep-rooted love for the game makes everyone an expert. Many Roughriders would prefer to hole up and hide once they leave Mosaic Stadium at Taylor Field, and some do…but not Mr. Hall. Good, bad, or tormented, he still goes out in public. This could cause even the best of souls to have trust issues.

As Georgia born and raised Rhett Dawson says, "Canada is a hockey country, but Saskatchewan is a football province." And we're passionate about hockey, so what does this tell you? Goodness, I grew up in a town of 1,350 people, Langenburg, playing for the Golden Eagles (nine-man version). For one of our playoff games, over half the stores in the town closed athletes from our rival hockey town, Churchbridge, showed up with their girlfriends; cars were lined up around the field; the sidelines paralleled the school; and there had to be a couple hundred people standing on the roof of the school. Maybe it's an exaggeration, but one of the local businessmen swore there had to be 1,000 people at the game. All I know is this—the next week every person I bumped into was talking about that game (we won), including people I never saw at previous games. Big fish—small little pond… But a little glimpse into Saskatchewan's passion for football and how much they love their Roughriders.

Trust has been a side benefit for Richie living in Saskatchewan's fish bowl for Roughriders and the province's over-the-top passion for football:

The more I have lived here and got involved, it was easy for me to fall in love with the culture. Yes, there are critics, but really I have found they are few and far between. Most people here understand the whys and hows of our ups and downs as a team. Maybe it's the farm or rural culture, in that there are seasons for everything, and how the economy is up and down. The longer I have lived here, the more I see the support trumps the negative voices by far. Living in a climate like this has built up my trust factor in people and also in God. Sure I have been burned a few times, so to speak, and it would have been easy to grow cynical, but the positives far outweigh the negatives.

In some ways I have taken risks, but the side benefit has been how my trust in so many different aspects of life has grown. On the football front I think of all the head coaches I have had. Ten in Regina alone. Coaches who have trusted me enough to keep me around when the standard procedure is to release most, if not all, of a staff and start fresh. I just try and do my best, keep learning and growing, put the team first, and trust that things will work out. I understand there are no guarantees, but it's nice to know most people look at your entire body of work and the circumstances that surround it. In the majority of cases people will judge you fairly when it comes to work. Sometimes philosophical differences or a fresh voice is what a head coach or management wants regardless, but I have learned that most coaches, especially the ones with longevity at this level, try to be fair. Trust really does build loyalty and I have been fortunate.

6. Strength

Spending the vast majority of his adult life in Regina, Richie is quick to point out he has matured in the area of mental toughness and a stronger faith:

From a football perspective I have learned to hang in there. I have been through a few rebuilding processes. Three Grey Cups, but in each case there was a maturation process. I came in the middle of the process in 1988, lost a tough semi-final against BC in Regina. It was their first playoff game since 1976. Disappointment! Then our roller coaster 1989 season when we eventually won it all.

The foundation for the 2007 Grey Cup started when the team brought in Mr. Shivers and Danny Barrett in 2000 to rebuild after a couple of horrible seasons. In many ways it's a shame they weren't able to reap the benefits of their foundation building as they were released after the 2006 season. The team brought in Kent Austin and Eric Tillman, who are great football men. Barrett and Shivers in this scenario remind me of long-time NBA coach Larry Brown who was known for being a builder. Yes he won that one championship in Detroit, but he never really inherited a team, but in time his teams become championship contenders. Austin and Tillman in this case seem a little like Phil Jackson, who wasn't known for building teams but had a knack of building upon strong foundations with the Bulls and Lakers who hadn't got over the hump in winning championships. For me, it's almost too bad all four of them couldn't have celebrated that Grey Cup win. You could see each year us getting better and becoming a championship-calibre team. We made four out of six Western Finals, lost that heartbreaker in overtime in 2004 in Vancouver with Shivers and Barrett. Would we have won with the same GM and coach in 2007? We'll never know, but they were capable. Patience!

Our 2013 Grey Cup was also preceded by a missed playoff berth in 2011. Changes were made, though not as drastic as back in 2000. We had way more of a core to work with, with that 2013 team, than we did back in 2000 working toward 2007. But there were growing pains. You've been through this enough you have to be patient, silence the outside voices, and believe in the systems or processes you are putting in place. You have to stay strong.

One of my favorite scriptures I share now and then is 2 Chronicles 15:7, "Be strong, do not give up, for your work will be rewarded." Generally speaking, this works if you stick to your convictions, work hard, and make decisions that are based in integrity. Football in Saskatchewan has sure taught me this, and now I am part of a rebuild in Winnipeg, where I can see the improvements step by step. I just hope I'm there long enough to see the reward.

7. Gratitude

As mentioned earlier, I first met Richie in 1988 while doing an Athletes in Action chapel service in Edmonton where the Riders were about to face the Eskimos. I was already a fan and was hoping he might be one of the players to show up. He was one of the last players to show up and he sat in the very back row. I remember saying something in my talk, and Richie smiled that big, disarming smile of his. Honestly, it calmed me down for the rest of my talk.

After the chapel a number of players came up and thanked me. I noticed Richie kind of lingering around, waiting to come over. As the room cleared he walked over and shook my hand and said, "Thank you for the chapel. You mentioned in your introduction that you have a social work degree. I have one too." And then we chatted for a spell.

What stood out was his humble, grateful demeanour. A lot of entertainers and athletes, quite frankly, have a sense of entitlement. There was none of that with Richie. I was hoping our paths would cross again as I sensed he was more than just a football player; his identity was clearly deeper than that.

Richie says living in Saskatchewan then moving to Edmonton for two years to be the head coach deepened his level of gratefulness:

As I was preparing to leave Saskatchewan, I felt so much appreciation from my friends and the province in general. I felt like my life had or was making a difference. You hope you are, but really you don't always know. I felt the province giving back in such a meaningful way. That first game back in Taylor Field still gives me chills and it gave me chills back then, and believe me it was one of those real hot Saskatchewan summer days. I wasn't expecting the response the fans gave me. Actually I thought I'd get some good-natured booing. The fans stood up for over five minutes giving me this ovation. I was stunned, humbled, and filled with such gratitude.

I recall that game like it was yesterday, as well. The ovation reminded me of the one we gave George Reed when he broke Jim Brown's all-time rushing record. That was about a five-minute ovation. I remember the *Leader-Post* saying something to this effect, "That may have been the longest ovation ever at old Taylor Field. It had to be at least five minutes long."

Did Richie set the record for standing ovations at Taylor Field? I don't know; I Googled and Googled, but could not find out the record times.

Regina and the whole province of Saskatchewan has been good to me. The longer I stayed the more grateful I became at how they embraced me, not only as a Roughrider but a man. I'll never regret getting involved in the opportunities they gave me to give back. I think every time I had one of those opportunities it made me a more grateful person than I was before. The more grateful one becomes I believe makes one want to give back even more so.

CHAPTER 24

Edmonton

Richie Hall makes you want to be a better person. I enjoyed his time as head coach here and learned so much observing him and working with him. Obviously we wish he had more time to finish what he started.

Three things really stand out for me as I reflect on his time here:

1. He is not an agenda person. He was here for the betterment of the team period.

2. Solid integrity.

3. Poise—he doesn't panic when he is in a tough situation.

- Dan McKinnon, former assistant GM, Edmonton Eskimos

In the previous handful of years Richie had interviewed for a few CFL head coaching positions. He finally got his opportunity in 2009 to coach arguably his most heated rival during his entire tenure in the CFL, the Edmonton Eskimos. One of the oddest spinoffs of his time in Edmonton was how Roughrider fans softened their extreme dislike toward this team. Richie had become more than a fan favourite in Saskatchewan as he was considered one of their own, just as Ron Lancaster or George Reed were.

Many long-time Roughrider fans have often wondered why Richie going to Edmonton softened the blow for Rider fans, more than when Lancaster went to become their head coach. Maybe it was because he went straight from Saskatchewan to Edmonton, whereas Lancaster had those few years in between as a CFL analyst on CBC before becoming their head coach. Or Richie went to Edmonton in the uber-technology age where social media and media in general had him more on the radar. Whatever the reason, Edmonton became for many Rider fans their very quiet second favourite team.

In some ways Richie was following a unique pattern, being the third all-star Rider player to coach in Edmonton. Hugh Campbell of course is still considered the greatest coach in Eskimo history with his five in a row Grey Cup champions, and other wins as their GM. Richie had only two years in Edmonton but looks back on them fondly for the most part. He uses the word opportunity a lot when talking about Edmonton. He was able to be the man in charge and says he learned a ton.

1. Leadership

Richie's brother Michael played NCAA football for two seasons at the famous Grambling University for coaching legend Eddie Robinson, who retired at the time with the best win/loss record in Division I football. At one time Grambling produced more African-American football players than any other college in the game. This is one time the hyperbole for a football factory applies. Michael enjoyed his time with Robinson, learning many of the life lessons he has taken to heart as a Denver policeman and father. The following Robinson quote captures the core of Richie's style:

Leadership, like coaching, is fighting for the hearts and souls of men and getting them to believe in you.

As Richie looks back at those two seasons in Edmonton, he stresses that leadership at the top is so much more than the X's and O's; it's getting the players and staff to believe in the head coach's philosophy. Dan McKinnon believes Richie accomplished that, but suffered through a tough second season, losing starting quarterback Ricky Ray and other key playmakers early in the campaign. The team had a strong finish just falling short of a playoff spot.

Richie summed up being the head man for the Eskimos:

I understand you have to take the good with the bad. We missed the playoffs in that second season. Getting fired is a blow to the ego for anyone. You are being told you weren't good enough to get it done by decision makers above you. Everyone has their opinion. And that cliché that coaches are hired to be fired is true for the most part. But I appreciated the opportunity the Eskimos gave me; not every coach gets this chance. Would I put myself out there again? Probably.

I felt I, or we the staff, won the players over. They believed in what we were trying to do or how we were trying to win. The game itself is all about execution and putting the players in the best positions to have success. There is so much more going on behind the scenes you have to deal with. I honestly tried to just focus on the things I could control as far as my future went. On the whole I was pleased with the job we had done. I learned so much about what works and what doesn't work.

What's often not talked about is how many factors go into making a championship team: skill at all the positions, depth, chemistry, morale, consistent execution of the fundamentals, Canadian content, health, all the three phases being playoff calibre, quarterbacking, coaching, the overall mental toughness, learning how to finish as a group, breaks, officiating, the list could go on. This is not to make excuses by any means, but the reality is that the Eskimo team was a team in progress, and a good team.

Sometimes all the parts just aren't there. Or the parts are there, but they haven't fully developed individually or as units, or enough as an overall team. I understand things will never be perfect, but the factors have to be good enough, and that "good enough" is subjective many times.

2. Peace

Edmonton didn't go as planned, but typical Richie, he walked away with lesson learned or relearned. There were highs and lows and he was proud of the way his team fought through that ugly start in 2010, just falling shy of the playoffs. I asked him how he slept at night—was there tossing and turning?

Really my faith was tested somewhat, but I was somehow able to find solace back at my condo. I slept well. I think of my mom and dad and all they have been through, and they really modelled faith in the midst of storms. They always seemed to have that "peace that passes understanding," as the Bible talks about. Perspective. I was still living the dream. As much as we all want to win, I understand that wins are hard-earned, especially at the pro level. It's not going to always go your way even if in your heart you feel you are doing all the things right to create a winning team.

Like my parents taught me and instilled in us kids, they were always happy where they lived. They made the best of things and we always knew we were loved and cared for. I knew in my heart that regardless of whether I got fired or not, I'd be okay. I might not always know how, but there was a peace in my soul that God would take care of me, even if I never coached again. I mean those thoughts do go through one's head.

Knowing Richie for over 25 years, I have seen a contentment or peace in him from knowing that there is a bigger picture than simply football. He knows it is a kid's game, and he has been blessed to make a long career out of something he has loved as long as he can remember. His faith in Christ really does centre him, or give him that big picture perspective.

3. Lack of Stability

Life is a paradox in so many ways. Richie did have a deep-down peace when things weren't going well in the win column and when the losing streak hit, and the thought did cross his mind if they'd ever win again. There was some instability he had to deal with—not so much instability in his heart, but around the whole structure of the Eskimos during this era.

As we mentioned earlier Bill Parcells, the NFL Hall of fame coach, was adamant... reality, you must discern between what a valid reason for failure is, and what is an excuse to abdicate responsibility. This is not always easy in football or sports in general, let alone life.

Richie acknowledges there was some inconsistency and confusion with the administration, coaches, and players and how this broke down and affected success on the field. Looking back, he felt these three facets weren't always on the same page. At times, for whatever reasons, he never felt that consistent trust after leaving the room that the team or whole organization would be unified. Richie would ask himself was he part of the problem or part of the solution? Were there hidden agendas taking certain decision-making out of his control? How could he try to fix some riffs that he was aware of? He is a strong believer that a team divided is eventually going to fall. He says:

I learned a ton about leadership, about trying to keep morale at a high level with the organization. There were a lot of things we couldn't overcome. Losing Ricky Ray, other key injuries, bad execution, which I felt is my job to minimize as a coach, especially a head coach. We accomplished and overcame a lot of tough obstacles, but it didn't always show on the scoreboard, and it is hard to explain all the factors to some people or making lame excuses.

There is always adversity and obstacles you face as a team. You just don't want to add more adversity than is necessary. That's part of beating yourself. Not just with this Eskimo team but various times on other teams the same issues would rear their ugly head. The solutions aren't easy. And I'm not the first head coach to coach a losing team like I did in 2010.

4. Endurance

Running the race, I felt like I learned a lot about endurance. Being the head coach you obviously have more authority and responsibility. I liked the challenge. In some ways I felt like I thrived, especially in that second season as we went through the tough start and tried to turn it around. I really wanted to finish that season, and hopefully be around the next season to continue where we left off. We started to turn things around, but we never had a chance at a third season to try and finish what we started. Frustrating? Yes, but that is pro sports.

Richie left Edmonton with his head held high. He endured one of the worst starts in Eskimo history and almost snuck them into the playoffs. He got caught in that tension between trying to live out his philosophy and not winning enough games, and wondering what he could have done better or differently.

Nothing really caught him by surprise. The toughest aspect was knowing in his heart he was still who he was, and was loved the same by his close friends and acquaintances and by the God he loved. The flip side was that he was being questioned and criticized in some corners and sometimes through the press and media. It's hard not to take some things personally, but in the deep places of his soul, he knew he would be okay regardless Occupational hazard.

Richie endured a losing season, missing the playoffs, upheaval around the team, and getting fired. Within a month he had four offers from other CFL teams. Those in the know always know.

5. Proud

Richie felt privileged to be coaching what many felt was the cornerstone franchise in the CFL. The Eskimos still hold the North American pro sports record of 34 straight playoff seasons and all those Grey Cups. Seldom, if ever, were they out of a playoff chase or playoff berth. Not just Edmonton, but northern Alberta passionately follows their Eskimos. Richie felt good about how his Eskimos competed. No one quit, coaches or players. They were a proud bunch who cared about winning. This makes it easy coming to work. Richie elaborates:

I am so proud of how we hung in there. We never rolled over, when we could easily have been out of the running by the end of September. Sometimes you are more proud, or just as proud of a team that doesn't make the playoffs as a Grey Cup champion. You have to admire people who give it their all, yet the results might not be showing up in the win column. We could see we had the core and pieces to compete, and we really showed it as we started to jell and some of the vets started coming back.

On a personal level I learned a ton. If I got another opportunity I know there are some things I would do the same all over. Of course there are some things I'd do differently. Our schemes and playbook were okay, although you always want to innovate and learn. I love that part of the game, especially in the CFL with its quirks or uniqueness. It is hard to have a complete shutdown defense on a CFL field, so you are always tinkering and picking people's brains. I had good coaches with me, players who bought in. But we also had to deal with transition in both seasons. After that first season I took on more defensive responsibilities. Sometimes those changes are enough to turn it around, but looking back we were a team in transition, and it was coming.

6. Inner Strength

Richie talked about how he found an inner strength he hoped he'd have if he was put on the firing line as a coach under siege, or in the spotlight. He came through with flying colors. Battered and bruised a tad, but not discouraged, or feeling like a failure. In all the interviews I was able to do around this section, I kept hearing over and over how Richie's faith was a source of hope and strength and how he came out of this even more determined to follow Christ. None of his inner circle was surprised.

His wife (or wife-to-be during his Edmonton years) Helen, said:

Yes, Richie was frustrated at times and felt a bit like a failure. Who wouldn't? All normal human emotions, but overall he was the same old Richie. He is so secure in himself, and because of his faith, he always, and I mean always, goes back to the big picture. He knows life is about faith and relationships, and making a difference with his life. He was still doing that, never wavered. But I wasn't surprised. His primary identity is not as a football coach and honestly I don't think ever has been. He is a Christian first and foremost and that is not in some trivial way. He lives it so naturally. He modelled to me and those around him that faith does make a difference in all parts of life.

7a. Delegation

Richie learned the art of delegation at a whole new level of responsibility while in Edmonton. As an assistant coach he was responsible for "his" assistants on the defensive side of the ball, and even then, the head coach was the main person to answer to, or where the buck stopped. Delegating was a challenge because it often involved more than his assistants. As he reflected on delegating, Richie said:

I realized going in to the job that I can't do everything. The head coach is making so many more decisions, and decisions that are final in many cases. But to be honest it was tough at times. I found this hard. The last thing I wanted to do was to give someone a meaningless job, just so they looked busy, or to use my authority in some kind of egotistical manner.

Ryan Wagner was Richie's administrative assistant in Edmonton. Richie found Ryan extremely helpful. Ryan was always asking Richie what he could do to make his life easier. This was new for Richie. He had an expense account that he hardly ever used. As Ryan would remind Richie, no one was going to question his use of the expense account unless it was something drastic, really drastic. The accountant and Ryan often laughed because he would remind Richie he had an expense account.

One time Richie actually used the account and took his coaches out for dinner. The bill came to about $500, which was not unusual at all for a pro football team on either side of the border. In the NFL with coaching staff of 20-plus coaches a bill like that could easily run $2,000–3,000, or even higher. Richie said the response from Ryan and the accountant was almost one of relief that he used his expense account.

In so many ways this is typical Richie. He didn't want to feel any sense of entitlement, or be seen as taking advantage of the team.

7b The Chain

When I first visited Richie in Edmonton in June 2009, he took me into his office the day before a pre-season game versus his former Saskatchewan team. Richie always has a motto for the year, and often includes a metaphor to remind the team of the process of winning or what it will take to win. He pulled out a chain link that was in his pocket. He explained that he gave each coach and player a link that would form a chain, a bond, and if the players all chose to be part of that chain they could form a strong, almost unbreakable bond as teammates. He used the chain throughout his two seasons in Edmonton. It is a great reminder of how football is a team sport, and how each player needs the others to be successful. Life is about relationships. It was Richie's way of saying, "No person is an island."

Sometimes the press would pick up on his chain link metaphor. It was something that seemed to resonate with people outside of the team's inner circle, as life is so much like that chain. I had friends in Edmonton who were die-hard Eskimo fans who brought up the chain metaphor when we visited. Richie often says his mottoes and metaphors are corny, but I am always amazed how almost everyone I interviewed referred to these saying and metaphors, and how they have stuck with them, influencing their lives in hopeful and motivational ways.

I'll always remember Richie playing with the chain link in his fingers, as I tuned into that final press conference two years later when he said his farewells to Edmonton the day after he was fired. He pulled out his piece of the chain from his pocket and showed the press his link, and said, "This is my link." Then he explained how he was dealing with his being fired and the lessons and encouragement he received and was receiving:

Emotionally, it's tough, but we also understand the business. When I think of this chain, the interlocking is permanent, not just because I'm an Edmonton Eskimo. It's something that is very special. There will always be that link because we are always there to support each other, and a reminder that we are only as strong as our weakest link.

One of the things I wanted to teach these guys and teach myself is that the things we learn in football are life principles about believing in each other, about supporting each other, about our struggles and our difficulties. I'm not the first person to lose a job as a head coach. There are people getting fired every day. It's what do you do? Do you pick yourself up? I've had ex-coaches call me, players call me, friends call me, and they are part of my chain, even though I'm going through my tough times.

I'm a corny guy, but it means a lot to me. It's just a constant reminder that we do need each other, that we're always linked to something, whether it's family or co-workers or teammates or your friends. We're all linked to something and we need somebody to provide that uplift for us. And when I returned to Saskatchewan in 2011, and even today in Winnipeg, I carry a chain link in my pocket.

As Richie left the press conference I thought to myself how he lives what he believes and reads on a daily basis. Richie was choosing to take the high road, not to become bitter or resentful. Yes, he was hurt, but he was also making choices not to live in any bitterness or resentment. The Bible verse that popped into my mind was from Hebrews 3:13:

Encourage each other daily, so long as it is still called today, so that none of you may be hardened by sin's deceitfulness.

CHAPTER 25

Regina II

You can count on Coach Richie Hall to take a bad situation and turn it in to a positive one. What makes him a good coach you ask? His leadership skills, loyalty, hard work, fairness, and perseverance. That's what makes him a good coach. I have heard him say to me, this is more than a job to me. I enjoy what I do.

- Helen Hall (Richie's wife)

You can go back home! If the CFL teaches us anything, it's that a player or coach can always return to where he once played or coached. I think most of us have been sold the mythology that going back home never works, or that it seldom works at best. The CFL, probably as much or more than any other league around, demonstrates that going to a former home is an occupational hazard, and often creates a thriving situation. In chatting to Richie about this CFL culture over the years, he has hit on the following.

He reminds me that the Bible says in a number of spots that God gives grace to the humble. Pro sports create situations for people to be humble whether they want to be or not. So many championship teams have a large core of journeymen, players who have been cut, told they weren't good enough anymore. Being the top athlete at your school, then being told for the first time in one's life that you don't make the grade is extremely humbling. Or getting to the end of one's career and having someone else make the decision for you that your time has expired. Most players and coaches were standouts in high school and college, so being a mainstay was almost expected for them all. Then they get paid to play professional football, and everyone is as good or better than they were. Primarily it's a business, pure and simple. For most CFL'ers, if they can stay in the game they will, because that is what they have grown to know best.

Richie often says, "We'll stay in the league and humble ourselves. I couldn't even begin to tell you how many CFL head coaches are currently assistants somewhere, and how many this has happened to. You really try to keep the doors open because what goes around usually comes around. We fell in love with this game as kids, and everyone deep down wants to stay young at heart."

So after getting fired by the Eskimos, the Riders made Richie an offer to return as the defensive coordinator. Other teams were interested, but Richie felt Regina was the place; he liked Greg Marshall, the new head coach. And he was about to get married to Helen. So Richie Hall came back to the city and province where he has spent the most years of his adult life.

What lessons did coming back home crystallize for Richie?

1. Memories

I started to reflect more as I came back to Regina. One of the most used words in the Bible is "remember." I know I need to reflect on my blessings and develop a grateful heart. When I think of Regina it really is where I grew up. Coming here in 1988 and being the one to recover the fumble in that late game of the regular season that clinched our playoff spot. The Riders had finally ended their longest drought in their history—eleven straight seasons out of the playoffs.

One year later winning the Grey Cup. To be part of a roller coaster 43–40, second-last play of the game victory on Dave Ridgway's thirty-five-yard field goal.

Ten years later being part of an awful 3–15 season, not knowing if I'd get hired by another new head coach. Then watching Roy Shivers and Danny Barrett rebuild the Riders. Every season you could see us getting closer. It was quite fulfilling to be part of building something almost from scratch.

The 2007 Grey Cup season. A lot of people don't know this but we set a record that year for man games lost to injuries. We had so much depth and character. What a lesson in learning to overcome and not give up. The celebration in Rogers Centre after beating Winnipeg for the Grey Cup was unbelievable. The place was GREEN and the fans never wanted to leave. The city of Toronto even turned the CN Tower green for the night.

And now new football memories after Edmonton. Being part of that 2013 Grey Cup in Taylor Field [he always refers to "The Shrine" as Taylor Field]. *I had been through so many highs and lows football-wise in Regina.*

But, more than football, I grew as a man, matured as a Christian, found Helen here, and got re-married. I have so many lifelong friends in Regina and Saskatchewan. Regina will always feel like home. The memories and the life lessons can never be replaced or forgotten.

2. Love

Richie honestly feels a part of the community and the province beyond football. He has probably been to more communities in Saskatchewan than the average born and raised Saskatchewanite, and that is saying a ton. He loves the people and feels the love. He met Helen here and married her, and her adult children have accepted Richie as part of their family. He understands the love Riders fans have for their only major professional sports team, until the Saskatchewan Rush joined the National Lacrosse League this past year. Here's some oddball Canadian trivia: Saskatchewan has just over a million people living within its borders, so is only the sixth most populated province in Canada of the ten. Only about 1/36 of the country lives there. Yet Saskatchewan has more communities—hamlets, villages, towns, and cities—than any province in Canada. I have seen it while with Richie in Regina, Saskatoon, Marsden, Artland, Yorkton, Dafoe, Fort Qu'Appelle, Neilburg, Lloydminster, and Langenburg, where he is always recognized and people's eyes light up when they see him and meet him. He is so grateful to have played and coached most of his career in a place that bleeds football green.

And to add to the oddball trivia, but it explains Rider Pride and the love Saskatchewanites have for their beloved Roughriders, well over two million people in Canada have been born there, and they infect their children born beyond the borders with Rider Pride. I'll give a personal example that Richie felt illustrates this point:

My son is named Reed, after George Reed. He was born in Provost, Alberta. He always thought he was born in Provost, Saskatchewan, until Grade 2. It was understood in our family that this little green lie was only a venial sin at best. I got a call from his Grade 2 teacher one night. She seemed a tad uptight. She said she got in an argument with Reed as he insisted he was born in Provost, Saskatchewan. He was almost moved to tears as she pulled out this giant map of Alberta. I tried to explain to the teacher about Rider Pride, but she couldn't wrap her educated brain around this phenomenon. Reed got home and he was ticked. He asked me if the teacher was right. I knew this day was coming. I put him to bed that night and he said, "I can't cheer for the Roughriders anymore. I still love you but you lied to me. I'm going to start cheering for the Stampeders."

A week later I was putting him back to bed and we said some prayers. I had since repented. As I was leaving the room, Reed called me back in, saying, "Dad, I made an important decision." Being a minister at the time, I thought he was going to say he invited Jesus into his heart or something like that. Reed said, "Dad, I can't be a Stampeder fan, I just can't. I love the Roughriders too much. They'll always be my team." Almost 20 years later he is still true to that decision, born in Alberta, but bloodlines in Saskatchewan.

Richie is easily one of the most popular Roughriders of all time. He may never have set records as did Lancaster, Reed, Elgaard, Narcisse, and company, but he won the hearts of the province by embracing their city and province. It was a comforting feeling coming back to a place he was appreciated and accepted.

3. Contentment

Richie never thought he'd spend the bulk of his adult life in Regina. And maybe it's a good reminder that even while he is currently working for the Blue Bombers, his home is still in Regina. He rents an apartment during the CFL season in Winnipeg. Richie talks about being content or growing in contentment:

This isn't meant to be disrespectful, but I don't want to die in Saskatchewan, but I can still see myself here fifteen to twenty years from now. I work in Canada, Helen has a job in Regina, and her children and grandchildren are here. I have always thought I'd live somewhere warm in my retirement years. That may or may not happen, but that's how I see it playing out. I also know things don't always play out as you envision them. Like many players who first come to Saskatchewan, they don't see themselves living here that long. But there is a long history of Roughriders born outside the province who stay here for good. It's nothing against the people, because you do fall in love with the people, but I hate cold. But a lot of Saskatchewan people say this as well. I mean winters can be harsh. But it's home and you make the best of it. And I have learned to be content wherever I am. I have learned to enjoy wherever I have lived. Some people think I might not have liked Edmonton because I was only there for two years and fired. But I like the city.

As Richie was sharing how he has grown content living in Regina, it hit me that he has spent 28 years with Saskatchewan as his home address. I have always seen myself as a pure Saskatchewan person because I was born and raised there. In my mind I was more Saskatchewan than Richie because he is from the United States. Yet I have only called Saskatchewan home for 23 years of my life. I have called Alberta home for 28 years. Who is more of a Saskatchewan person? But to be fair, I have been a Rider Prider my whole life.

You feel a sense of home where you make connections with people. I have made more deep connections with people in Saskatchewan—both on and off the field—than any other state or province I have lived in. The older one gets you do understand that life at its fullest is about relationships. Where are the bulk of my relationships? Even while I was in Edmonton, I began to realize Saskatchewan would always hold a dear place in my heart because of the memories and ongoing relationships. I was content in Edmonton but moving back to Regina I had this content feeling in my soul, which I know was related to relationships.

Richie has always had family and friends from the south come and visit him in Regina. They all observed how much Richie was embraced and accepted as one of the province's own. They were happy for him. This helped him feel more and more a part of his adopted home. Loved ones are always happy when they see their loved ones loved in a new locale.

4. Second Chances

Coming back to Regina after his two years in Edmonton was "okay" in Richie's often "aw shucks" kind of way. Usually okay was code for more excited than not. Richie came back to his city and province of second chances. He was about to marry Helen and found himself rehired by the Riders. As he came back to Regina, Greg Marshall was the eighth Roughrider head coach he served as an assistant with. This is one of the quirkier, yet highly significant records in pro football for an assistant coach. And an unofficial record in all of pro sports as the Google search couldn't find another assistant coach in any professional sport that served under eight different head coaches with the same team. Maybe there is a person on some soccer team in Moldova or the Maldives, but we couldn't confirm. Respect!

I see Saskatchewan as symbolic of second chances for me. We talk about the province's ups and downs over its history with farming and the economics. And it is a province with grit, quiet strength, and support. And true to Saskatchewan's persona, I was welcomed back with open arms both on the field and off the field.

My second marriage happened when I came back to Saskatchewan. It was a second chance at love for myself and Helen. And the Riders were fairly quick to hire me back on staff.

I have always been conscious of not burning bridges and trying to find the positives in whatever negative situation life throws at me. I believe this has helped keep doors open for me with second chances in life. My parents taught me well that there is always a big picture in life, and more goes on behind the scenes than we usually see. I have slowly learned to not take things one hundred percent personal when I am caught in the crossfires of football or life breakdowns. I usually have a part to play in these things, as do others. There are always so many factors in involved, some within your control, and so many more outside your control. Striving to not burn bridges has served me well. It has kept my attitude healthy and steered me back toward perspective, and has forced me to keep my eyes on the bigger picture.

5. Listening to My Heart/Gut

Richie is big on following his heart or gut instincts. He doesn't rush into major decisions and takes time to think, pray, ponder, and consider with trusted friends. There is a Proverb that says, "There is wisdom in the midst of counsellors." Over the years he has been approached by various teams to interview for head coaching or other defensive coordinator positions. Twice he was interviewed by Winnipeg before accepting his current position. His alma mater Colorado State approached him, as well as the University of California. These are geographical locations that more than appealed to Richie's love of the mountains and ocean. But something never felt right. Not that they were wrong places, but for whatever reasons, the timing wasn't right. As he reflects, he says:

I know where I'm supposed to be right now. I really do. I'm learning to better trust my intuition and God as I understand my relationship with Him. Moving back to Regina and having it as my current home base, even though I am coaching with the Bombers, I feel I have grown better in understanding where I am supposed to be.

I have always tried to listen to my gut feelings. I haven't always made the best decisions, but I do feel I am getting better at listening. I look back over my life and am so grateful for those moments where I have listened. It has never steered me wrong. But like everything in life, it is a learning process and still is.

6. Quiet Time Development

How can I describe my husband and his spirituality? Let me think for a second... Hmmmm, this may sound funny, but it describes Richie. He is a holy man. [She laughs]... But it's true, I don't know if I have ever met anyone else whose walk with Christ matches his talk as much as Richie. Believe me, he is human. He is a man. But he is so authentic. He really tries to match his walk with his talk as well as anyone I know. I can't believe I just called my husband a holy man. I have never called anyone this, but it's pretty accurate. Why wouldn't I be attracted to a man like this? A holy man! Can you believe I said that?

- Helen Hall, Richie's wife, in an interview

Richie has taken the time over the course of his life to develop his spiritual, emotional, and mental quiet time. He craves it as much now as he ever has. His quiet time is his strength, the inner food he knows he can't live without. It is part of his DNA.

My quiet time is probably as good as it has ever been. It keeps me balanced and keeps life in proper perspective. I make better decisions as a result, treat people better; I'm more content on the inside, and more aware of God. I'd like to think I have matured more spiritually and simply as a human being because of this. I have noticed since my second stint in Regina how much more it is simply part of who I am. As humans we all battle with self-will and selfish choices; it's human nature. I know this helps me manage me better.

7a. Outreach and Humanitarian Work

Close to the end of writing *Smoke and Mirrors*, I attended Richie's 25th anniversary of the Red Cross fundraiser in Yorkton, Saskatchewan. This was only a couple of weeks removed from the brutal forest fire in Fort McMurray, Alberta, when all 88,000 residents had to evacuate for almost a month. His fundraiser has raised over half a million dollars in the last quarter century. Even while Richie was with Edmonton, and now currently Winnipeg, the fundraiser continued. He has often joined charitable causes over the course of his career as a participant and/or guest speaker.

In 1990 Richie won the CFL's Tom Pate Memorial Award as Humanitarian of the Year. It is an award a CFL'er can win only once. This is an award Richie is extremely proud of, and when he sees it, it is a reminder about the importance of loving and serving others. Richie would be the first to acknowledge that striving to be a humanitarian was exemplified by his grandparents, parents, his faith, and other positive examples of people involved in his profession. To say he was inspired by some high-character people is a huge understatement. Richie told me that this desire to give back keeps growing, and he sensed the call to be a humanitarian even stronger as he moved back to Regina for a second time.

God has blessed me in so many wonderful ways. How can I not want to give back? I think the more you are blessed, regardless of who you are, you feel this urge to bless others if it is in your power to do so. You learn fairly quickly to appreciate whatever this game has brought to you. The awards, the rings, the memories, the friendships are all amazing, but what brings the most satisfaction is knowing your life can make a difference to others. If I can plant spiritual and emotional seeds of hope and motivation in another's life, my life has so much more meaning and purpose.

7b. Reflections at the 25th Richie Hall Red Cross Golf Tournament

While in Yorkton I was able to gain five more interviews. I hopped on a golf cart, feeling like I was in *Caddyshack* driving all over the course, probably killing thousands of armyworms in the process, tracking down ex-CFL players who joined the fundraiser for the day. I watched them putting on greens that from a distance looked like they had little waves from the thousands of worms they were literally putting over. I wanted to get their impressions of Richie from their friendship over the years. The players, along with CTV/TSN's Lee Jones, couldn't have been more cordial. The players would hop on the cart with me for a couple of holes and answer my questions.

Lee Jones, CTV/TSN:

I have enjoyed getting to know Richie over the years. Coming to his golf tournament is an easy decision for me. You want to support good people. When I first met Richie I knew he was a nice person, but what surprised me was as interested as I was in him, he shows that same interest back to whoever he is with. It's real, his character and commitment. This tournament is a prime example of this, I mean 25 years!

I was genuinely happy for him; especially when he was part of that 2007 Grey Cup win in Toronto. He is always so cool, calm, like nothing rattles him. My favourite image of him is when they won the Cup, and he is down on the field as part of the presentation and he raises his hands in victory with that big smile on his face. I knew right there this was the culmination of years of rebuilding that Rider team. I think everyone that knew him was as happy for him as his expression showed.

Luc Mullinder, part of the 2007 Roughrider Grey Cup defence

Luc was born in New Zealand and is a huge All Blacks rugby fan, but was raised in Toronto, moving to Canada at nine years old. He fell in love with football, eventually attending Michigan State before joining the Riders:

This game is a business. One of the things Richie brings is he makes the team feel like a family as much as you can in this game. That's hard to do. You know he cares about you as a person and he'll be fair in his decision-making. You might not always agree of course, but you know he will be fair. When I look back on that 2007 Grey Cup, Winnipeg had a very good team, but we were a family. Richie was a big part of creating that atmosphere. He was fun to play for and so poised. We could be up by forty points or down by forty points, but he was the same Richie. The way he communicated with you, wouldn't know what the score was. No one lost their edge with guys like Richie coaching the team. He never panicked, so we seldom, if ever, as players panicked. This was a big part of our success.

Scott McHenry, Saskatoon born and raised, and an integral part of the 2013 Grey Cup champion Riders as a special teamer and backup receiver:

Richie had a soft spot for Scott and said, "He was a big part of our success. His attitude and making clutch plays often went unnoticed to the average fan, but give me a team full of Scotts. He was a difference maker."

Scott had these thoughts as we chatted on the golf cart:

Guys wanted to play for Richie, the way he treats people. There are so many personalities in this game and how they coach. I like Richie's way as much as any coach I respected. The way he treats people is the right way, maybe the best way. He wasn't my position coach as I was on offence and special teams. But before every game, Richie would go around during the pre-game exercise warm-ups and shake everyone's hand and have a word or more of encouragement. I have never seen another position coach do that. He knew us all. You really felt that as a person you were more important to him than just a player that could be moved around on a whim. Boy, when he spoke up you listened. He is so calm and matter of fact, but when Richie was emphasizing something, everyone listened, because you knew he knew what he was talking about, so smart.

Marcus "Chunky" Adams, DT on the 2007 Rider Grey Cup team:

Adams is an Indianapolis born and raised, eight-year veteran Roughrider. He literally grew up within earshot of the Indy 500 racetrack. His best statistical season was that 2007 Grey Cup championship year:

Wow, one of the smartest coaches I ever played for, just an honest, real man. You learned early on he really cared about you as a man. I know it's a cliché but I would have gone through a wall for that man. He empowered you as an athlete. That's good coaching. He prepared you, never over-coached you, and told you to go out there and just play football. He really trusts his players. He made the game simple, the sign of a brilliant teacher.

I loved how he taught us to "Trust your eyes. If you see it, it's really happening— react accordingly. If I see it, I see it." So often in sports we don't step out of the box of our position and it hurts the team, even though we may be playing our position. Yes, there are parameters, but he emphasized to us that we are all football players that can be a difference maker and playmaker. Of all his coaching, this one sticks with me the most. I think of it often, even outside of the game. He helped teach me how to win. Not just play the game.

"The Raz," Dan Rashovich, a 16-year CFL veteran all-star LB and special teamer, and part of the 1989 Grey Cup Roughrider team:

Mr. Rashovich understands the history of the game and the honour of playing a professional sport. He was a long-time teammate of Richie's and a player on Rider teams Richie coached. I hope I capture Dan's emotion as he talked about the game. As he said "I loved playing football. I loved this game," his eyes came alive as he talked about his 16 years in the CFL and his long-time association and friendship with Richie:

When I think of Richie, I think of a warrior, a battler, passionate and smart. No wonder he's a good coach. He really knows the game, but his edge is he knows people and genuinely cares for the people he is in contact with. He bridges that gap from employer to an actual human being, bringing that emotional connection. When that happens your care level goes up on the field.

I'm glad to be part of his fundraiser. You don't mind supporting a person like Richie and being associated with whatever he is involved with. He's such a giving, generous guy. And he was that way on the field. He gave one hundred percent. What's the old saying? "It's not the size of the dog in the fight, but the size of the fight in the dog."

CHAPTER 26

Winnipeg

So Gate 31A was Hawaii and Gate31B was Winnipeg. So…
Going to Winnipeg!

- The popular Fountain Tire television commercial
advertising their Air Miles rewards program

Winnipeg is a nice city—the riverfront area, the music festivals, a historic downtown, friendly people. I tease my Manitoba cousins that it's just a larger version of Regina, and how my Roughriders own Labour Day, but I must be somewhat careful as the Riders tend to struggle in the Banjo Bowl a week later. My roots are from Beausejour, about 45 minutes northeast of the Peg. This is where family reunions will congregate. As the years have gone on, the Saskatchewan Scholzes are undefeated versus the Manitoba Scholzes in touch football. This is important!

Because Winnipeg is uber-cold in the winter, scorching hot in the summer, has the prairie flatlands like Saskatchewan, is the windiest city in all of pro football, and the smallest city in the NHL, it can get a bad rap in pro sports circles, including the CFL. No mountains, no oceans nearby, no Broadway, Hollywood, or funky Country Music capital, the Siberia of the NHL, yet some of the world's best talent comes out of those Siberian zones in both hockey and football. Go figure!

Gordie Howe—Richie—Jeremy Roenick—Winnipeg—Gordie Howe—Richie

As I was typing this chapter, Saskatchewan born hockey legend Gordie Howe passed away. Richie in his interaction with the fans has always reminded me of Mr. Hockey. I always thought it was ironic that Richie has spent all those years in Saskatchewan and was loved by the public in the CFL like Saskatchewan born Gordie Howe. Richie was born in Texas and is seen as an adopted Saskatchewanite. Howe was born in Saskatchewan and was seen as a lifelong resident, yet spent his entire adult life in the USA. Obviously, Gordie Howe is more of a household name with his worldwide appeal, but the thread runs through Saskatchewan. In my interaction with professional athletes, Richie Hall and Gordie Howe stand out as two of the most fan-friendly, genuine men I have ever come across.

I haven't forgotten about Winnipeg. Follow the segue…Jeremy Roenick is an 18-year NHL veteran and future Hall of Famer, one of only a handful of players to score 500 goals in his career. He said he missed road trips to Winnipeg after they moved to Phoenix. The following line endeared him to Winnipeg fans when he said, "I was upset when Winnipeg moved the Jets. Maybe it's just me, but I looked forward to Winnipeg; they seemed to have an unusually high percentage of good looking blonds, and they all seemed to get dressed up for the games. The female esthetics in the arena was nice." Just for the record Roenick is known as a happily married family man who takes time for the fans. When he described his philosophy of catering to the fans he reminded me of Richie Hall. Roenick describes the influence a high-profile athlete can have on someone's life.

When Roenick was a kid growing up in the Boston area, he often attended Hartford Whaler games. During one game, Gordie Howe picked up a pile of snow off the ice and threw it over the glass on top of Roenick's head. Howe continued to skate around for the warm-up, but looked back at Roenick and winked. Roenick recalled in a number of interviews the lasting effect it had on him, saying:

I thought that was the coolest thing that ever happened in my whole life. It took about three seconds. It was me, Gordie Howe, and no one else. That moment stuck with me for years and years. It was a little gesture, it was small and it took nothing out of his time, but it resonated with me my whole life. So, as a player, as I got older, I tried to reach out to fans, reach out to kids whether on the ice or on the street or in a restaurant. I try to do little things where I can make the same impression on a young child that Gordie Howe made on me. That's a gift that was given to me. And I made sure I did it, every single day. Without the fans, without their support, the NHL would be nothing, the NFL would be nothing, basketball, baseball, you name it right down the line. The two or three seconds you give each day to make sure you appreciate the people who appreciate you, goes a long way.

Richie understands this as well as any celebrity or athlete. Early in 2015 Richie's role with the Saskatchewan Roughriders was unclear as he knew he wasn't going to return as the defensive coordinator. The door was left open for him to field offers from other teams. Many, like me, saw this as a backhanded way of showing Richie respect for his years of involvement with the Roughriders and the affection the team knew he had from the province and fans. No one could deny his popularity or his football acumen. So what would happen to Richie Hall?

Within days Mike O'Shea, head coach of the Blue Bombers, called to see if Richie would consider the defensive coordinator job with Winnipeg. Richie was intrigued with the offer and the direction the Bombers were headed in their rebuilding phase. It had been four long years since the Bombers had made the playoffs, one of the longest droughts in their franchise history. Richie would still call Regina home as Helen had a full-time career in the city. Richie, like a few other CFL vagabonds, would rent an apartment in Winnipeg during the season.

Richie was going to Winnipeg!

1. The Past Is the Past

Richie knew that going to Winnipeg was definitely a new chapter in his football life. His fourth CFL city, and now he had played or coached in all four CFL prairie cities. He reflected on one of his favourite Bible verses from Philippians as he was about to journey a few hours east of Regina:

But one thing I do: Forgetting what is behind and straining toward what is ahead. I press on toward the goal to win the prize...

Always grateful for new opportunities, he said:

I don't like to live in the past, or dwell in the past. I reflect on the good times I had in Regina, but I often reflect on my good times, as well, as a player in Calgary, and as head coach in Edmonton. I have friendships in each of those cities that I treasure. I already had some special relationships in Winnipeg before I got here and would be reunited with some former coaching colleagues, too.

Joining the Bombers reminded me that the past is the past and to embrace my new opportunity in Winnipeg. If the CFL teaches you anything, it is change. Even if you stay in the same place with the same team every year, there will be changes, big or small. This change is just a little more pronounced by joining a once-rival team.

2. Confidence

If there has been a phrase that has coloured my thinking every day since coming to Winnipeg, it's having an unconditional mindset.

As a DB I had to learn a long time ago to develop a short memory and to block out misfortune. You get beat. Consistently good quarterbacks have to develop this mindset as well. Sometimes it's your fault and sometimes your opponent simply makes a great athletic play, which to the casual viewer can look like your fault. I took a bit of a personal hit with the Riders; my confidence was tested somewhat. A little doubt crept in. And from my daily readings and times with God this phrase popped into my heart: unconditional mindset.

Things happen. Life happens. Life isn't always fair or doesn't go our way, but I'm always learning to do my best, do my job, be true to myself, and let the chips fall where they may. Perspective! Looking at the whole body of work, not just an isolated play or an isolated bad season. There are so many factors that go into being a contender in pro sports, but also in my everyday living. We can only control what we can control.

What keeps Richie going regardless? He focuses on that word "perspective" and looks at the big picture. He is great at looking at the big picture and considers all the factors involved. He knows you don't lose your ability to coach overnight. He knows you don't lose your true essence unless you make a consciously bad series of choices. But he is human and he admits his emotional health was knocked around a bit after Saskatchewan. This was similar to being traded from Calgary to the Riders in 1988 and being fired as head coach of the Eskimos in 2010.

But his DB background helped restore his confidence. No one is perfect. Regroup, learn from your past, and incorporate the lessons learned or relearned. Take it as a challenge. He has a litany of successes both as a player and coach; he has accomplished much in his three and a half decades of college and pro football. So many others in his field of work have gone through the same ups and downs. He knew he could still coach and coach successfully at a high level.

Unconditional mindset! What is true? What is real? Look at the big picture. Focus on those realities regardless and confidence may take a shot or three, but it will revive itself.

3. Patience

The older I get the more patient I am becoming. It takes time for things to develop, especially if you are trying to build something for the long haul. For me coming to Winnipeg has felt similar to when we started our rebuilding process in the Danny

Barrett/Roy Shivers era in Saskatchewan. We started in '01 and eventually won it all in '07, with the core of that team, but we started to contend after a couple of seasons. For me Winnipeg feels much the way I did in 2001, the newness of building something solid.

Coming to Winnipeg for Richie wasn't something new but a new situation for him. He knew that Winnipeg had missed the playoffs in the previous three seasons and were getting closer. This would be head coach Mike O'Shea's second season with the Bombers, and he was still trying to find the missing pieces throughout the organization. He believed hiring Richie with his extensive CFL experience would improve their defence. The team didn't make the playoffs in 2015, but the team was improving and by the end of the season the defence was one of the better ones in the league, but it was a process to get it to where Richie and O'Shea were somewhat satisfied. Richie knew there would be growing pains in getting the D to jell and find all the right pieces and the depth to go with it, but patience was the key.

Beyond the Bombers, coming to Winnipeg and trying to help build a consistent contender reminds me that my own personal and spiritual growth is not instantaneous but always an ongoing process. My marriage with Helen is an ongoing process. I'm really learning that for good things to last you must try and develop a patient heart. It can be frustrating in sports, sometimes, in this day and age where the tendency is for quick success. But I remind myself how the successful teams have some longevity to their core staff and players. In the NFL you have Pittsburgh, Green Bay, New England as the examples who have stick-to-it-tive-ness to them. Montreal and Calgary are pretty steady in our league. Look at those five teams: they are usually in the playoffs, and if they miss, it's only for a season or two at the most.

4. Transition

The CFL or pro sports in general are quite transitory in nature. One has to embrace change or transition to a certain degree. The normal coach's CV usually will have half a dozen to a dozen or more coaching locations listed. One of the primary reasons is coaches usually gain more responsibilities as they stick around. Richie has had more stability than most, but even for him he started as a DB coach, moved up to coordinator, head coach, and back again to coordinator. The other reasons often involve the infamous coaching carousal of impatient organizations, justified or not. As Richie would say, "It all depends."

But for Richie transition wasn't just on the football front:

I'm still a bit of a newlywed. Helen has a full-time career in Regina that she enjoys and has been at for a long time. It's a new family dynamic for us. Believe me, it's an adjustment for us. We want to be together, but to Helen's credit she understands the nature of what I do. This is the first time since we have been married, and I have a second home for half the year in another city. She comes out to Winnipeg as often as she can. There is more than a handful of us in the CFL that coach in one city and call another city home. I think it's a bit tougher on a guy like Greg Knox, Bomber linebackers' coach, who calls Toronto home with his wife, Robin. Regina isn't that far from Winnipeg.

Mentally it's just different being in this transition. It's an adjustment period. New team, new coaches, new city, new stadium, new team culture. It takes a little while for things to feel at home or stable. But I understand these things do take a little time, and having that understanding and a supportive wife does make the transitions easier. The new job is exciting, yet I often feel like I am living out of a suitcase.

I spent almost a week with Richie in his Winnipeg home. He had a small one-room apartment about 15 minutes from the stadium. It was a nice place. But I did laugh when he showed me his fridge. There was some water, ketchup, mayo, butter, three eggs, a soda, some jam, and some bread. Richie told me it was more than normal and laughed. Helen brought it up when I interviewed her:

I shake my head when I visit Richie. He keeps a nice place. It's clean and tidy—probably because he's never there. I fill the cupboards and fridge with food. When I come back there is nothing really new in the fridge or cupboards but the stuff I bought from the previous visit. I know he cooks a bit when I am not around, and he's fully capable and pretty good at the cooking. But I also understand he's by himself and eating out after a long day is so much easier. But it's like going to an extended stay hotel, not an apartment. [She laughed.]

5. Journey

Moving to Winnipeg got Richie doing a lot of reflecting on his career, his faith, and his life in general. He sees life a lot like seasons, football seasons. You have cycles, ups and downs, setbacks, surprises, and always something in process. He may have a better grasp on this than most of us because he does get a schedule every year to keep or to follow.

It's really hit me moving to Winnipeg, the journey I have been on. I'm grateful, very grateful and thankful for all my blessings. This is my thirty-first year in the CFL, my thirty-third year in Canada. I'm in a new environment; I'm part of building or rebuilding something new in Winnipeg. The Bombers have a pretty cool history when you look back. They have been to and won a lot of Grey Cups. I can't believe it's almost twenty-five years since their last Grey Cup win. I'm part of another storied franchise. In some ways it has brought freshness to me.

I can't believe I've been at a kid's game I love for thirty-one years at the pro level. Looking at the CFL, who would have thought that twenty-two of those years were mostly in Regina? That's a long time with the same team. I have made so many friends on the journey both in and out of the game. But football opened a lot of doors. I was such a baby Christian when I moved up here from Colorado. My faith has grown more than I ever dreamed it would. God has been my best friend and I have seen His faithfulness and grace in all aspects of my life. Through it all, the ups and downs, I know God is good. How can I not be grateful?

6. Faith

When you get to know Richie it doesn't take long to see that his faith is extremely important to him. He does not wear it on his sleeve, but lives it in his choices organically. I have met so few people in my travels who have as deep a commitment to Christ as Richie does that draws people rather than repels them. In a good handful of my interviews, I'd hear a similar: I'm not religious or I'm not very religious, but Richie governs his life around his beliefs. He is so non-offensive yet firm in his convictions. He lives it as best as he can. Once you get to know him, he makes it easy to talk about spiritual issues. He won't force it, but he won't shy away from sharing his heart if you give him an open door. He doesn't judge or condemn, and you often come away with the feeling you want what he has. The way he lives makes God believable.

I found it interesting that almost every person, it might have been every person, I interviewed brought up the fact that faith is critical to understanding what makes Richie tick. And almost everyone made reference to how Richie's walk with God is so natural and appealing.

My year and a half in Winnipeg I have given a lot of thought about my relationship with Christ. Like I have said, moving here to coach has caused me to reflect on many things. I understand more than ever life is about relationships. And to keep cultivating the ones I have. I met the Kiezik family in my playing days. They are huge Bomber fans. Helen and Ed, along with her sister and husband, Irene and Mike Bozynski, go to games together. They were teasing me as I would come off the field when playing for the Riders. So after one of those games I made a point to meet them. We have been lifelong friends ever since. On home game weeks in Winnipeg, they always invite me over for a beautiful meal the night before game day. It's one of my highlights. They are one of God's gifts I treasure. They are like my second family in Manitoba.

I miss Helen and so value her input. We talk and text every day. In some ways I feel this has made us closer. I'd rather be with her every day, but thank goodness for technology. I feel God has made time for me and I need to make time for those around me. I have my circle of friends going back to my Colorado State days, and many I have made since, that I keep in constant communication with. I see that faith is rooted in love and God works mostly through people.

One of Richie's favourite Bible verses we quoted earlier from Hebrews 3:13 seems apropos once again in capturing Richie's style.... in connecting his faith with relationships "But encourage one another daily, as long as it is called today, so that none of you may be hardened by sin's deceitfulness."

7. Evolution

As we were finishing the first rough draft Richie and the Bombers were about to open the season in a few days versus Montreal. This will be Richie's second season in Winnipeg. He says he is excited and feeling opportunities arising. There is stability on the defensive side of ball. There have also been a couple of new additions that should make them stronger. Drew Willy, the starting quarterback who went down early last season has been given a clean bill of health, and he has some new weapons to utilize, including another former Roughrider #7, dynamic, multiple all-star Weston Dressler (whom Richie claims he is at least one inch taller than). Number 7 in a Roughrider jersey sure symbolizes speed, shortness, fan popularity, and all-star calibre. Richie was hopeful a tipping point was about to occur in the team's evolution:

I want to use the word evolution for season two in Winnipeg and the life lessons I am learning. I thought we could make the playoffs last year. We were evolving as a team. We had structures and schemes in place, along with the right fits with our players to be successful. Growing pains, but we were growing.

In my own life I feel like I am evolving more as a man, a husband, a coach, and a Christian. I'm growing and have my own growing pains. The older I get, the more I realize I will always be learning and growing both in my vocation and outside of it, as well in my personal life.

When I was with Richie in Winnipeg, Mike O'Shea popped into Richie's office at the end of the week to chat. They were processing the week and trying to evaluate if all the hay was in the barn for the next day's game. They were talking about the team's growing pains. Mike said he wants to see more "speed and violence," having the players get to the stage where they are reacting more than thinking about what they are supposed to do. By violence he simply meant being more physically imposing than their opponents. Both Richie and Mike hated stupid penalties. Then Mike said something that seemed to resonate with Richie: this whole idea of watching the team evolve into a consistent contender. That was the goal. Mike said the following would be key to the team's evolution or growth. Richie was quick to elaborate. I instantly thought what he was about to say captured so much of the inner spirit of Richie Hall:

We need more consistency with resiliency.

2007

2013

2013 Grey Cup Champ 3 –Ron Hopkins 0.

Coach Chamblin and I, Champions.

3 rings, Coach Barron Miles 2013.

Sherman Wilson (my barber), roasting me before leaving for Edmonton.

Winnipeg vs Sask, Labour Day Classic – yes, we can be friends.

Hello, Winnipeg. Chantel (stepdaughter), Michael, Me, Helen (wife), Richard Sr. (Daddy), Janice.

Dinner with my adopted Winnipeg family before a game.

Helen and Richie.

Vonnie and Joe Schmidt, and Helen (future wife). Friends are family.

Family at Keri's (niece) graduation from Hampton University.

EPILOGUE

We'll Go Till the Hay Is in the Barn

"I never cared much about making headlines—
I wanted to make history!"

- From the movie *Breach*. Actor Chris Cooper says this line
in light of the Cold War.

When I first heard this line in this 2007 movie, I immediately thought of Richie. He cares about winning, he embraces a championship ring, but he is motivated by a higher purpose. He wants his life to count in ways that could conceivably last forever, on an eternal level. Richie is satisfied, very satisfied, when he knows he has planted seeds in another's life or in the greater culture. At the tail end of 2007 Richie invited me out for a pre-game breakfast visit at the hotel the Saskatchewan Roughriders called home for Grey Cup week in Toronto. Richie's Riders were about to meet their long-time rival, the Winnipeg Blue Bombers, in the Grey Cup. It is a morning I'll never forget—ever. Here I sat with one of my good friends, a player I loved to cheer for when he joined my favourite childhood team, in any sport with all due respect to beloved my Detroit Red Wings.

If I could go back in time, and this breakfast occurred—something as a kid I'd have died for, Grey Cup Sunday having breakfast with a CFL legend—I would have thought I had won the sports lottery of a lifetime. Now here I was, not talking football at all. Seriously, and I didn't mind one little bit. Richie wanted to talk about the goodness of His Heavenly Father and what had gone on that season. And now I was at a stage of life where I could honestly say this was more exciting than football. Now, don't get me wrong, when James Johnson intercepted his third pass of the game to clinch a 23–19 win for the Green, I shed a few tears. Rider Pride runs a tad deep in my blood.

Richie then revealed what makes his soul tick:

This may go down as my favourite season ever. I hope we win today and I like our chances. But even if we don't win today, this season has been amazing from a spiritual perspective. I think it will go down as my favourite season ever, regardless. Kent Austin told me at the beginning of the year he was going to base his pre-practice talks and pre-game talks primarily on scripture without being preachy or saying where he got his stuff from. The players really liked his talks. This created an interesting atmosphere around the team. Nothing churchy, believe me. His talks resonated and related to the task at hand.

I had a ton of players come up to me throughout the season asking where Kent got so much of his good material. Some of the players were surprised where he based his talks upon. This opened up so many conversations about spiritual realities in the most non-threatening ways. I have never seen so many seeds planted in a team situation. I don't think one soul was offended. Not even close. And everyone enjoyed the direction he was taking us. This created a team that cared about each other and was willing to do all those little things both on and off the field that make a team great. What I saw and what the players saw was a team that didn't just talk the walk, but a team that walked the walk.

What happened this year and what may happen today may or may not make big headlines, but in God's eyes history was and is being made.

Richie is never one to seek the headlines, but he has a heart that wants to make history in people's lives. Billy Graham once said:

A coach will impact more people in a year than the average person will in lifetime.

Richie is in the business of making history regardless of how many accolades or rings come his way.

****

"But if we win, on our budget, with this team…we'll have changed the game. And that's what I want. I want it to mean something."

- Billy Beane (played by actor Brad Pitt in *Moneyball*), long-time GM of the Oakland A's, known for getting more bang for his buck than any team in pro sports.

When I read the book *Moneyball*, by Michael Lewis, then saw the Academy Award-winning movie in 2011, I once again thought of Mr. Hall. Small market teams, undersized pro football player, underdog perception. Richie has a heart that desires to be a difference maker not only on the field but also in life—period. He is a big picture person, a process person, a builder that knows it takes time to build a foundation or for a team to jell.

We have talked about one of our favourite football teams in history, the four in a row AFC Super Bowl champion Buffalo Bills led by Pro Football Hall of Fame and two-time Grey Cup winning coach Marv Levy. As Richie has said:

Think about it, really think about it, four straight trips to the Super Bowl. That is a lot of winning key games along the way. Other than that first Super Bowl they were underdogs in the other three. Shoot, they were underdogs in some of those AFC playoffs. But that team did something no team has yet to do, four in a row. And, that K-Gun no-huddle offence built for Jim Kelly has changed the game in so many ways. A lot of teams have won championships on the Buffalo Bill template on both sides of the border. History!

Richie's story is an ongoing story. Much of his life template has been documented in this tome. When I approached Richie I wasn't thinking so much about his CFL odyssey, although I knew this was a natural segue into his life philosophy, which is a good foundation for anyone who wants to deepen their own spiritual and personal growth, and desires to create strong teams in any field of life. Richie is at the core a man who desires to be a difference maker more than a headline maker. Richie's heart echoes what Ray Lewis, the former Baltimore Ravens LB and two-time Super Bowl winner, articulates:

Success is one thing—
Impact is another

OVERTIME

November 2016—Takeaways and Faith

The key coordinator positions, all three, I give the edge to Winnipeg, particularly on defence…in the CFL because there's such a distinct disparity in the rules for offense against defence… I have the utmost respect for Richie Hall, and I don't think there's better people than him that I've ever met in my lifetime. Paul Lapolice, Winnipeg offensive coordinator, is strong—I wouldn't put him in the same category as Richie—but I think he's strong.

- Gary Etcheverry, long-time CFL coach and consultant being interviewed on Rod Pedersen.com, twice voted Canada's #1 sports blog, and radio voice of the Saskatchewan Roughriders prior to the 2016 playoffs

Most of *Smoke and Mirrors* was researched during the 2015 CFL season. The Blue Bombers were a team in transition after missing the playoffs the previous four seasons, the longest stretch of missing the playoffs in Bomber history. After spending my week in Winnipeg with the team in 2015 and having weekly chats with Richie since then, one could sense the excitement and hope as the team was starting to jell. They were so close. One could see this was a team in the process of building toward something positive.

A missed tackle here, an untimely turnover there, a dropped pass here, a late game penalty killing drive there, inches away from a key first down to secure a victory here, a last-minute field goal there, an unexecuted scheme here, and maybe one significant player away there.

In so many of the losses it came down to one or two key plays. Was it a sign of a young inexperienced team growing together, or were they not that good? Richie was convinced it was that close. He had seen this scenario play out before in rebuilds as a Stampeder and Roughrider player, and a Roughrider coach. He could observe it in Ottawa when they rejoined the league and two years later represented the East in the Grey Cup, and then winning it all in November of 2016.

The 2016 season started out as the 2015 concluded. Losing close games and feeling like they were one or two plays a game away from turning the corner. The team started at 1–4 and the city and province were getting restless: 2016 was looking eerily similar to 2015. The team was now 6–17 since the beginning of 2015. Mike O'Shea's job seemed to be on the line. Then…the team turned it around and went 10–3 down the stretch to clinch a playoff spot in the Western Semi-Final versus BC. After leading that entire playoff game, they lost a heartbreaker 32–31. In my 30 years of knowing Richie, I don't know if I have ever seen him as despondent after a loss. High hopes! But Winnipeg finally has the core they were building and are hoping 2017 will take them those of couple extra steps to a Grey Cup berth.

Sometimes a coaching staff and the players know they have the parts necessary to be a playoff contender, and the patience it takes can cause a team to doubt themselves. But that is human nature. Richie felt this strongly about the Bombers. It was a combination of those little things. The effort was there, the players' morale was surprisingly very good, the coaching staff was on the same page. But the wins weren't coming. And of course the city of Winnipeg and the province of Manitoba was growing cynical in many corners.

And then a quarterback change was made, with Matt Nichols given the reigns over Drew Willy. It definitely made a difference to have Nichols at the controls, but the defence then went on a tear of their own, tying an old Blue Bomber record of 59 takeaways. That is a tad over three takeaways a game. It wasn't the CFL record, but it was in the top one percentile! The points against started going down dramatically and the offence and special teams started to produce. Takeaways energize a team and a crowd. Takeaways create instant hope.

Who says football isn't an emotional game? Well, for the record, probably nobody because even to the casual fan, when a takeaway occurs they tend to stay in front of the TV and stop any channel surfing to see what happens, or stay in their stadium seat after standing and cheering.

As Richie and I put this manuscript together we wanted each chapter to have a takeaway life lesson that not only applied to football, but also applied in a general sense. Takeaways tend to be remembered because they are momentum shifters. It is amazing at any level of football. When a takeaway occurs, well over 65 percent of the time a team will get a score—off that takeaway. And over 90 percent of the time the takeaway will create a good field position, which often leads to a score in the next position. We hope the takeaways from our tome will be difference makers in your own life.

To go along with the takeaways is faith. Faith can be seen as a metaphor, but can also be taken literally in football. Faith in the process is a common term in football parlance. Winnipeg has a plan that Mike O'Shea and his staff started to put together in 2014. Richie joined the team in 2015 as part of the process with the experience and knowledge he brought to the team. The pieces and execution were a work in progress. The hard-core Bomber fans could see the steps of growth, even though at times they probably had their faith shaken somewhat. Many casual fans, of course, wanted drastic changes.

Then the Bombers went on their first seven-game winning streak in almost a decade. The pieces were starting to fit, the execution was becoming more consistent in all three phases of the team, and the aggression on defence with takeaways was starting to produce. The team was starting to see the fruits of their faith in their game plans. Now the fans of the Bombers and fans throughout the CFL were seeing a team who was climbing up the standings. The Bombers had faith in their system and the process to get there. The overall takeaway was what I have been hearing from Richie for 30 years—significant changes and learning how to win and become a championship contender is a process. This takes time and jelling. As Richie says:

Sometimes a team will know they are many steps away from becoming a contender. But I could see along with our team even in 2015, even though we weren't producing the wins as we expected, we were only one or two plays per game away from being that contender. We were so close.

When I was in Winnipeg after that frustrating 1-4 start to the 2016 season, Richie put on a brave face when he came out to meet me at the Bid Grant statue in front of the Stadium.

We are so close! Consistency! We have the players we need; we're just not getting the results—yet! All we need is to be more consistent and we can turn this thing around. We have the players, we have the schemes, and we don't need to make many changes, if any. These guys are capable. We need to keep believing in the process, the system, and each other.

I walked away with a couple of friends, including my CFL writer friend from Chicago, Chad Rubel. Chad was born and raised in the USA but fell in love with the CFL. One of his bucket list items was to attend a game in each CFL city, which he has done. Also with us was an old family friend Karen Schmidt, my younger sister Holly's best childhood friend, who was raised on Bomber football. They both commented on Richie's class but also the look of frustration in his eyes. I think it was Chad who said, "He really believes they can be okay. It has to be frustrating when they lose so many close ones. You can see they are a good team."

And Karen, being the softy, said, "You can see how much his players love and respect him. I hope they can turn it around. Winnipeg is getting so frustrated with this team. My goodness Richie is a nice man." (For the record I hear that all the time when new people meet him.)

On the drive back to Saskatchewan the next day, I was processing the game and thinking about Richie. I couldn't shake the image of the players touching him as they walked by after a pretty disheartening defeat. I knew we'd talk soon; I had already received a couple of texts. I remember thinking if I was a betting man I'd put some money down that this team would find a way to get in the 2016 playoffs, against some pretty significant odds. I never said it out loud, because sports are so fickle. My only concern was, I hope the Winnipeg decision makers on the coaching staff will show just a little bit more patience. I would have made a bundle in hindsight because who knew they were going to go on a seven-game winning streak, knocking off many of the contenders.

When Richie retires, I, along with many others, believe he is a candidate for the CFL Hall of Fame. His resume speaks for itself. He is a man who sticks to the process and has seen the fruits of his labours, along with his teammates and fellow coaches. The rebuilds as a player in Calgary and Saskatchewan. The other rebuilds in Saskatchewan as a coach (three times), and now the current rebuild in Winnipeg. It would have been interesting if he had had one more year in Edmonton, but we'll never know. But as the Moosomin, Saskatchewan, curling club used to post in very large letters at the back of their curling club:

"IF! The biggest little word in sports."

Through the writing process and reflecting on Richie's 31 years in the CFL, I feel like I have learned so much about faith, and about how faith is an organic, living process. Not a blind silly faith, but a reasoned out trust in what one is trying to accomplish before you may see the fruits of that faith. Richie and I have talked about this extensively. Both of us take life refuge in a handful of verses out of what theologians nickname the "Hall of Faith" chapter in Hebrews 11.

These few sentences from the book of Hebrews chapter 11 capture so much of Richie's life and football philosophy. They are a pretty good takeaway as we close his story:

Now faith is being sure of what we hope for and certain of what we do not see... And without faith it is impossible to please God, because anyone who comes to Him must believe that He exists, and that He rewards those who diligently seek Him... And all these people were still living by faith when they died. They did not receive the things promised they only saw them and welcomed them from a distance... By faith he persevered because he saw Him who is invisible.

ACKNOWLEDGEMENTS

This book was a joy to research, and it was a joy to meet so many fascinating people from Richie's life. My only regret is that we have so much material that this book could have easily been quadrupled the size. So many wonderful stories aren't being included, but the spirits of those stories have added to the flavour of the overall manuscript. The extra stories were muses.

In no particular order we want to thank each of the following people for being so generous with their time and often phoning or emailing us back with more stories or insights:

Dan McKinnon was the assistant GM of the Eskimos during Richie's tenure with Edmonton.

Ventson Donelson, whom I played with and coached in Saskatchewan, and Stacey Hairston, whom I played with in Saskatchewan and coached with in Edmonton.

Cindy Kearse of Regina kept me laughing with so many Richie stories from both on and off the field.

Jim Daley was the first coach to hire Richie in 1994. He saw something in Richie before Richie saw his own coaching career take off.

Ron Hopkins was the most elusive phone tag person in this whole process. One of Richie's oldest and dearest friends ever since meeting Ron in their rookie seasons in Calgary.

I see where Richie Hall Jr. gets so much of his sweet yet deep conviction-like spirit from—his father, Richard Hall Sr.

Helen Hall is the women who keeps Richie happy, fulfilled, and on his toes. Her humour and insights into her husband were priceless.

Janice Watley, Richie's sister from Baltimore, was a true pleasure to visit with, as was his brother Michael Hall from Denver. Their stories from childhood through to the present revealed a family connection that is so rare.

Steve Hisamoto was Richie's high school teacher and baseball coach. As long as I have known Richie he has talked glowingly about Mr. Hisamoto being the most influential person in his life outside of family.

The CSU gang known as "the Creepers": Dwane Kelley, his CSU roommate; Jr. (Jowel) Briscoe, his longest childhood friend from 1973; and Joe Porter, one of his closest teammates on that Ram team.

Kelly Martin, whom Richie met in 1979 at CSU, his running partner and the female perspective he would often need, navigating his way through college.

And, from the village of Rama, Saskatchewan, the Dutchak family: Darrell and Monica and their son Greg, with whom Richie developed a lifelong relationship. Uncle Donn joined me in an interview with Greg. I think I filled up an entire journal from their Richie relationship.

Joanne McClenahan, the ongoing contact person for the 25 years and counting Red Cross fundraiser in Yorkton, Saskatchewan. She provided us with a handful of historic scrapbooks and sweets.

Randy Goulden, a long-time season ticket holder from Yorkton who shared her enthusiasm and how Richie exemplified Rider Pride and was a natural for Saskatchewan.

Heather Hodgson (Richie's knitting guru) and Bela Szbados, long-time friends of Richie's in Regina, sent me articles, emails, and stories that enriched the manuscript. We sat together at Richie's first-ever game as a Bomber coach, ironically in Regina. The three of us were conflicted Rider/ Richie fans.

Eddie Davis was like the professor in his insights on playing for Richie as his defensive coordinator. He blew apart the misconception of Richie's defenses being "bend but don't break," and shared insights into his aggressive nature as a coach.

Ron Estay coached with Richie for a number of years in Saskatchewan. The old "swamp dawg" was a CFL Hall of Fame member of that famous five in a row Edmonton Eskimo juggernaut, always entertaining and insightful.

Kyle Walters, GM of the Blue Bombers, was gracious in letting me have access to all thing Bombers for my four days in Winnipeg. Forever grateful.

Mike O'Shea, head coach of the Blue Bombers, who was nothing but generous and welcoming to my access hanging out with the team. I enjoyed watching him operate and seeing his passion and smarts. He should have his honorary PhD in "Team."

The Bomber assistants were all friendly, engaging, and made me feel at home. I almost walked away from the week a Bomber fan. Almost! Todd Howard (tomahawk man), Bob Wylie (loved his jokes), Buck Pierce (he could still be playing), Marcel Bellefeuille (enjoyed your book), Markus Howell (the best laugh in football), Barron Miles (appreciate you sitting with me during the opening morning meetings—always a pithy insight), Paul Charbonneau (friendly and smart), Greg and Robin Knox (I did remember your playing days, and Robin and I drank wine together in section 11 while watching the Bombers battle Calgary…she also told me gingers are worth pursuing).

Glen Suitor, teammate, pro football's #1 analyst. I could have talked with you another two hours.

Dave Ridgway gave me the gist of the 89ers that captured the spirit of the team that won the most exciting Grey Cup in history. And a friendship I will treasure forever.

Lee Jones of CTV and TSN in Regina was a wealth of information and stories.

Scott McHenry was part of the 2013 Rider Grey Cup team. I enjoyed his perspective on being a Saskatchewan born and raised Roughrider, and his insights into playing under Richie.

Luc Mullinder is not only a very good analyst for Roughrider radio, but shared some of his insights into the 2007 Grey Cup champions. His roots are from New Zealand and his passion for the All Blacks came through loud and clear.

Marcus "Chunky" Adams, Grey Cup champion with the 2007 Roughriders, kept me entertained and shared insights that were invaluable for this manuscript. I enjoyed his stories about growing up blocks from the famous Indy 500 track.

Dan Rashovich, "The Raz," 16-year CFL veteran, we could have talked for hours about Richie and life in the CFL. Between Dan and Glen Suitor, these two were on the field for so many of the 1989 defining moments. What a treasure! Appreciate the emails and pictures he sent our way. Mr. Raz, you need to write a book; you are like a walking historian that brings the colour.

Thank you to our four CFL Hall of Fame writers, Darrell Davis, Terry Jones, Allan Maki, and Ed Tait, for taking the time to endorse our book. We have enjoyed each of your writing and journalism over the years. Always entertaining, inspiring, fair, and insightful. Mr. Peter King, the premier football writer of *Sports Illustrated*, the *MMQB (Monday Morning Quarterback)*, and *"Football Night in America,"* and his ongoing coverage of the CFL. Thank you.

Maxine Galger, who endured about 38 football games, countless football conversations, and proofread most of the chapters.

Kim Staflund, our very patient publisher. We love your style and did I say—patience. Appreciate you and the team at Polished Publishing Group. Tia Leschke and Pierre Joyal the arduous job of indexing the manuscript. Our proofreader Susan Chambers who did a fabulous job. Our graphic designer, Jordan Schlachter, and his outstanding creativity. And our copy editor, Tania Cheffins who made more catches in the manuscript than the entire CFL. This is the kind of team Richie is inspired by.

Horizons Café and Boutique in Langenburg, Saskatchewan, where the majority of this book was written. To Kim Mitschke and her staff, a huge shout-out and thank you. We'll do a book signing at your locale.

Herb and Arni Scholz, who always support my dreams and sometimes crazy detoured life, you are the best parents. Love!

BIOGRAPHIES

Richie Hall

Richie is a 31-year CFL veteran. He played nine seasons as an all-star defensive back and punt returner with Calgary and Saskatchewan. For the last 22 years he has been a head coach and a defensive backs coach, and is currently a defensive coordinator. The bulk of his coaching career has been in Saskatchewan, with stops in Edmonton and currently in Winnipeg. He has a genuine soft spot for all four cities he has coached or played in.

Born into a military family, Richie moved around as a youth. He was born in San Antonio, Texas, with stops in Okinawa, Japan, Wyoming, and Maine, before settling in Denver for junior high and high school. He attended college at Colorado State in Fort Collins as a walk-on, eventually earning an athletic scholarship and a degree in social work.

Richie holds the distinction of three unique CFL records or milestones. He is the only player/coach of the Saskatchewan Roughriders to have earned three of their four Grey Cup rings. He is the only CFL assistant coach to go through seven head coaching changes with the same team and to get rehired by the new head coach starting a new tenure. And he is the only 31-year CFL veteran to have never finished in first place in his career. He has been part of rebuilding projects in Saskatchewan (three times), Edmonton, and now Winnipeg.

Known as a humanitarian and proficient public speaker, Richie has spoken at all sorts of functions ranging from sports banquet motivational talks, to men's groups, women's groups, an inspiring voice from a church pulpit, charity fundraising events, and high-performance sports talks in schools and for sports teams. He has been invited to speak in a number of Canadian provinces, and estimates in at least half of Saskatchewan's many communities large and small.

Richie calls Regina home. He is married to Helen and inherited two stepdaughters, Sara and Chantel, along with step grandsons Tristan and Nathan.

Guy Scholz

Guy is an award winning, national bestselling author and journalist. His first book, *Gold on Ice: The Story of the Sandra Schmirler Curling Team* was on a number of bestselling charts for a full year and was the #1 selling non-fiction book by a Canadian author in Canada the year it was released. His second and third books, *Between the Sheets: Creating Curling Champions* and *Between the Sheets: The Silver Lining*, have been Amazon bestsellers in the winter sports and sports psychology genres for the past five and ten years, respectively, hitting #1 on sports psychology as recently as October 2016.

More than 50 World, Olympic, and/or National curling champion teams from 15 countries have incorporated his book's principles into their training. Guy has written for a variety of magazines on a number of topics and has been published over 170 times with 30 cover features.

Guy's fourth book, *The Masterpiece Within*, was released in 2015, co-written with Nashville singer/songwriter, actor, and model Claudia Church. This is an entertaining, story-driven life skills book that falls under the spirituality, psychology, and motivational genres.

Since 1978, Guy has conducted workshops and seminars on topics such as writing, recovery/addictions, high-performance sports, motivation, spirituality, sexuality, trauma, and transition in a multitude of settings in over 200 communities throughout North America. He is also an ordained minister, certified social worker, and communications manager.

Guy was born in Saskatchewan and recently moved back to his home province after a three-year writing sabbatical in Colorado and Tennessee, where he made time for his favourite sport of curling and lead Colorado to a US Arena Curling National Championship. He lived the bulk of his adult life in Calgary training his two adult children, Anah and Reed, to pledge their allegiance to his beloved Roughriders, with partial success.

INDEX

Indexers notes:
The abbreviation RH in subheadings refers to Richie Hall
The letter 'p' after a page number means a photo page

A
Adams, Jeff
  On RH, 41
Adams, Joe, 23
Adams, Marcus "Chunky"
  On RH coaching, 200–21
Albright, David, 72, 73
Aldag, Roger, 23
Anderson, George, "Sparky," 69
Arena Football League (AFL). see Gregory, John
Athletes, gifted
  And mental aggression, 124
Athletes in Action
  RH speaking on behalf of, 29, 145
Austin, Kent, 3, 23, 73, 107p, 160, 181, 217. see
    also Saskatchewan Roughriders
Australian Open 2016
  Angelique Kerber defeats Serena Williams,
    141
Ayatollah Khomeini, death, 20

B
Babcock, Mike, 125
Backup quarterbacks. see Canadian Football
    League (CFL)
Banjo Bowl
  Labour Day Classic, 202, 213p
Barrett, Danny. see Saskatchewan Roughriders
Baseball
  Batting stance, swing and hitting, 121, 122,
    123, 124

Perfect game, 165, 170
BC Lions. see Saskatchewan Roughriders
Beethoven, Ludwig, von, quotes, 28
Belichick, Bill, 66
Berlin wall falling, 19
Bernard, Cheryl. see Curling
Berra, Yogi, 87
Between the Sheets (Bernard, Scholz), 103, 229
Bibby, Dr. Reg, 36, 37
Biblical references, 63, 66, 133, 135, 161, 162,
    164, 182, 191, 192, 193, 204, 209, 222,
    223
Biletnikoff, Fred, 27, 38
Block, Ron, 97, 115
Bozynski, Irene and Mike, 208
Brady, Tom, 143
Breach (Ray), 216
Briscoe, (Jowel) Junior
  On RH coaching potential, 22–23
  RH Friends, "The Creepers", 110p
  RH high school friend, 135, 136
  On RH playing the angles, 126, 136
Brown, Albert, 13, 17
Brown, Lloyd
  On RH as motivational speaker, 26
Brown, Paul: The Man Who Invented Modern
    Football (Cantor), 64
Bryant, Bear, 73
Buffalo Bills, 218
Bulgaria, end of communism, 19
Burgess, Tom, 3, 23
Bush, George Sr., first act as President, 20
Byers, Royal (Rev.), 23–24

C

Calgary
RH perspective on, belonging, 168, 170,
173, 175, 178
Calgary Stampeders. *see also* Saskatchewan
Roughriders
CFL Chapel service, 168, 169, 182
Financial troubles in the late 1980s, 1, 172
RH traded to the Saskatchewan
Roughriders, 27, 150, 151, 163, 205
Calipari, John, 74
Cambodia-Vietnam War ending, 20
Campbell, Hugh, 87, 185
Canadian Football League (CFL). *see also*
Grant, Bud
Attendance per game, 21–22
Backup quarterbacks, practicing for set
amount of time, 88
Cities, charm of, 173
ESPN, ESPN3 covering, 6
Game day roster, number of eligible
players, 86
Games to remember, 10–11
History and charismatic personalities, 22
National and International player rule,
90, 91
NBC coverage, 6
NFL comparison, 20–21, 22, 144
Players returning to a former home, 192
Players taking to curling, 128
Underdog league, 30, 31
Canadian sport history
Where were you moments, 11
Carolina Panthers. *see* Super Bowl 50
CFL Chapel Service. *see* Calgary Stampeders
Chamblin, Corey, 211p. *see also*
Saskatchewan Roughriders
Champion, Tony, 10
Chapdelaine, Jacques, 38
On RH, 38
Charbonneau, Paul, 53
Chicago Cubs, heartbreaking losers, 11
Coaching. *see also* Ryan, Rex
Peer teaching, RH emphasising, 102
Colorado State University. *see* Hall, Richie
Communism, fall of, 19
Constantine, Kevin, 119
Contact sports
And communications, 103

The Creepers
RH friends, annual getaways, support
system, 111p, 135, 136, 137, 171
Crosby, Sidney, 11
Curling. *see also* Canadian Football League
(CFL); Football
Canadian prairies, hotbed of, 127–128
Cheryl Bernard team, 127
Confidence building strategies, 132
Ernie Richardson team, 128
Kevin Martin team, 127
RH discussing with Scholz, 128–129
Ron Northcott team, 127
Schmirler, Sandra, World and Olympic
champion, 128
Winnipeg, home of countless World and
Olympic champions, 128
Curling references, 7, 8, 23, 30, 41, 50, 58,
59–60, 93, 111p, 115, 123, 126–127,
128, 129, 130, 131, 132, 133, 138, 141,
147, 163, 169, 179, 222
Czechoslovakia independence, 19

D

Dalai Lama. *see* Nobel Peace Prize
Daley, Jim, 34
Davis, Eddie, 114
On RH, 114, 115–116, 120–121, 123
Dawson, Rhett, 180
Denver Broncos. *see* Super Bowl 50
Donelson, Ventson
On RH, 45–46
Dunigan, Matt, 12, 13, 17
Dutchack, Greg, 38
On RH, 38

E

Edmonton Eskimos
1989 season, 10, 12, 72–73
2010 season, ups and downs, 154, 155,
156, 157, 185–186, 187, 188, 189
Coach expense account, RH using, 190
Grey Cup, five in a row dynasty, 87
RH firing, reactions to, 41–42, 188, 191,
193, 205
Elgaard, Ray, 8, 15, 23, 72
Eligible players. *see* Canadian Football
League (CFL)

ESPN. see Canadian football League (CFL)
ESPN3. see Canadian Football League (CFL)
Estay, Ron, 87, 107p
Etcheverry, Gary, 116
   On RH, 219

F
Fairholm, Jeff, 72
Faith. *see also* Football; Life lessons; Life
   lessons, Calgary; Life lessons,
   Edmonton; Life lessons, takeaways;
   Life lessons, Winnipeg
   Authentic, woman in Tennessee example,
     64
   Inner city church woman example,
     153–154
Fans. *see* Richie Hall
Field of Dreams (Robinson), 20
Flutie, Doug, 43, 124
Football
   Confidence building strategies, 132
   Faith, metaphor for, 221
   Successful teams and longevity, 206
   Unorthodox quarterbacks, 124
   Wind and weather conditions affecting
     decision-making, 131–132
Football IQ, 90, 91, 92, 93, 96, 99, 101
   Controlled intensity, 73–74
   Difference maker, 101
   Energy and focus, 100
   Mental mistakes, coaches confronting,
     timing, 80, 91
   Playmaker mindset, 72, 73, 75, 76, 93, 200
Football metrics, 71
Football playbook
   Bible metaphor, 52, 62, 63, 64, 89
   Players understanding, importance, 102,
     103
Football plays, schemes and fundamentals
   Basics, importance, 79, 92, 115, 116
   Communicating, 58–59, 68, 74, 75, 81,
     100, 101
   Execution, 52, 67, 74, 75, 89, 156, 157
   Good eyes, adjusting, 58, 68, 72, 75, 78,
     81, 82, 101, 200
   Opposition tendencies, recognising, 78
   Quarterback, pressuring, 143
   Reacting to the hips, 82
   Repetition, 86, 87

Staying in the receiver's window, 82
Takeaways vs turnovers, subtle difference,
   93
Tomahawk chop, 79, 87, 93
Urgency, 59, 67, 70, 72, 73, 74
For Love of the Game (Raimi), 170
Fountain Tire Air Miles Award commercial, 202
Frankl, Vicktor, 35

G
Gabriel, Tony, 43
Geopolitical events in 1989, 19–20
Gibson, Mike, 107p
Global Positioning System (GPS), 20
Golden Eagles. *see* Langenburg,
   Saskatchewan
Goldsmith, Vince, 145
Google references, 1, 7, 22, 85, 183, 196
Grant, Bud, 8, 21, 31, 128
Great Plains of North America, players and
   coaches originating from, 8
Gregory, John
   Iowa Barnstormer (AFL) team coach, 23
   On the September 30, 1989 game, 14, 15
Gretzky, Wayne, 126
Grey Cup. *see* Edmonton Eskimos; Hall, Richie;
   Ottawa Redblacks; Ridgway, Dave;
   Saskatchewan Roughriders; Suitor, Glen
Grey Cup 1989. *see* Ridgway, Dave;
   Saskatchewan Roughriders

H
Hajrullahu, Lirim, 88
Hall, Cheryl (former wife), 105p, 149, 173
Hall, Helen (wife), 30, 148, 149, 206, 207, 213p,
   214p, 215p
   On RH, 189, 192, 207
Hall, Jean (mother), 105p, 135
   Passing away, 149
   Hall, Michael (brother), 116, 135, 213p
Hall, Nickie, 174
Hall, Richard Sr. (father), 105p, 135, 213p
Hall, Richie. *see also* Curling
   1989 Grey Cups champion, 105p
   1989 Grey Cups champion with family,
     105p
   2007 Grey Cup champion, 210p
   2007 Grey Cup champion with family, 106p

2013 Grey Cup, 210p, 211p
After a game, 109p
Angles in sport, thoughts on, 125–126
Aw shucks style, 40, 45
Baseball, outstanding player, 75
Before leaving for Edmonton, 212p
Big plays, 2
Born in San Antonio, Texas, 1
Calling the play in the huddle, 3
Certified social worker, 30, 37
Coaching philosophy
    Empowering players, 114, 115
    Fundamentals and creativity, 116–117,
        119, 123–124
    Leveling the playing field, 5, 8
Coaching style, 4, 99
Colorado State University defensive back, 1,
    104p, 170, 171
Curling with Guy Scholz and daughter, 111p,
    130–131
Difference maker, 2, 27–28, 217, 218
With family members, 213p, 215p
First quarterback pick and touchdown, 174
Football metric, knowledge of, 71
With friends, 214p, 215p
Golfing, 109p
Grey Cups (Three), 7, 8, 22, 43, 44, 211p, 212p
With Helen, 214p
With Helen, friends and family, 215p
Hope, cultivating an atmosphere of, 165
Influences, 3, 116
Inner circle, friends, importance, 134, 137,
    143, 171
Last year as a player (1991) with his parents,
    104p
Matt Dunnigan sack, 108p
Mentor, teacher and motivator, 38, 93–94, 117
Motivational speaker, 28, 29, 37, 99, 129,
    153–154, 169, 178
Motivational words, office whiteboard filled
    with, 51–52, 58–59
Parents, relationship with, 171, 186
Passion for the CFL, 1
Personality, 93
Popularity, reputation, fans' favourite, 22, 40,
    41, 140, 177, 179–180, 183, 184, 185,
    195, 204
Punt return with Calgary Stampeders, 108p
Released by Saskatchewan Roughriders, 27

Resilience, durability, 27, 38, 178, 197,
    207–208, 222
Romantic heartbreaks, first marriage, 149,
    173
Sport IQ, decision-making ability, 130–131
Undersized player, 2, 28, 30, 31, 40, 104p,
    120
Unorthodox, unconventional style, 120–121
Winnipeg, moving to, 206–207
Work ethic, 2, 54, 57, 90, 164
Yoda analogy, 8
Ham, Tracy, 72-73
Hansen, Steve, 92
Henderson, Paul, 11
Hip2Knit
    RH joining, 177
Hisamoto, Steve
    On benching RH, 150
    With RH, 110p
    On RH coaching potential, 22
Holland, Johnny, 144–145
Hopkins, Ronnie, 211p
    On RH coaching potential, 23
    RH on, 170, 171
Hopson, Jim
    On RH, 41
Howard, Todd, 56, 67, 77, 78
Howe, Gordie, 31, 203
Howell, Markus, 53
Hungary independence, 19
Hurl, Sam, 101

I
I feel like Going On (Lewis), 161
Improvisation. see Jazz
International player. see Canadian Football
    League (CFL)
Internet, development, 20
Investors Group Field
    Coaches lounge, 50
Iowa Barnstormer. see Gregory, John

J
Jackson, Phil, 66
James, Gerry, 128
Janikowski, Sebastian, 88
Jazz,
    Improvisation, fundamentals, importance
        in, 97, 115, 116

Jones, Lee *(CTV/TSN)*
  On RH character and commitment, 199
Jones, Terry *(Edmonton Journal)*
  CFL, Japanese baseball league comparison,
    21
  On RH firing from Edmonton Eskimos, 41–42
Journeymen, role players in sports, 126
Julien, Claude, 123
Jurasin, Bobby, 15–16
  Northern Michigan (NCAA) coach,
    reputation, 23–24
Just Once (Ingram), 151

K
Kansas Jayhawks, 72–73
Kearse, Cindy, 154
  On RH, 35
Kearse, Tiffany, 154
Kelley, Dwane
  On RH coaching potential, 22–23
  Kelley, Dwane RH Friends, "The Creepers",
    110p
  RH Colorado State teammate, 135
  On RH overcoming the odds, 136
Kerber, Angelique. *see* Australian Open 2016
Kiezik, Helen and Ed, 208
King, Peter
  On the CFL, 21
  On RH as defensive coach, 6, 21
King Solomon, 34, 35
Knox, Greg, 56
Krause, Alison, 115

L
Labour Day Classic. *see* Banjo Bowl, Labour Day
    Classic
Lancaster, Ron, 8, 128, 185
Langenburg, Saskatchewan
  Centennial Park, 85
  Golden Eagles games attendance, 180
Lapolice, Paul, 219
Leave No Doubt (Babcock), 125
Levy, Marv, 31, 146, 147, 218
Lewis, Ray, 218
Life lessons
  Balance, striving for, 145–146
  Failure, setbacks, learning from, 148, 149,
    150, 151, 152

Faith, spirituality, Christianity, 31, 32–33,
    34, 51, 64, 80, 89, 130, 133, 162,
    164, 171, 174, 179, 185–186, 189,
    197, 198, 208–209, 217–218. 223
  Leadership by example, 99–100
  Life equilibrium, maintaining perspective
    and balance, 158, 159
  Old soul, making a difference, 26, 28–29,
    30, 31, 32, 35, 37, 39
  Overcoming odds, adversity, inner
    demons, 40, 42, 44–45, 140, 141,
    142, 147, 152, 153, 154, 155, 156,
    157, 158
  Repetition, 83, 87
  Support system, Faith, family and friends,
    134, 135, 142–143, 149, 156, 157,
    171
  Unconditional mindset, 51, 52, 72, 151,
    152, 205
  Views on love and marriage, 51, 96, 103,
    138, 142, 148, 152
  Winner mindset, 88
  Wisdom, learning from others, 36, 37
Life lessons, Calgary
  Accomplishment, named to the CFL West
    Division all-star team, 174
  Business, pro sports as a, 172
  Courage and fear, test of faith, 174
  Dreams come true, 170
  God as Friend, relationship with, 171
  Joy, gratefulness, 173
  Loneliness, overcoming, 170
Life lessons, Edmonton
  Accomplishments, 188–189
  Adversity and obstacles, overcoming, 187
  Chain link metaphor, believing in each
    other, 190–191
  Delegating, art of, 189–190
  Enduring a losing season, 187
  Inner strength, faith a source of hope, 189
  Leadership, more than X's and O's,
    185–186
  Peace, faith and contentment, 186–187
Life lessons, Regina
  Family, Saskatchewan becoming, 177
  Gratitude, opportunities to give back,
    182–183
  Growth and maturity, becoming a man,
    179–180

Longevity builds credibility, 178
Strength, rebuilding process requires,
    181–182
Trust builds loyalty, 180–181
Vulnerability, lasting influence and impact
    outweigh, 178–179, 180
Life lessons, Regina II
Contentment, a sense of home, 195–196
Following heart and instinct, 197
Love, Rider Pride, 194–195
Memories can never be replaced, 193–194
Outreach and humanitarian, 198
Quiet time, spiritual, emotional and mental,
    197–198
Red Cross Golf Tournament (25th),
    testimonies to RH, 199–200
Second chances, 196–197
Life lessons, takeaways
Change, embracing, 163
Emotion, removing, 159–160
Faith, God, refuge and strength, 162, 221
Gratitude, becoming a better person,
    164–165
Learn from the negatives, setbacks,
    162–163
Learn to regroup, 161
Life as seasons, new starts, 161–162
Life is messy, 165–166
Quiet time, spiritual, emotional, mental,
    163–164
Win and learn vs win and lose, 160
Life lessons, Winnipeg
Confidence, unconditional mindset and
    perspective, 205
Consistent contender, evolving toward, 209
Faith and relationships, importance,
    208–209
Journey, resilience, endurance, 207–208
The past is the past, 204
Patience, rebuilding takes time, 205–206
Transition, change, adjusting to, 206–207
Lombardi, Vince, 31, 65
Lowe, Eddie, 73

M
Mandela, Nelson, 20
Manning, Peyton, 141
Man on Fire (Scott), 33
Maris, Roger, 8

Martin, Billy, 7–8, 148
Learning from bad coaches, 148
Martin, Kelly, 116, 130, 135, 154
On RH, 130, 135
With RH, 110p
Martin, Kevin. see Curling
Matthews, Don, 147
Releasing RH, 27, 150, 151, 163
McHenry, Scott
On RH and the way he treats people,
    1999–2000
McKinnon, Dan
On RH, 184
Memphis Tigers, 74
Miami Dolphins (1972)
Perfect season, 144
Miles, Barron, 56, 74–75, 81, 82, 93, 94, 95, 96, 97,
    212p
Miller, Ken, 107p
Mitchell, Bo Levi, 67
Montreal Alouettes. see Saskatchewan
    Roughriders
Moosomin Curling Club, 222
Mullinder, Luc
On RH fairness, 199
Mund, Gail, 163–164
On HR, 164
Murray, Allan, 76

N
Narcisse, Don, 23
National Collegiate Athletic Association (NCAA).
    see Jurasin, Bobby
National Football League (NFL). see also Canadian
    Football League (CFL)
Attendance, 22
National Hockey League (NHL). see Saskatchewan
National player rule. see Canadian Football
    League (CFL)
NBC. see Canadian Football League (CFL)
New England Patriots, 31
New Zealand All Blacks Rugby Team, 92
Nichols, Matt, 220
Nietzsche, Friedrich, 158
Nobel Peace Prize
Dalai Lama winning, 20
North Carolina Tar Heels, 73
Northcott, Ron. see Curling
Northern Michigan. see Jurasin, Bobby

O

O'Day, Jeremy, 144

Olympic Games 2002, men's hockey gold medal, 11

O'Shea, Mike, 49, 55, 59, 61, 66, 90, 91, 92, 103

Ottawa Redblacks
  2016 Grey Cup, 220

Ottawa Renegades, 31

P

Paper Lion (Plimpton), 56

Parcells, Bill, 155

Parker, Jackie, 128

Peer teaching. *see* coaching

Playmakers (ESPN), 70

Poland independence, 19

Poley, Bob, 15

Pomeranz, Sheila, 110p, 135

Pop culture
  Used to relate to an audience, 34, 36, 37

Pope John Paul II, quote, 28

Popovich, Gregg, 66

Porter, Joe, 135, 136
  On RH as a coach and a person, 136

Porter, Joe
  RH Friends, "The Creepers", 110p
  On RH playing the angles, 126

Q

Quarterbacks. *see* Canadian Football League (CFL); Football

R

Rashovich, Dan
  57 days in 1989, 16
  On the September 30, 1989 game, 16–17

Red Cross Golf Tournament. *see also* Life lessons, Regina II
  RH involvement, 16, 111p, 179, 198–199

Reed, George, 8, 183

Rice, Jerry, 84

Richardson, Ernie. *see* Curling

Richie Hall: A Football Yarn (Hodgson), 177

Rider Nation, 10, 194–195

Rider Pride. *see* Life lessons, Regina II

Ridgway, Dave, 15, 23, 73
  Grey Cup 1989, field goal, 15, 17–18, 193

Rip Van Winkle (Irving), 143

Robinson, Eddie, 116

Robokicker: An Odyssey through the CFL (Ridgway, Poulsen), 177

Robots (Wedge), 134

Rocky IV (Stallone), 166

Roenick, Jeremy, 203

Romania, successful coup, 19

Roy, Patrick, 120

Rubel, Chad, 222

Rugby. *see* New Zealand All Blacks Rugby Team

Running the Riders: My Decade as CEO of Canada's Team (Hopson), 41

Russell, Bill, 36, 121, 122

Russia independence, 19

Ruth, Babe, 36

Ryan, Rex
  On coaching decisions, 83

S

Saskatchewan
  CEOs, authors, artists from, 44
  Deep-rooted love of football, 180
  NHL Players from, 44
  Pro football players from, 44
  And RH, underdogs, 42, 44–45, 46
  Smallest professional sport market, 40
  Winters, 195

Saskatchewan Roughriders. *see also* Calgary Stampeders
  The 13th man! Grey Cup loss to the Montreal Alouettes, 43
  1963 playoff comeback against the Calgary Stampeders, 42
  1966 Grey Cup, 43
  1972 Grey Cup loss to the Hamilton Tiger Cats, 10, 43
  1989 Grey Cup win, 3, 10, 11, 17, 20, 105p, 107p
  1989 season, 3, 10, 12, 17193
    57 days in the, 12, 13–14, 15, 16, 18
    Players other achievements, 23
    Ring finger taping, 14
    September 30 game, 3, 11–18
    September 30 game, I can't believe it!, 11, 13, 20
    Team chemistry, leadership, 24–25
    Western final against the Edmonton Eskimos, 72–73

2004 season, Western Final loss to BC Lions, 151
2007 Grey Cup win, 71, 106p, 107p, 193
Shivers and Barrett era legacy, 160, 181–182, 193, 205–206
2007 season, Kent Austin scriptures references, 217
2013 Grey Cup win, 71
Rebuilding, growing pains, 182
2014 season, head coach Corey Chamblin calling defensive plays, 149–150, 151
History, 42–43
Longest playoff drought and playoff run, 43
Rod Pedersen.com, voice of, 219
Silent Killers, 143–144
Team Health Program, RH player participant, 29
Saving Private Ryan (Spielberg), 147
Schmidt, Karen, 222
Schmidt, Vonnie and Joe, 215p
Schmirler, Sandra. *see* Curling
Scholz, Guy. *see also* Curling
Friendship with RH, beyond football, 6–7
Heartbreaks, 137–138
Inner demons, conquering, 141–142, 147
Nostalgia about high school football, 85
Shadowing RH in Winnipeg, 50–54, 56, 57–61, 84, 85, 86, 90, 98, 103, 165
Slo-pitch baseball, playing, 75, 76
Speeding in Neepawa, Manitoba, 49–50, 51
Visit to TD Boston Gardens, 121–122
On writing *Smoke and Mirrors,* 7
Scholz, Reed (Guy Scholz son), 11, 194–195
Self, Bill, 73
Shaw, George Bernard, 61
Shivers, Roy. *see also* Saskatchewan Roughriders
On RH, 45
Sleepy Hollow (Irving), 143
Smith, Alex, 107p
Solti, Georg, 115
Spiritual truisms
Theory and practice, closing the gap, 64
Sports
Game as angles, 126
Super-learners, 125

St. Augustine, 152
St. Louis, Martin
Unorthodox style, 124–125
St. Louis Cardinals, 31
Suitor, Glen
Coach/player relationship with RH, 4
Friendship with RH, 2–3
On RH as defensive coach, 6
With RH before 1989 Grey Cup, 104p
On RH fighting for the Calgary Stampeder survival in the 1980s, 1–3, 172
September 30, 1989 game, pass interference penalty, 12–13, 14, 15–16
Sit-up routine with RH, 2–3, 16
As a *TSN* analyst, 4, 23
1972 Summit Series, 11
Sunter, Ian, 10
Super Bowl 50
Denver Broncos defeat Carolina Panthers, 141, 143

T
TD Boston Gardens. *see* Scholz, Guy
Teams
Caring attitude translating on the field, 33
Chemistry, trust, building connections, 94, 95
Finding players with good character, 92
Overachieving by getting the best of your players, 5
Support system, 65–66, 91–92
Teen Challenge Curling Charity, 115, 128, 130
The 7 habits of Highly Effective People (Covey), 158
The Bible, book of love, 52, 62, 63
The Gladiator (Scott), 37
The Guardian (Davis), 62
Their Life's Work (Pomerantz), 103
Theismann, Joe, 124, 143
The Replacements (Deutch), 48
The Satanic Verses (Salman Rushdie), 20
The Science of Hitting (Williams, Underwood), 122
Thomas, J.T., 103
Thomas, Tim
Commonality with RH, 118, 119, 123
Goalie philosophy, 119–120
Unorthodox style, 119, 120, 125

Tiananmen Square protests, 20
Tom Pate Memorial Award
    CFL's Humanitarian of the Year award,
        163, 198
Toronto Argos
    Scoring 21 points in 90 seconds, 17
Toronto Maple Leafs, 31
"Turn! Turn! Turn"!(The Byrds), 161

V
Van Gogh, Vincent, 22, 28, 29, 78, 130
Vespaziani, Bob, 165

W
Wagner, Ryan, 190
Walsh, Bill, 31, 54
Watley, Janice (RH sister), 28, 135, 213p
Weather conditions. see Football
West, Jerry, 126
Where were you moments. see Canadian
        sport history
Williams, David, 15
Williams, Roy, 73, 74
Williams, Serena. see Australian Open 2016
Williams, Ted, 121, 122, 123
Willy, Drew, 209, 220
Wilson, Russell
    Marriage breakup, 142
Wind. see Football
Winnipeg, 202. see also Curling
Winnipeg Blue Bombers
    2015 season
        Defensive takeaways, 220–221
        Rebuilding, 219, 220, 221, 222
    2016 Season, 1-4 start, 137, 138, 209, 220
    Coaching staff, 51
    Coaching staff, pranking RH, 53
    Defensive teams meetings, 57, 66, 67, 68,
        71, 75, 78, 81, 82, 87, 93, 98, 103
    Head coach meetings, 59, 60, 61, 91
    Locker room humour, 60, 65, 67, 81, 94
    On-field practice, 85, 88
    Special teams, onside kick practice, 88, 89
    Team slogan, tough-stingy-opportunistic
        (TSO), 67
Wooden, John, 66
Worman, Rick, 42, 145, 150
Wrigley, P.K., 119

Y
Youkilis, Kevin, 121
You've Got Mail (Ephron), 20

CPSIA information can be obtained
at www.ICGtesting.com
Printed in the USA
LVOW10s1543020218

565061LV00010B/788/P

9 780995 819306